"Carey Perloff, [quite literally, raised a vibrant new theater from the rubble of an old one. This refreshingly honest account of her triumphs and misfires over the past two decades is both a fascinating read and an invaluable handbook for anyone attempting such a labor of love."

—Armistead Mau[

"*Beautiful Chaos* is an extraordinary journ
theater, A.C.T. Their continued evolution
define themselves with courage, tenacity
confront what seem like insurmountable odds. I his continues to shape
and inspire Carey and those who work with her."

—Olympia Dukakis, Academy Award–winning actress

"Carey Perloff's lively, outspoken memoir of adventures in running and directing theater will be a key document in the story of playmaking in America."

—Tom Stoppard, playwright

"Carey Perloff's marvel of a book is part memoir—of a working mother, a passionate artist, a woman flourishing in a male-dominated craft—and part lavish love letter to theater. It is as lively, thoughtful, and insightful an account I have ever read about the art form. This one is for any person who has ever sat in the dark and been spellbound by the transformative power of theater."

—Khaled Hosseini, author of *The Kite Runner*

"This is an engaged, engaging, deeply intelligent, and passionate account of why the theater matters and how it works in a city and in a society. It is also a fascinating and essential chapter in the history of San Francisco itself, as well as the story of a committed theater artist's determination and vision."

—Colm Tóibín, author of *Nora Webster*

"When did we forget that theater is more than sedate art or bottom-line entertainment? How exhilarating to be reminded by Carey Perloff that it is still a grand adventure and a high calling. In *Beautiful Chaos: A Life in the Theater*, we follow her quest to give San Francisco's renowned American Conservatory Theater a present and future as glorious as its past. A life in the theater demands vision and conscience, not to mention improvisation. A playwright, says Perloff, makes contradictory beliefs 'collide in real time and with equal force.' That's the pleasure of this book. We see her think, plan, persuade, and fight; balance the personal and the political. We watch as art and history collide and collaborate. 'I'm a beast of the theater,' Perloff declares. She's a noble beast. And she's a heroine."

—Margo Jefferson, Pulitzer Prize–winning cultural critic

"Carey Perloff writes as she talks: with passion, profound insight, and a warm and accessible style. The story of A.C.T. under her stewardship is linked with her own growth as an artist and a citizen. She raises some questions vital to the American theater and offers some provocative and innovative strategies for survival and success. This is not just a great read, it is an important book that demands attention."

—Joe Dowling, director, the Guthrie Theater

"Carey Perloff is one of the very few remaining artistic directors who have remained faithful to the original ideals of the American resident theater, and her new theatrical biography, *Beautiful Chaos*, is an engrossing account of how difficult that has been for her in the current economic climate. Her devotion to global theater, to reanimated classics, to the most penetrating new plays, and to rigorous theatrical training was hardly an easy thing to preserve during the last few profit-centered decades, which makes *Beautiful Chaos* both a readable adventure and a heroic narrative."

—Robert Brustein, former drama critic, *The New Republic*

"Carey Perloff is a veteran of the regional theater wars. *Beautiful Chaos* is her vivacious account of her ambitious work commanding San Francisco's American Conservatory Theater (A.C.T.). The book exudes Perloff's trademark brio: smart, outspoken, full of fun and ferment."
 —John Lahr, author of *Tennessee Williams: Mad Pilgrimage of the Flesh*

"In my mind, it is indispensable reading for anyone who cares about theater art, values its profound impact on the quality of human life, and may be curious about how it is made. The book is an inspiration on many levels. First, because it is truly a memoir and necessarily personal. To gain access to the mind and heart of a genius, to survey with her the ordeals and revelations of a historic tenure as the leader of one of America's greatest theater companies, to hear her authentic voice articulating the 'state of the art' and speculating about its challenging future is to be a privileged companion on an adventure of breathtaking scope. Second, it provides deep insights into those mentors and colleagues who shaped Ms. Perloff's aesthetic (as they shaped the art and literature of the last century): Martin Esslin, Samuel Beckett, Harold Pinter, Tom Stoppard, and Robert Wilson. Perloff studied with Esslin; at A.C.T. she worked closely with Pinter and Stoppard, and she collaborated with Robert Wilson. Her mastery of the classics, devotion to the Greeks, intimate acquaintance with international theater artists like Ariane Mnouchkine, Simon McBurney, Peter Brook, Giorgio Strehler, Andrei Serban, Liviu Ciulei, and Jerzy Grotowski, and her embrace of the legends and theatrical conventions of Asian theater art exemplify the range of her aesthetic. And perhaps most thrilling of all is her personal story and its intersection with the harrowing job of rebuilding a ruined theater and reimagining a collapsed institution while remaining a devoted wife, mother of two, and citizen of a city and country in the throes of economic and political crisis. Carey Perloff is a lucid and penetrating critic, a passionate and at times hilarious raconteur, an erudite scholar, and a warm and generous heart. Her memoir is moving because it is courageous. She tells it like it is and her assessment of the current state of liberal arts and our accelerated and mediated age is a fair warning. She cherishes what the theater brings and what William Ball envisioned when he created A.C.T., and she aptly quotes Lorca: 'We must always remember . . . that our task is to offer a cup of beauty to the public so that, in drinking, they will understand themselves.'"

—Frank Galati, actor, writer, and director

Beautiful Chaos

A LIFE IN THE THEATER

Carey Perloff

City Lights Foundation
San Francisco

Front cover photo: Carey Perloff contemplates the stage of The Geary Theater at a technical rehearsal in 2006. Photo by Jeremy Harris

Library of Congress Cataloging-in-Publication Data
Perloff, Carey.
 Beautiful chaos : a life in the theater / Carey Perloff.
    pages cm
 ISBN 978-1-931404-14-3 (pbk.)
 1. Perloff, Carey. 2. Theatrical producers and directors--United states--Biography. I. Title.

PN2287.P393A3 2014
792.023'2092--dc23
[B]

eISBN: 978-1-931404-16-7

City Lights Foundation books are published at the City Lights Bookstore
261 Columbus Avenue, San Francisco, CA 94133
www.citylights.com

Contents

Preface

It's a peculiar thing to write a memoir while one is still in the middle of it all. But this book is not really a memoir; it is the result of what happened to me during the beautiful chaos of a life in the theater, when I paused long enough to try to take stock of where I was and how I got there. I have always wrestled with the evanescence of live theater, with the way the work consumes every ounce of one's creativity and then disappears overnight, almost without a trace. But though I have always kept a journal and held tight to mementos like opening-night cards and letters from playwrights, I had never stopped working long enough to gather my thoughts and consider whether and how the whole endeavor adds up. On the occasion of my twentieth anniversary as artistic director of American Conservatory Theater, I mentioned to Jim O'Quinn (editor in chief of *American Theatre* magazine) that I was thinking of writing an essay about my experiences at A.C.T.; he was encouraging and said he would consider publishing what I wrote in the magazine. Once I began, I couldn't stop. The first two chapters of this book were indeed excerpted and published in *American Theatre* (January and February 2013), and I remain deeply grateful both to Jim and to Terry Nemeth (publisher of Theatre Communications Group), who not only urged me to write but introduced me to Elaine Katzenberger, executive director and publisher of City Lights press. For any literary-minded San Franciscan, the thought of being published by City Lights is a dream come true. Just to sit in Elaine's office, where the anniversary edition of Frank O'Hara's *Lunch Poems* was being prepared and Lawrence Ferlinghetti's old wooden desk still holds pride of place, was worth the entire process of writing the book. I am honored to be among their authors, and to throw my lot in with the intrepid publishers of Ginsberg's "Howl."

Beautiful Chaos is an attempt to articulate not only why I chose a life in the theater, but how being in the theater has given shape to the rest of my life. It is also something of a polemic about the state of the American theater today and the urgency with which I feel certain aspects of it must be addressed if the field is to flourish. It doesn't pretend to be an objective account, although my treasured colleague, A.C.T.'s education director (and former publications editor), Elizabeth Brodersen, has tried to bring the chronology and details in line with the actual facts. But if it is true that the particular yields to the universal, then it is my hope that this very subjective and particular story about a particular artist in a particular city at a particular time will yield some broader truths about the state of culture and the world we live in today. I hope it will make people long for the beauty of live performance, as it offers a glimpse into the often byzantine inner workings of making theater.

I also hope the book will encourage women in this field, particularly women with children, to stick with it in spite of the punishing hours and relative paucity of female voices rising to the top of our profession. The logistics of the life of a working mother in the theater are ridiculously complex, but to my mind the effort is utterly worth it. I vividly remember a T-shirt that circulated around our household when my children were young; the lettering on the front declared, I CAN'T, I HAVE REHEARSAL! in bold capitals. Indeed, rehearsal is the great maw that devours Fourth of July picnics and Christmas Eve celebrations, family visits and school performances. I spent over twenty years wishing that I could clone myself and be at home and at work simultaneously, worrying that my bereft family would disown me if I rehearsed one more play or cultivated one more donor. The beauty of hindsight is the realization that much more is possible than one thinks, and that it's never worth torturing oneself for failing to subscribe to some artificial norm of marriage and parenthood.

Much of this book is concerned with the artistic collaborators that have meant the most to me in my creative life, and I hope that those artists will forgive me if I have pulled the curtain back on conversations and rehearsals that were essentially private and occasionally difficult. At the same time, the book makes no attempt to cover the entire time period comprehensively, so I make apologies to many treasured colleagues who didn't end up being mentioned. In trying to stitch a narrative out of many disparate threads, some have inevitably ended up being more visible than others.

The next few years are filled with new adventures: At A.C.T. we are opening our long-awaited second stage (The Strand Theater); we are starting an initiative called Stage Coach to bring theater on a mobile unit to neighborhoods across San Francisco; we are developing an unprecedented number of major new theatrical projects; and we are launching the San Francisco Semester to introduce undergraduates from across the country to A.C.T.'s unique form of actor training. Several of my plays are having productions around the country and in Europe that I look forward to enormously. Perhaps this book will help to frame and catalyze many of these initiatives; I know I will learn a great deal in the process.

In researching stories for this book, I reread hundreds of letters from A.C.T. subscribers and notebooks full of press clippings, and I am eternally grateful both to Bay Area theater audiences and to the *San Francisco Chronicle* and Bay Area theater critics for their ongoing dialogue with our work. For reading sections of the manuscript in process, I want to thank James Haire (who patiently guided me through much of A.C.T.'s complicated history and explained the earthquake and many other touchstone moments with his incredible memory and wit), Alan Stein (who reminded me of many things I had forgotten about our early years of working together and continues to be my gold standard of arts patronage), and Sue Yung Li (whose taste and wisdom have guided me from the day I arrived at A.C.T.). Olympia Dukakis read the book cover to cover and responded with her characteristic passion about the artistic journey it represents, and Robert Brustein encouraged me to tackle the big issues of acting companies and classical repertoire that he has championed so brilliantly in his own career. Graham Beckel dared me to be provocative, and Liz Perle's well-honed narrative instincts helped me lift my personal observations toward something more universally applicable. Michael Paller applied his razor dramaturgical eye to the proceedings; Craig Slaight urged me to think rigorously about my dreams for the future; and Ellen Richard made sure my frequent hyperbole was grounded in the truth. Nancy Livingston gave me the invaluable perspective of a longtime Bay Area arts lover and trustee, and Caresa Capaz held the rest of my life together while I tried to remember what happened when. My parents, Marjorie and Joseph Perloff, and my sister, Nancy Perloff, all three among the most incisive critics I know, were happily patient and incredibly perceptive as I attempted to become the last person in the family to finally write a book.

For being my companions in this long theatrical journey, I thank the tenacious and talented staffs of Classic Stage Company and A.C.T., as well as so many remarkable board members whose faith and generosity have sustained the work. For helping me shape and conceptualize the whole project, for talking me through every argument and interrogating every assumption, and for mitigating my sense of the dramatic with doses of reality, I thank my editor, Elaine Katzenberger, and my right hand, Elizabeth Brodersen, for their wisdom, tenacity, and wit.

Most of all, this book is for my husband, Anthony, and my children, Lexie and Nicholas, the three people in the world whom I always long to come home to, and who always make me laugh, no matter how bad the review or how difficult the actor. They are the luckiest things that ever happened to me.

CHAPTER 1

The Beginning

The voice on the other end of the phone is modulated with the faux calm unique to consultants and headhunters. "The theater does indeed lie in ruins, but the potential is enormous. The rebuilding campaign is a thrilling opportunity to reintroduce A.C.T. to the community. The cost is estimated to be upwards of $30 million."

Behind me on the floor, my two-year-old daughter, Lexie, is drinking soy sauce directly out of the bottle, gurgling happily. It is 7:00 PM in New York and she hasn't been fed yet. I cradle the phone with one cheek and deftly swipe the soy sauce from her hands, substituting an animal cracker to buy five more minutes of transcontinental conversation.

"The search was well under way when we got your letter, but the board is definitely intrigued. We think you should come out immediately and meet the search committee."

It was August 1991. I had a babbling two-year-old, a job I loved at a beautiful but indigent small theater in New York, and a husband whose career in Soviet foreign policy had been prematurely cut short by the fall of the Iron Curtain. (END OF THE COLD WAR: THERE GOES MY CAREER read the T-shirt I gave him at the time.) I also had a lovely teaching position at Tisch School of the Arts at New York University, which meant there was a pool and a superb library at my disposal. I lived two blocks from my theater, and my life seemed about as full as it could get. Yet something in me had instinctively sent a brief letter of introduction to the search committee of a famed but troubled institution in San Francisco to suggest that I might be an appropriate candidate to helm American Conservatory Theater.

I was not a stranger to destitute nonprofits. The day I took over Classic Stage Company in 1987, I discovered to my horror that no payroll taxes had been paid for several years and Con Ed was about to turn off the power due to outstanding bills. My first task as artistic director was to hire the heaviest actor I knew (no names named) to sit on the sidewalk grate outside the building to prevent eager meter readers from descending to the basement to quantify our negligence. I attempted a crash course on tax law at night while directing Tony Harrison's *Phaedra Britannica* by day, and bit by bit we wiggled out from under our disastrous tax burden. Over time, CSC had come back to life through blind chutzpah, a great deal of cajoling, and a Harold Pinter premiere. I figured A.C.T. would just be worse on a magnitude of five. . . .

Thus, two days later, I found myself on a plane to California with my loquacious two-year-old in tow. I told my beloved CSC colleagues that I was going to see my mother, a Stanford professor, for the weekend. The chances of anything materializing at A.C.T. were so slim it seemed unnecessary to tell them the truth.

On the plane, Lexie played Pat the Bunny and I conjured up everything I knew about A.C.T. A few years before, while visiting San Francisco on a Theater Communications Group (TCG) observership, I had attended A.C.T.'s production of Chekhov's *The Seagull*. I remembered sitting in the last row of the second balcony of The Geary Theater, while those booming, well-trained voices carried all the way back to the deeply uncomfortable wooden benches that constituted the cheap seats in that otherwise spectacular playhouse. (I still remember that there was no sound barrier between The Geary and the commercial theater next door, and when their musical finished that evening at the quietest moment of Chekhov, right before

2

Kostya shot himself, the crowds tramped loudly down the fire escape stairs outside, and the moment was lost. That was one of the first things I wanted to fix when we renovated The Geary Theater years later.) Because my Stanford drama professor Martin Esslin (author of *The Theatre of the Absurd*) was also a resident dramaturg at the Magic Theatre in the 1970s, I spent more time during my undergraduate years going into the city to see experimental theater at Fort Mason than attending A.C.T. productions. But a few years after graduation, when I found myself interning in the casting office at The Public Theater, I auditioned recent A.C.T. alumni and learned more about the theater's famed graduate-level training program for actors (then known as the Advanced Training Program, the antecedent of today's Master of Fine Arts Program). It was around that time that rumors began to circulate that Bill Ball, founding genius of A.C.T., had died of a drug overdose in Los Angeles—he had departed A.C.T. a few years earlier, leaving it in the hands of his capable second-in-command, Ed Hastings. Of course I also knew that on October 17, 1989, the company's gorgeous 1910 Beaux-Arts theater had collapsed in the Loma Prieta earthquake. Clearly, A.C.T. was in a financial crisis and on shaky ground in more ways than one. But I knew, too, that in the mid sixties something legendary had happened with the founding of A.C.T., something idealistic and pure and brave that focused on great actors, great literature, and lifelong learning.

I got off the plane on that late summer day in 1991, deposited my daughter with her soul-mate grandmother, Marjorie, in Palo Alto, and drove up Interstate 280 to interview with the A.C.T. search committee in an office at the Bank of San Francisco. As I drove, my mind flashed back to September 1976 and the first time I had driven that particular route, but in the opposite direction, heading south from the San Francisco airport on my way to Stanford as an incoming freshman from Philadelphia. As soon as I landed in California that day, having never lived anywhere but the East Coast, I felt I had discovered a little piece of heaven. It was the year of the Big Drought, which meant perpetual sunshine and water-saving communal showers, students typing under palm trees and riding bicycles into the hills, watching the nascent Pickle Family Circus cavort around White Plaza (never imagining that years later Pickle members Bill Irwin, Geoff Hoyle, and Lorenzo Pisoni would become beloved collaborators), declaiming Greek tragedy in the back garden of Helene Foley's house, and watching Professor Jack Winkler climb out of the chimney as the deus ex machina Athena at the end of my first-year Greek class. It was bliss. I was an East Coast girl; I had never encountered the "other" that is California before leaving the protective confines of Germantown Friends School and Philadelphia (a city that at the time seemed inordinately filled with Biddles and Cadwaladers whose claim to fame was the number of generations since the Mayflower that they had parked themselves on Wissahickon Drive) and arriving at San Francisco International Airport, two suitcases in hand, to board a bus to the campus. My college counselor had desperately tried to dissuade me from my California ambitions by informing me that the last GFS graduate to go west had joined the Moonies at Berkeley and never returned, but this had only made the whole venture even more tempting. As we drove south, I saw signs for Half Moon Bay above a glistening blue reservoir and wondered where I had been all my life. This was my coast.

So here I was in reverse, fifteen years later, driving north in a rental car and an ill-fitting borrowed suit, trying to look vaguely professional and rehearsing a few key declarations of principle in my head as I navigated my way downtown. It's a tiny city, San Francisco. I was an inveterate New Yorker by then, accustomed to colliding with a million people as I shoved my way through turnstiles to jump on the subway in a desperate attempt to get home in time to relieve the babysitter and make dinner before blood sugar levels plummeted and tears ensued. San Francisco seemed like a toy city that day, intimate and charming and somewhat inscrutable. The original Bank of San Francisco is now defunct, but at the time its headquarters sat in a grand pile on a distinguished street corner across from the Transamerica Pyramid, a reminder of the robber baron days when Leland Stanford and Collis P. Huntington ruled the city. In a big, sunny boardroom, six trustees were waiting for me. The head of the

4

board was a smiling man named Patrick Flannery, who was as honest and disarming that first day as he continued to be throughout the many disasters and tribulations that followed over the next five years. Next to him was the imperturbable Ellen Newman, daughter of the legendary Cyril Magnin, who, along with Mortimer Fleishhacker Sr. and Melvin Swig, had selected A.C.T. to be San Francisco's resident flagship theater back in 1966 when the company first arrived from Pittsburgh. Beside Ellen and her giant glasses was a small, wry man wearing a cowboy belt and a quick grin who introduced himself as Shep Pollack, and the lively and frank Joan Sadler, whose devotion to A.C.T.'s conservatory was legendary. I was captivated by the woman across the table from me, a striking woman with bright eyes and extraordinary chunks of jewelry around her neck and wrists. This was Sue Yung Li, a landscape architect who worked with the legendary Lawrence Halprin and who would become one of my saviors throughout my A.C.T. career. Finally there was Mary Metz, brilliant and businesslike, the former president of Mills College, with just a hint of a Louisiana accent and a seemingly endless supply of pointed questions. I began to reply.

A confession must be made right up front, one that will come as no surprise to those with whom I have even a passing acquaintance: I enjoy talking. Bruce Weber, in an interview with me in the *New York Times* some years later, labeled me a "world-class talker," and indeed talking is probably the only activity in the world at which I am world class. There are so many things in life I have no talent for: I cannot intuit anything on a computer, back the car into our garage, build a fire, remember the passwords for my internet accounts, read music, analyze data, follow sports, or read Brecht in the original. What I can do is set a trail of words in motion and watch them quickly find their way into complete sentences, paragraphs, speeches. I have never had a fear of speaking in public, because there is something about standing before a group that feels liberating to me. I love to extemporize, in front of an audience, about any number of things I care about, and theater and culture most particularly. So the talking part of my first A.C.T. interview was easy. I believe in the transformative power of theater, I have a great love of dramatic literature, I revere great actors and I am willing to fight for them, and I know what it is to run a cash-strapped theater and to fundraise as if my life depended on it. I also knew even then that, unlike many theater people for whom the freelance gypsy life is most congenial, being part of an institution suits my particular temperament. From my first day at CSC, the institution had functioned like an envelope into which I could place my appetites, my questions, my interests; it was the village well around which I could contextualize what I saw happening in the field and contribute to the larger art form. I shared this with the A.C.T. board. They asked questions. I replied. We laughed. We shook hands, and it was over. Two hours later I was back on the highway heading south toward my mother and my two-year-old. The two of them were so delighted with each other (as they have continued to be ever since), that the entire trip seemed worth it just for their pleasure, and I never expected things would go any further than that conversation in the boardroom of the Bank of San Francisco. I was in every possible way unlike the standard profile of a LORT (League of Resident Theatres) artistic director: I was young, female, classical in bent, noncommercial, and way too opinionated.

Two months and several visits later, the phone rang. It was Alan Stein, the gentle and heroic chair of the A.C.T. board. He wanted to see me at his apartment in New York; could I come up tomorrow? Within two minutes of my arrival at East 77th Street, he offered me the job. He was extremely sober about the current condition of the organization, and extremely passionate about its future. He said that if I'd commit to helping resurrect A.C.T., he'd be with me every step of the way. It had all happened so fast that I had no time for self-doubt, self-reflection, or even self-congratulation. I said yes. And so the adventure began.

CHAPTER 2

What Do You Have for Free?

B ritish director Emma Rice, who has created work with the experimental Kneehigh theater company in Cornwall for two decades, uses an expression about theatrical investigation that struck me as invaluable as soon as I heard it. Whether she is talking about a particular actor or about a piece of theater, she begins her investigation by asking, "What do you have for free?" Not "What is your type?" per se, but "What qualities exist innately in your being that others can instantly ascribe to you?" I teach a class to A.C.T.'s first-year master of fine arts students titled "Why Theater?" in which we borrow from Emma and begin by exploring what each of those young artists has "for free" before we move on to discuss what might stretch them beyond their natural givens. We then do an exercise about our hometowns, in which we try to imagine what a given community has for free, to try to determine what kind of theater might thrive there.

When I took the job at A.C.T. I thought I understood what San Francisco had, as it were, for free. This is critical when you are thinking about running a major arts institution. Despite the fact that the American theater is often in danger of becoming, in the words of Steppenwolf Artistic Director Martha Lavey, a kind of "McTheater" in which institutions across the country often produce the same five plays in the same packaging, I have always believed that great theater grows out of a very specific time and place, with specific artists in service to a specific audience. Repertoire is most interesting when it is determined by the unique geography, demographics, mood, and history of the given community.

After all, it was not a coincidence that A.C.T. ended up in San Francisco to begin with. When Bill Ball first conceived of the notion of a permanent company of classically trained actors committed to staging a diverse repertoire of plays to be produced on a large scale for a literate audience, he traveled across the country looking for the perfect home. Pittsburgh proved difficult because of power struggles with the Pittsburgh Playhouse; Chicago extended a hand, but the deal was never closed. It was San Francisco in 1967 that became Bill Ball's natural partner in crime. In his book *The Creation of an Ensemble*, John Wilk quotes the *Minneapolis Tribune*'s Mike Steele about why San Francisco proved to be the perfect match for A.C.T.: "It's a city of theatricality. Every street corner is a stage and every fourth person seems to be either a manic actor out of Genet or a street musician out of work. It's the obvious city for the American Conservatory Theater, America's most flamboyant regional theatre and one of its best. It reflects San Francisco exactly, erratically brilliant, vain, diverse, perverse, and very exciting." The Actor's Workshop founder Herbert Blau, in *The Impossible Theater*, described San Francisco in the fifties and sixties (with the arrogance and slightly patronizing tone of a transplanted New Yorker) as "a gilded boom town grown urban on a fissure . . . two great universities nearby, and a trolley college of high caliber; a great park of eclectic fauna; a Chinese ghetto which feels affluent and no conspicuous slums; sick comics in the bistros and a Bohemian Club of unregenerate squares . . . withal, a city reposeful and august . . . the old Pacific Union Club on Nob Hill, home of the railroad kings, lording it over the new arrivals: the students, the dockworkers, the doctors of the Kaiser Plan, the Hadassah ladies, the vagrants from the valleys, the junior executives of the new Playboy set, the Beats from Tangiers and North Platte, all the questing intellectuals . . . a city with a nervous graciousness, upholding a worldwide reputation for a culture it doesn't quite have . . . a city that is a myth, with the golden opportunity to live up to it." The audacity and elegance of the new American Conservatory Theater in the late sixties and early seventies matched both the appetites and nascent sophistication of San Franciscans, and elicited the kind of financial generosity necessary for a nonprofit venture of that scale to survive. During those initial years, San Franciscans fell in love with Bill Ball and he with them; Ball won their hearts with an unparalleled sixteen-play rotating repertory in the initial twenty-two weeks. As Ball told Wilk: "The idea was to have so much, such a splashy repertory that it was an undeniable experience. We had to dazzle our audience and overwhelm them."

Alas, despite its glorious beginnings, A.C.T. failed to create an infrastructure to match its ambitions, with the result that by the time Ball departed in the eighties, there was precious little to hold together the brilliant idea he had created. The man who adored casts of thousands and staged legendary curtain calls (called "walk-downs") at the end of each season (in which actors bowed in the costumes of one show and then madly changed into costumes for the next until the entire season's repertoire had been represented in one fabulous and continuously swirling bow) had been reduced to producing *The Gin Game* and other small-cast plays for an increasingly disaffected audience. The story of Ball's downfall is complex: He rarely engaged with his San Francisco fundraising group (originally called the California Theatre Foundation and later the California Association for the American Conservatory Theatre, or C.A.A.C.T.) in any substantive discussion about the direction the company was taking, because he viewed A.C.T. as a national theater and resisted outside input of any kind. Meanwhile he became more and more fanatic about his own power and need for control. This situation proved unsupportable, particularly when major foundation funding began to dry up, and according to all accounts, Ball became increasingly volatile, unpredictable, and isolated. Rumor had it that he locked Cyril Magnin, his largest and most passionate benefactor, out of the theater for alleged disloyalty, and that, nervous about the future, he had taken a large portion of an A.C.T. Ford Foundation grant and invested it in gold to create retirement accounts for himself and his trusted lieutenants. In 1986, the California Attorney General stepped in and forced his resignation. Critic Sylvie Drake described the end in her *Los Angeles Times* obituary for Ball in 1991: "Well-known bouts with booze and pills exacerbated [Ball's] intemperate personality and growing reclusiveness. By the early 1980s, the work at A.C.T. began to slip. So did the finances. And Ball had lost perspective on it all. He seemed no longer to differentiate between himself as an individual and the institution he had created, dismaying associates with infuriating behavior and alienating the very people who had invited him to San Francisco in the first place. In typically flamboyant (and prophetic) style, he abruptly announced his . . . resignation while staging a crucifixion scene." This final story may be apocryphal, but it was the beginning of a heartbreaking demise. In 1991, at the age of sixty, Ball died of an overdose in Los Angeles, "an apparent suicide."

Ball's successor, Edward Hastings, was a compassionate leader and an able director who mounted a major effort to move A.C.T. forward, diversifying the acting company, stimulating A.C.T.'s commitment to new work through the creation of Plays in Progress, building bridges with small local ensembles, stabilizing the finances, and staging major productions of American classics. But for many reasons, it was difficult to keep the ambitious dreams of A.C.T.'s beginnings alive.

By the time I arrived in the early nineties, A.C.T. was so complicated, so troubled, and so dysfunctional that I failed initially to grasp the depths of its paralysis. Ignoring its fraught past (and earthquake-destroyed building) for the moment, I focused instead upon the present day, and tried to envisage what A.C.T. still had for free by being housed in the very specific arts ecology that was the Bay Area in the late twentieth century. This exercise led to some disastrous assumptions that plagued my first year of programming, but it was not done without real thought. Outside of the hermetic bubble of A.C.T., here's what I assumed 1992 San Francisco had "for free," in no particular order:

- A tradition of physical comedy, clowning, and vaudeville dating from the San Francisco Mime Troupe's

10

beginnings in 1959 to the inception of the Pickle Family Circus in the mid seventies and the ongoing presence of such amazing clowns as Bill Irwin, Geoff Hoyle, Joan Mankin, Sharon Lockwood, and Jeff Raz.

- A love for the radical, aggressively acted work of such directors as Robert Woodruff at the Magic Theatre.
- A cultural pluralism that has permitted a wide range of ethnic and cultural traditions to be represented equally around town, from African drumming to klezmer music to Russian Orthodox liturgy to Filipino parades to Japanese tea ceremonies.
- Gay culture—I assumed the presence of a politically powerful gay culture that made its presence felt would be a major plus in programming a season.
- A European feel—I've always believed that it's easiest to make theater in a place where people can walk in off the street and find it. San Francisco's origins as a European-style city can still be felt in its urban planning and in the intimacy of its streets and sidewalks, to say nothing of its population of Russians, Irish, and Italians. It is a city where many people get around on foot or by bicycle. This seemed to me a helpful thing when building a theater community.
- A highly literate book-reading population.
- A love for the experimental and the multidisciplinary in performance, evidenced by the presence of such visionaries as George Coates (whose new take on the *Alice in Wonderland* story, *Right Mind*, had just opened at The Geary Theater before the earthquake brought the building to the ground), Chris Hardman, Lou Harrison, David Harrington, Anna Halprin, and more.
- A sense of pride in being three hours behind New York but always with an eye to the future, a city of endless technological and social revolution, looking to the East instead of the West.

Some of these assumptions proved in the long run to be true and valuable as guiding principles. Others turned out to be misleading. What didn't occur to me was that, although it had arrived in San Francisco as the brash, brilliant, and exciting new kid on the block, by the early nineties A.C.T. had become a bastion of culture, a somewhat intimidating monolith housed in a gilded structure out of another century. Its relationship to the city as a whole was oblique; from the beginning, Bill Ball wanted to create a national rather than a regional theater (hence the name "American Conservatory Theater" rather than "San Francisco Conservatory Theater"). Ball was grateful for local philanthropy, but his biggest support came from the Ford and Rockefeller foundations, and under his leadership A.C.T. became a self-contained entity within the cultural landscape of San Francisco. Ball brought his acting company with him from Pittsburgh, trained them in the confines of his own very private institution, and produced a repertoire heavy on classical literature without requiring much collaboration from the community at large. Despite the fact that Ed Hastings was an intensely generous community builder who helped spawn many smaller companies (including Turtle Island Ensemble, Asian American Theater Company, and Encore Theatre Company), it was startling to me when I arrived at A.C.T. to discover just how isolated the organization had become.

Trauma leaves its marks on a theater just as it does on a human being, and A.C.T.'s history was one of repeated glory followed by repeated trauma. By the time I arrived, the organization was twisted around its own pathologies like a strange family that has learned to live with its brilliant but transgressive father, its competitive angry siblings, and its wary jealous neighbors. It also seemed to be a very male institution. Few women had held positions of leadership at A.C.T. over the years; in addition to Ball, the power had been housed in the hands of such men as James McKenzie, Robert Goldsby, Allen Fletcher, and Ed Hastings. Some talented women directors had left their mark, including Elizabeth Huddle and Joy Carlin, but they were the exception rather than the rule. When I arrived, the atmosphere was grim. It was as if Daddy had killed himself, Uncle Ed had left town, and now the

12

potentially evil stepmother had arrived. No one had any idea what to make of me. I remember my first A.C.T. company meeting with horror: I walked into an immense studio in which the entire company, from actors to stagehands to stitchers to faculty members, had lined up to hear from the new artistic director. They greeted my words with complete silence and would barely meet my gaze as I looked around the room. It was clear that survival at A.C.T. had come to mean keeping one's head down so as not to make waves; everything was done by code, there were no policies on anything from maternity leave to sick days to parking, nor any clarity about how decisions were to be reached about play choices, casting, or academic admission. If the buzzword of the new millennium is transparency, the buzzword of A.C.T. in the nineties was secrecy. The very geography of the office space, a rabbit warren of small rooms inaccessible to each other and impossible to navigate, epitomized the culture in which I found myself when I first arrived, and the anxiety in the air was palpable.

It should be said at the outset that the recruitment process that led to my hire was anything but transparent. The board handled the search internally with great care, but very few people outside the small circle of the board had any say in my appointment or any knowledge of me or my work. When Producing Director James Haire, who had been with the company almost since its inception, was asked to give me a tour of the theater while I was in town for one of my interviews, he had no idea who I was or that I was a candidate for the artistic directorship of his own theater until Joan Sadler called him later and inquired, "What did you think of our girl?" To which Jim replied, "What girl?" The person most opposed to my appointment was supposed to be my closest colleague, Managing Director John Sullivan. I discovered halfway into my negotiations that during the search process John had proposed a new organizational scheme whereby he would be named general director and supervise two stage directors (Anne Bogart and Robert Woodruff), who would report to him. The board had considered but ultimately rejected his proposal. John had chosen to stay on as managing director regardless, a disastrous decision from my point of view, and probably from his.

He was, perhaps without quite knowing it, deeply invested in my failure, and my year's "collaboration" with him was among the hardest of my professional life.

Without giving me any real guidelines, Sullivan announced at our first meeting, in November 1991, that I would have to have the following season announced and budgeted by January. If I had been less naïve and compliant I would have refused; it takes at least six months to understand an organization and its culture well enough to begin to make remotely informed decisions about the work ahead. But I said yes, and made every mistake I could possibly have made.

It all went back to what I thought we had "for free."

In celebration of an artist whose work had had a dramatic impact on Bay Area theater during his distinguished career at the Magic Theatre (and to please Sullivan), I asked director Robert Woodruff whether he would like to be part of my first season at A.C.T. This seemed like an obvious way to bring younger, edgier audiences into the A.C.T. fold, to salute the city's cultural history, and to give us license to do more adventurous work. Woodruff eagerly accepted and chose a classic I loved that had strong meaning for him at the time: Webster's Jacobean masterpiece *The Duchess of Malfi*.

To honor the company of actors who had meant so much to A.C.T. over the past decades, I found roles for many of them in a 1930s American comedy I had always admired, *Dinner at Eight*, and in a new translation of Molière's *The Learned Ladies* that Richard Seyd had directed very successfully for me in New York. These two plays would give me a chance to see how I related to a whole raft of A.C.T. talent (including Peter Donat, Sydney Walker, Richard Butterfield, and Frances Lee McCain) and to do a few comedies on the grand scale that Bill Ball had espoused and adored.

To share my own personal aesthetic and theatrical training with my new audience, I chose to commission a new Timberlake Wertenbaker translation of Euripides' *Hecuba*, which was to star Olympia Dukakis in the title role. And to appease those who felt my tastes were not popular or American enough, I agreed to produce Ken Ludwig's Broadway farce *Lend Me a Tenor*, which was not a play that particularly spoke to me but which I thought might appeal to the opera lovers in San Francisco and balance out my Jacobean drama.

And finally, because it never occurred to me that Strindberg's dark psychological landscape might be a bizarre way to usher in a new theatrical era, I chose to begin my tenure at A.C.T. with Paul Walsh's new version of *Creditors*, which we had done so successfully at CSC the season before.

All this was thought through and decided on planes and phone calls between November 1991, when I was hired, and March 1992, when the season was announced. I was still living in New York, still running CSC, and still raising a two-year-old. It was hardly the calmest and most propitious way to plan an inaugural season. Not realizing until I had accepted the job how disastrous A.C.T.'s cash flow was and how complex the union contracts and administrative budgets were, I allowed myself to be railroaded into decisions that had far-reaching consequences. Many of these decisions were shepherded by a shadow marketing consultant whose salary was nowhere to be found on A.C.T.'s official payroll but whose Denver-based office seemed to be generating whatever thinking was going on about how to introduce new artistic leadership to A.C.T. and how to communicate with the audience. "If your theater were a vegetable, what kind might it be?" was one of her first questions to me. I think it was this encounter that led to my ongoing antipathy for consultants and my resistance to the kind of marketing speak so ubiquitous in the field today.

If I was surprised by what I discovered, so was the theater community when they learned that a thirty-two-year-old neophyte from New York had been hired to run one of the five largest companies in America, a once great institution with a theater full of earthquake rubble, a troubled school, a negative cash flow, a dwindling audience, and a traumatic history. Why did A.C.T. choose to gamble on me? Trustee Joan Sadler recently shared with me the letter she wrote to the full board that fall, in which she articulated her unqualified support for their candidate (me), not just "because she was capable, talented, experienced, committed to excellence—they all were. But because for A.C.T., with the special characteristics of its history and its special needs of the moment, she seemed uniquely suited, offering unusual strengths, skills, and understanding. First, because she communicated immediately the kind of passion, the 'fire in the belly' that will be a critical factor for us in our daunting task of capturing the public's imagination and rallying its support. . . . Furthermore, because she recognizes A.C.T.'s unique role . . . with its dedication to training and ensemble, and she is committed to furthering and enhancing both. . . . Thirdly, because she recognized immediately the particular challenge and opportunities offered by the enormous diversity of the Bay Area." It was a brave and unpredictable choice that this committed but beleaguered board was making. And San Francisco had little idea what it was getting.

Not that I have ever been secretive about my tastes and desires. I am passionate about complex dramatic literature, heightened text, big ideas, deeply invested acting, beautiful visuals, and international collaborations. I am woefully ignorant of pop culture, have little appetite for television, and have kept the remotest track of popular music only in recent years because my son is a musician. I realize this is a terrible admission, one that today would most likely disqualify me for the very job I have been doing for over twenty years. But I came of age at a time when live theater was meant to do something different from pop culture, and when success was measured in ways other than simply the number of people served. The current punishing fiscal climate and the challenge of attracting new audiences has led to a hunger for theater to aim more and more closely for the commercial center, in terms of subject matter, casting, and methods of outreach. The arts have come to rely on metrics that measure success according to the cost per person of producing a given play or mounting a given art exhibition. Obviously, broadening audiences in an era of niche marketing and the ability to self-curate any artistic experience is hard. But as Ezra Pound famously said, "Literature is news that stays news," and the converse can also be the case: those pop-culture phenomena that may seem on the cutting edge of cool one year may be obsolete the next. If part of the mandate of the nonprofit theater is to nurture and cultivate that which may have lasting value, I believe it's worth being cautious about the endlessly seductive pull of the trendy and the transient. Looking back on my years at A.C.T., the thing I am proudest of is that we have for the most part managed to consistently fill a large house by programming juicy literature with great actors, rather than by chasing every passing trend. But it's certainly been a long hard fight, and it's not over yet.

CHAPTER 3

The Postfounder Era

My generation of artistic directors sits somewhere between the visionary founders of the regional theater movement and the often refreshingly anti-institutional independent artists who have found homes either in the commercial or experimental theater worlds in recent years. We were idealistic enough to believe in a commitment to acting ensembles, classical repertoire, large-scale new work whose goal was not Broadway, subscription audiences with a love of variety, and federal funding for the arts. We were not disillusioned enough yet to despair of institutions and to hold the nonprofit movement accountable for the lack of access and adventure in the field, a charge one hears repeatedly (and often fairly) today. After all, the founding notion of the National Endowment for the Arts was that the future of a democracy is interlaced with the future of its art forms, and that to nurture the arts there must be a subsidy that protects risk and keeps artists' vision focused on the long-term growth of the art form rather than the short-term profitability of any given piece of work. Bill Ball articulated this beautifully in the souvenir program printed for A.C.T.'s inaugural season in Pittsburgh in 1965:

> The American Conservatory Theater has been founded as
> a non-profit, educational institution to bring together the

finest directors, authors, playwrights, and educators in the theatre arts. Its immediate goal is to awaken in these theatre artists a maximum versatility and expressiveness. And as they approach these goals, we hope that their audiences will be provided with a banquet rather than merely another dessert. . . .

The American Conservatory Theater exists not only for the benefit of the artist—but also for the benefit of the audience. In recent years, the metropolitan theatre audience has become more and more an audience of hit-followers. The thoughtful theatre lover is offered little in the way of a sustained, meaningful repertoire. The thirteen plays which comprise the first season of The American Conservatory Theater encompass every major dramatic epoch in the history of the theatre.

Ball understood that resident theaters were given nonprofit status because they were held in the community trust, and at the beginning, he took that charge very seriously.

I recently reread Arena Stage co-founder and longtime producing director Zelda Fichandler's words, written in a letter to the U.S. Department of the Treasury in the fifties (and later read into the Congressional Record), arguing that theaters should be accorded 501(c)(3) tax-exempt status: "Once we made the choice to produce our plays not to recoup an investment but to recoup some corner of the universe for our understanding and enlargement, we entered into the same world as the university, the library, the museum, and the church, and became, like them, an instrument of civilization." So beautifully put. The fact that many large-scale institutional theaters today have become roadhouses to incubate commercial productions headed for Broadway is a sad diminution of the original notion of the nonprofit theater, but in the face of declining contributions and audiences, some argue that this is the only means of survival.

I will never be entirely sure why the board of A.C.T. decided to risk everything on me, but I suspect it was that, on some deep level,

I shared DNA with Bill Ball: I believed in the uniqueness of A.C.T.'s mission, and I knew it was worth fighting for. Most important of all, A.C.T. was about lifelong learning. That's the piece of it I loved. The founding definition of A.C.T. stated:

> The American Conservatory Theater combines the concept of resident repertory theater with the classic concept of continuous training, study, and practice as an integral and inseparable part of the performer's life. . . .
>
> Our goal is to awaken in the theater artist his maximum versatility and expressiveness.

I hoped *her* versatility and expressiveness would be awakened as well.

Ball's company of forty-plus actors was engaged in constant artistic growth, taking and teaching classes while performing a repertoire of up to twenty-three plays in the first full San Francisco season. Modeled on the Comédie Française, A.C.T. was built around a large rotating repertoire, a permanent acting company, and a conservatory in which actors studied and students acted. The conservatory quickly became a major training program in which young actors apprenticed at the feet of master actors while performing alongside them onstage. As the critic Martin Gottfried explained it, "[Bill Ball] is training them to discipline flamboyance and then apply it to productions that he stages with all the devices of grand opera, ballet, mime, and magical full-throated theater. Combining these primary theater colors with an unrelenting demand for such basics as voice control, diction, movement, and facial expression, and pumping them up with the inspirational effect of his own genius, he blends directorial creativity with respect for a playwright's purposes."

The idea of a theater that sustained not only a permanent acting company but a multi-year actor training program was thrilling to me. This was how the ancient art of theater had always been carried forward. Educated actors and an educated audience meant the opportunity to do challenging work in a sophisticated way. San

Francisco's proud separation from the entertainment industry in Los Angeles freed A.C.T. from the oft-bemoaned requirement of hiring television and film stars to populate its stage: Bay Area audiences pride themselves on knowing good theater acting when they see it, and Ball had trained his audience to recognize talent. So although I was sad to leave the vast talent pool that was New York, there seemed to be the potential in San Francisco for a sustained and serious theatrical exploration.

As actor Ray Reinhardt, a member of the original A.C.T. acting company, explained, "No repertory company has been able to make it in New York over a length of time. APA [Association of Production Artists] did have some wonderful seasons, but the pressure becomes too much. It's more and louder and faster and funnier and—I don't know. The temptation is always there for other things. . . . I'll tell you why not Los Angeles. Obviously, in Los Angeles every actor would be going to Bill and every director saying, 'Oh, just one day out, just one day's shooting on a film, one day on a television program.' It would be impossible. Up in San Francisco, it is a very good choice because you are away from the commercial pressure. You're in a cosmopolitan city. It's still, as far as . . . social living is concerned . . . perhaps the best city in the United States to be."

In addition, the fact that San Francisco is an extremely small town compared to New York, Chicago, and Los Angeles makes cross-disciplinary collaboration far easier and quite natural: over the years at A.C.T. we have collaborated with such composers and musicians as Kronos Quartet, Chanticleer, Rova Saxophone Quartet, Nathaniel Stookey, Bonfire Madigan Shive, and Tracy Chapman; such dancers as Pascal Molat and Muriel Maffre of San Francisco Ballet, and Nol Simonse and Joe Goode; and local visual artists and video makers— all because we share the same town and, to some extent, the same philosophy of making art. We also share the frontier spirit that has historically characterized Northern California; after all, this is where the Gold Rush began, where Levi's were born, where many social movements, from black power to feminism to ecology to gay pride to ethnic studies to social media first found fertile ground in which to grow.

One of my happy discoveries when I took the job at A.C.T. was that San Francisco was the least corporate place I had ever been, and the kind of hierarchy originally envisioned by the NEA as good business practice for the arts, with organization charts for theaters and museums that looked like those of banks and corporations, seemed somehow less applicable in Northern California. A.C.T.'s precarious history as a one-man band with very little in the way of corporate structure or governance was also its saving grace: it had never become an institution in search of a mission; it was, rather, a mission in desperate search of a sustaining financial structure. In many ways, twenty years later, I feel as if we are still searching for that elusive formula whereby a thousand-seat theater company can produce serious and exciting work while at the same time developing new plays and sustaining a highly regarded training program in the most expensive real estate market in the world. I discovered early on that survival is never something one can or should count on; each play, each season, each young actor in training has to be its own event, its own journey, as if it might well be the last. This was the lesson of the earthquake.

CHAPTER 4

Urban Archaeology

"It's like seeing a dear friend in intensive care," actor Raye Birk said about The Geary Theater as it lay in ruins after the 1989 Loma Prieta earthquake. Indeed, my first glimpse of the destruction was an awesome sight. I can't remember upon which of my early visits to A.C.T. I was taken inside the ruined building, but I do remember how astonishing it was. And beautiful, in a kind of horrifying way. Truth be told, in addition to my love of talking, I love ruins. In fact, since the second grade I had longed to imitate Heinrich Schliemann, excavator of Troy, by reading Homer and finding lost cities on the plains of Greece and Turkey. I majored in ancient Greek at Stanford with the express purpose of preparing myself for this lifelong adventure, after having spent my teenage years in the Four Corners region of the American Southwest, digging up Anasazi ruins in the baking heat under the guidance of an archaeologist named Arch from the University of New Mexico, on whom, I recall, I had an enormous crush. I loved the puzzle-making aspect of archaeology—the process of finding isolated clues that, if pieced together correctly, could yield lost information about human behavior from remote times and places. In high school I had interned at the University of Pennsylvania Museum of Archaeology and Anthropology just when the rich cache of artifacts from the Ban Chiang excavation in Thailand was being shipped back to the museum. My best friend, Nora Winkelman, and I spent hours and hours in a dark basement piecing potsherds into recognizable shapes in order to help the team leaders explore the very first evidence of domesticated rice in history, one broken pot at a time. It was thrilling—our own private detective story. There was something about the mundane exercise of reconnecting broken pottery that allowed my imagination to run wild, and that sensation came back to me in powerful waves as I beheld the ruins of The Geary Theater in the fall of 1991.

The stories of that fateful October day were already legion. George Coates's experimental production *Right Mind*, a version of *Alice in Wonderland*, had just opened to strong reviews. It was the year of the all–Bay Area World Series, and anyone in town who could snare a ticket had rushed to Candlestick Park to watch the San Francisco Giants play the Oakland A's. The game was about to begin. The city was calm. The Geary was momentarily quiet—A.C.T.'s stage crew had just left the theater for the dinner break before coming back to set up for the 8:00 PM performance. The offices across the street were humming with activity, and the many children enrolled in the Young Conservatory were arriving for their afternoon classes. As often seems the case on days of epic disaster, the skies were blue and clear on October 17, 1989: a gorgeous afternoon promising a happy ending. At 5:04 PM the rumbling began. Still captured on ABC news footage is Al Michaels, in the midst of rallying listeners about the upcoming World Series game, slowly realizing that an earthquake of massive proportions was taking place. Within minutes, a span of the Bay Bridge had collapsed, the Marina district lay in disarray, a two-decker freeway in Oakland had crumbled onto itself, crushing cars and trapping commuters, buildings all down the Peninsula (including many in the Quad of my beloved Stanford University) had been shaken beyond repair, and the auditorium of the magnificent 1910 Beaux-Arts Geary Theater was covered in rubble.

Bill Ball, ever the stubborn impresario, had been warned by the San Francisco Fire Department for years that the accumulation of twenty years of costumes squeezed underneath the stage of the theater in a makeshift costume shop was a fire hazard that had to be resolved. He remained unconcerned. At the same time, board members had been warned that the unreinforced brick wall at the back of the stage could present a major hazard in the event of an earthquake. But in the random manner of most disasters, the culprit in the case of A.C.T.'s destruction was a loose fan housing on the roof that fell through the ceiling, bringing down the whole gilded proscenium with it. In an instant, the cables attaching the lighting grid to the ceiling moved one way and the arch itself moved another, tearing apart the surface of the proscenium like an orange peel and sending massive amounts of rubble tumbling down into the house in huge waves of destruction. It was a miracle that no one was in the theater: only a few hours later, hundreds of people would likely have been hurt. (Interestingly, the biggest destruction lay in Row G, the critics' seats. As someone who has never been a darling of the press, the irony of this was not lost on me.)

By the end of the twenty-second temblor, there was sunshine pouring through the roof of The Geary, the air was thick with plaster dust, and the extent of the destruction was impossible to gauge. Producing Director James Haire describes walking across Geary Street in trepidation and trying to see through the swirling dust to the damage within the theater. The first concern of A.C.T.'s management was to make sure that no one had been hurt and that the children in the Young Conservatory were reunited with their parents. Once that was accomplished, a kind of numbness must have set in. As streams of shell-shocked people made their way across town, walking all the way to downtown from Candlestick Park or trying to reach loved ones across the Bay, it became clear to the artists and management at A.C.T. that their playhouse had sustained devastating damage. Alan Stein, then chair of our board of trustees, likes to say that this was the moment he got to utter the immortal words "The show must go on!" as the staff gathered at Ed Hastings's house on Lake Street and tried to determine how best to proceed.

Within a mere few weeks, A.C.T. was in diaspora, and it would continue to be so for the next six years. It was a major turning point for the company, a moment that could easily have ended Ball's great experiment. But somehow in adversity the institution rallied: indeed, the earthquake quickly revealed the suppleness and survival instinct that has always lain at the heart of A.C.T. Alternative performing spaces were found, schedules altered, audience members notified, and, miraculously, the 1989–90 season continued to unfold. Perhaps because 1989 was a year of political eruptions and explosions all over the globe, the magnitude of the Loma Prieta earthquake barely penetrated my consciousness in New York: I had a needy infant and was more aware of the fall of the Berlin Wall and the exhaustion of early motherhood than the distress of Northern California. In fact, when Romanian dictator Nicolae Ceaușescu was shot on December 25, 1989, and my friend director Andrei Belgrader called the next morning to inform me of the news, all I could think about was the miraculous fact that my three-month-old baby had just slept through the night for the first time.

Thus, when I arrived at A.C.T. in October 1991 for my second or third interview, it was a shock to discover the extent of the earthquake-induced damage. The Geary lay in silent ruin, like a kind of modern-day Pompeii: nothing had been touched since 5:04 PM on October 17, 1989. The atmosphere inside was eerie and magical. The callboard backstage, covered in dust, announced the evening's schedule and the actors' calls; the stage manager's coffee cup and prompt script lay in waiting offstage right; wardrobe racks and prop tables were readied—it was as if the ghosts of A.C.T. past could rise up at any moment and begin a performance. Because of fears of asbestos, crews had stayed out of the building for months after the event. When the wreckage was finally surveyed, it was discovered to be extensive and structural. Ironically, the much maligned back wall with its unreinforced brick sustained virtually no damage. But the tumbling proscenium arch tore away the fabric of the ceiling and exposed the heavily damaged roof and interior structure of the building. Photographs and video shot right after the quake reveal the vulnerable bones and tissue of this stunning and delicate building, whose original architects (Bliss & Faville) had lavished loving attention on every corner, including delicately molded gold pineapples surrounding the high, round dome and repeated patterns of rosettes dotting the proscenium arch.

All of us who make theater are forced to acknowledge with every closing night how transient our art form is; nevertheless, it was startling to realize how transient the performance space itself can be. The Geary was one of the last fully operational hemp houses in America, its backstage walls lined with a rope system designed to raise and lower scenery by hand. The names of the many flymen of its storied history were graffitied on the walls; pieces of scenery and extraneous props were piled high in the corners; the life and breath of a thousand actors still permeated the air. I was overwhelmed by the beauty of this contemporary ruin. Perhaps because I had spent such a large portion of my younger life immersed in ancient Greek culture and traveling to sites like Epidaurus and Delphi, there was something both moving and strangely familiar about this semi-destroyed theater: it made me feel oddly at home.

The catastrophe had escalated the decision of Ed Hastings to leave A.C.T. He wisely felt that whoever was charged with rebuilding the theater should be committed to working in it afterwards, and that was more of an extended time commitment than he was interested in making at that stage of his long and successful career. Early plans for the reconstruction of The Geary called for a wholesale reimagining of A.C.T.'s operations: the corner property, owned by the theater but currently housing a greasy-spoon diner, a car rental business, and, upstairs, A.C.T.'s box office operations, was envisioned as a new unified campus that would contain the institution's offices, studios, and school. The architect behind this original inspiration, Joseph Esherick, was a visionary, but it quickly became clear to the theater's shaken board that it would be a monumental enough effort to rebuild The Geary without taking on an entire new institutional complex. In a sense this was an enormous shame, and twenty years later we are still wrestling with the imperative that an institution as complex and multifaceted as A.C.T. needs a central campus where its original vision of training, performance, and community-based education can truly be realized. Indeed, this is the work of the next decade.

It was clear that rebuilding The Geary was to become the top priority of whoever was chosen to be the new artistic director of A.C.T. For me this was the most exciting aspect of the job, and the most terrifying. I was a downtown director, steeped in alternative performance spaces and accustomed for the past six years of my career to staging plays on the intimate thrust of CSC's theater. I was a relative stranger to the kind of Broadway proscenium house that The Geary represented and had never imagined that an old-fashioned nineteenth-century theater would become my most treasured artistic home. The learning curve was going to be incredibly steep. Again, it astounds me in retrospect that I was selected for this task, given my lack of experience with building projects or even, indeed, with proscenium theaters; I continue to realize how lucky I was to encounter a board willing to bet on my potential rather than my résumé. I was also braver in those days. I was out around town raising funds to rebuild The Geary before I had any real working knowledge of what the restoration would entail or what kind of work the theater was destined to house. I suppose it is often true that what you don't know saves you: if I had had any inkling in November 1991 of the vast challenges that lay ahead, I would not have accepted Alan Stein's job offer with such a light heart. I had to raise almost $30 million in less than two years without an identified donor base or even a proper capital campaign plan, and I had to do this at the same time I was radically changing the aesthetic of the organization, reorganizing the school, rethinking the entire administrative structure, stretching my wings in new and surprising ways as a director, and raising a child. Maybe my naïveté was what saved me.

CHAPTER 5

The Issue of Children

I was raised by a working mother and a liberated father and was in high school during the height of 1970s feminism, so it had never occurred to me that of all fields least friendly to child rearing, theater had to be at the top of the list. I was running CSC when I got pregnant with Lexie, and I suppose it was the ignorance of youth that prevented my husband, Anthony, and me from making any sensible plans about how we were going to raise this child in the midst of our already crazy lives. Lexie was only ten days old when I started rehearsals for a double bill of Harold Pinter's *The Birthday Party* and *Mountain Language*, with the great man himself in attendance. This project had been in the works for some time; Pinter's agent, Judy Daish, had been phoning anxiously all summer to ask, "Have you had that child yet?" in her baritone smoke-filled voice, while I reassured her that the impending baby would in no way compromise our upcoming production. When rehearsals commenced, Lexie was hidden in the back dressing room of CSC, sleeping peacefully in her carry cot until feeding time, at which point Jean Stapleton, who was playing Meg, would sidle up to me and whisper, "The princess needs you now," and I would disappear for a brief spell to feed the baby. I had been told that Pinter was not fond of babies, so I made sure to keep Lexie well out of sight when he was at rehearsal. I thought I was handling the secret well, so it was astonishing when one day, while advising actor Peter Riegert about a particularly wrenching scene between the political prisoner and his mother, Pinter marched backstage, picked up the sleeping baby in her cot, deposited her (still sleeping) on the table in the midst of the rehearsal room, and said to Peter: "This is your baby. You have been needlessly prevented by the regime from ever seeing her. In fact, you will never see her. *Never*. Now play the scene." A startled Riegert quickly found the despair Pinter was looking for, and he and Lexie have been good friends ever since. When the Pinter plays opened at CSC in the fall of 1989, Pinter sent his friend Lauren Bacall to give a report of the proceedings, and the only picture I have left of that evening is "You Know How to Whistle" herself cooing at baby Lexie after the show and pronouncing herself delighted by the entire evening.

CSC had a tiny staff and was two blocks away from my apartment, so I could bring my daughter to work if necessary and (to some extent) set my own rules. The managing directors during my tenure at CSC included Ellen Novack and Patricia Taylor, both of whom had children themselves and were deeply supportive of working mothers, so I never felt I had to defend my decision to have a child and remain in the theater. Being a mother at A.C.T. was altogether a different matter. This was an enormous and complicated institution in which women were, as I have said, relatively absent (with the exception of dedicated employees like Dianne Prichard and Maureen McKibben, who mothered the actors and students with unflagging devotion), and staff children were virtually unheard-of. There was no precedent, and no template for how to behave. Meanwhile, Anthony was a full-time law student at UC Berkeley's Boalt Hall, competing with mostly younger students who certainly had no children. So we just made it up as we went along.

The subsequent eighteen years witnessed an often hilarious and endlessly complicated stream of nannies that became part of the fragile system we jury-rigged to keep our chaotic working and home lives together. Someday perhaps we should write a sitcom about our child-care adventures, which included a fanatic vegan who hid our defrosting hamburger meat under the sink and was consistently late to work because she "didn't believe in the tyranny of time," a narcoleptic Turkish woman who spent most of her working day fast asleep on our living room couch, and a wannabe rapper who blared her latest works from her car's CD player while the children cowered in the backseat with their hands covering their ears. We had a student of Marxism from Berkeley who read Lenin's "What Is to Be Done?" while feeding Nick, and a Southern pastry chef who taught Lexie to make perfect pie dough; we had a compulsive shopper who spent her whole salary on new sheets and towels, and a wise older woman who read the children Victorian stories and brought a big dress-up box to work every day. Throughout it all, Anthony and I shared the joys and tribulations of our mad lives with our two intelligent and often amused children, who were articulate enough to report back their child-care misadventures on a daily basis. I'm certain that if I hadn't had a remarkably patient and intelligent husband who happened to be a superb cook, and children in whom I delighted, I never would have survived the vicissitudes and setbacks of running a theater like A.C.T. There is nothing like a sweet face smiling up at you as you read your bad review in the morning to provide reassurance that you haven't completely failed in the world.

But in so many ways I knew I could never compete with my male and/or childless colleagues, who could jump on a plane at a moment's notice to see a show they'd heard about or an actor who was receiving attention halfway across the country; my rehearsals always had to finish in time to relieve the babysitter, and sleep was in short supply. It was also clear to me, from the moment I arrived in San Francisco, that the way I was written about in the press would have been different if I'd been a man. No one could wait to prove that this little girl was ill-equipped for the job. When I look at photographs of myself from that first year, I am astonished at how I dressed, in severely tailored suits that had nothing to do with my personality or my taste. I must have been desperately trying to look like I had a degree of authority that internally I felt I lacked.

So I was grateful for every encounter with, and encouragement from, the women who had come before me: producer Lucille Lortel, who at age eighty (when I met her) had more appetite for theatrical adventure than people a third her age; JoAnne Akalaitis, whose imagination captivated me as soon as I moved to New York and who took me under her wing and supported me early on; Women's Project Theater founder Julia Miles, who taught me how to develop new plays; founder and director of La MaMa E.T.C. Ellen Stewart, who had a genius for rallying audiences to embrace unusual work; Manhattan Theatre Club's Lynne Meadow, who urged me to become an artistic director; and Fran Smythe, who chaired the board of CSC and took a huge leap by hiring me as artistic director when I was twenty-seven and knew nothing.

Much has been written about the paucity of female voices in the contemporary theater, and about how rarely stories by and about women dominate. Yet it was only in the process of writing this book that I began to realize how long it actually took me to stop playing at being a man and to acknowledge my own personal point of view on the world and on the work. The juggling act required of female artists in the theater, particularly those in positions of authority, is acute, and our failures are often seen as failures of our entire gender. We have little power to fall back on. One of my first experiences as a young director came back to haunt me: When I returned from England to the United States in 1981, I brought back a pile of plays I wanted to direct, including Steven Berkoff's classically inspired *Greek*, which I managed to persuade L.A. Theatre Works to let me stage. When Berkoff himself arrived on the scene two weeks into rehearsal, after I had cast, designed, and prepared the entire production, I was suddenly relegated to driver and junior acting coach, while the great man took over and directed his play. The producer said nothing. I remember Berkoff asking me in extremely patronizing tones whether I would like to warm up the cast before he began work. His behavior was never questioned; I was simply supposed to be a good girl, accept the authority of the great man, and support his wishes. I realized then that I could never take for granted that it would be assumed I knew what I was doing. I would have to prove that, again and again.

In the early days at A.C.T., I was often quizzed about why my choice of repertoire had a "feminist agenda," when I knew full well that if I did a season of Mamet and Shakespeare no one would ever accuse me of having a male agenda. I watched female students in our school struggle to take center stage, and I thought long and hard about power and how uneasily it is granted to women. I also learned how women personalize failure, and how hard it is for us to be resilient in the face of a doubting culture that rarely believes we have it in us to succeed at the highest levels.

I have given a lot of thought to the live/work conflict of working mothers in the theater, as I try to support my younger female staff members in their efforts to raise children on the schedule and uncertainty of a theatrical life. When I look into their eyes, I remember the incredible exhaustion of trying to get through a day that often begins at dawn with tearful babies and ends at midnight with tearful actors after a rocky tech rehearsal or first preview. So many times during those early years, I felt like a guilty failure for leaving home after dinner to go back to the theater while my toddler son stood on the front porch and howled with his arms stretching out toward my disappearing car (a true drama queen, he!). Many evenings I would call my own mother in tears and worry that my children would begin to think that the nanny was their mother. ("Don't worry, they'll figure it out," she always reassured me.) If I hadn't had as my own role model a mother who worked throughout my upbringing and managed to be remarkably present and engaged as a mother at the same time, I'm not sure I would have attempted it. I kept her good humor at the back of my mind on the occasions of maternal failure, when in my haste I sent Lexie to the Jewish Community Center preschool with a ham sandwich for lunch (and received a note back in her lunchbox alerting me to my faux pas) or missed her starring role in the Shabbat service while other mothers turned up with homemade challah. ("Just tell them you don't compete on that level," my mother was fond of advising me.) Attempts to separate my roles as mother and artistic director were rarely successful and often yielded comic results, as when I went to a photo shoot for *Hecuba* wearing an expensive borrowed "Grecian" gown and proceeded to lactate all over it because I hadn't nursed Nick on time. This was the same small boy who had been in utero and ready to emerge while we were casting our epic production of *Angels in America*; my casting director, Meryl Shaw, famously called me between contractions while I was in labor to make sure that she could issue offers to the actors before I gave birth. So it went. In the days before cell phones it was especially hair-raising; I still remember with horror a board retreat during my first season, in which I was being excoriated for *The Duchess of Malfi*, when I suddenly realized there was no one to pick up Lexie from child care at six o'clock; unable to reach Anthony, and panicking that my sweet three-year-old daughter would be left wandering on Arguello Street, I interrupted the meeting to find a pay phone and beg my assistant, Larry, to go fetch her, earning the opprobrium of both my board and the JCC for months afterwards. Now that my children have grown up, it is almost impossible for me to figure out how I and they managed to survive those years in one piece, but we did.

Both of my children were weaned on the theater and grew up within its institutional embrace, riding the waves of euphoria and despair with their mother almost instinctively. (I am somewhat ashamed to admit that whenever an obituary was read at our breakfast table, the children would immediately inquire whether that person was a member of A.C.T.'s Prospero Society, the group of donors who commit planned gifts to the theater after their deaths.) I was constantly reassured by my friend Veronica's dictum: "Just remember that the days are long, but the years are short." My own counsel to young women in the field who get discouraged and are tempted to give up is that a career is long and children are young for a very short time. It's worth sticking it out during those chaotic sleepless few years, because in the long run, if you stay with it, you may have a career that will sustain and nurture you later on.

Interestingly, I never thought about my struggles and compromises as "women's problems"; I always thought they were *my* problems.

I tried not to share these problems with anyone else, as clearly they were mine to solve and they only made me vulnerable to attack. It has only been in recent years that I have begun to pick my head up and realize that the challenges of being a woman in this field are serious and continue unabated. Indeed, few of the women directors I knew and admired in New York in the eighties (particularly those with children) have gone on to run major theaters (which one might have expected to be the trajectory, as it has been with our male colleagues), and I have slowly begun to understand the depth of the gender-disparity issue in the American theater.

Still, when A.C.T. Executive Director Ellen Richard returned from a League of Resident Theatres (LORT) conference in the fall of 2012 and informed me that the percentage of women running LORT theaters had not increased in the past twenty-five years, I was completely taken aback. How could that be? There are huge numbers of women in the lower echelons of the theater—directors, writers, administrators. Why were they not making it to the top? The answer to this question is complex and will require serious study. Indeed, A.C.T. recently entered into a partnership with the Wellesley Centers on Women to undertake comprehensive research on this subject. Clearly there are a number of factors at play: For one thing, as I have already mentioned, having children is extremely challenging when you are living a life in the theater, a problem exacerbated by long hours and low pay. In addition, the two major search firms in charge of hiring artistic and executive directors in the United States are run by middle-aged white men, who perhaps replicate themselves in their search lists. (It astonished me that in June 2014, when the Women's Project in New York was seeking a new artistic director, its board immediately contacted one of these two men to lead the search, instead of seeking out a female headhunter who might have had a better track record in recruiting female leadership.) Furthermore, I would hazard that boards unwittingly play a role in the paucity of women leaders. This is a difficult thread to tease out, and leads to the larger and often thorny issue of nonprofit governance in the arts. American nonprofit theaters are led by boards of directors who are responsible for their fiscal health; because this is a country with little government subsidy for the arts, a theater rises and falls on the generosity and tenacity of its board. Theater boards tend to be comprised of individuals who have been successful in their communities and have a desire to give back by supporting a civic organization. These are not necessarily individuals with a deep knowledge of theater, yet in addition to fiscal oversight, the primary responsibility of a board of directors is to hire the leadership of the organization.

So by what criteria are those hiring decisions made? The disturbing truism is that men are typically hired on their *potential* and women on their *résumés* (a practice thankfully not employed by A.C.T.'s board when hiring me). As long as that is the case, it is no wonder that theater boards hire men far more often than women. No résumé can adequately measure an individual's ability to engage with a community, appetite for public speaking, imagination and resilience in tough times, or, most important, aesthetic and artistry. So when looking for an artistic director, boards tend to rely on a given director's track record in the commercial theater, where things like a *New York Times* review and proximity to celebrity are comfortable metrics. Again and again, interesting women get passed over for artistic director jobs because they have fewer such credits and relationships to their name, yet these are often the artists who would be most adept at charting a long-term relationship with an audience, investing deeply in local artists, and sustaining interesting work over time. Furthermore, it seems to be a commonly held assumption that men are better fundraisers than women. Perhaps this goes back to the days of solicitation on the golf course, but I am here to tell you that being nine months pregnant and walking up a steep San Francisco hill to a fundraiser is also an effective means of encouraging donor participation! In hindsight, I recognize that it wasn't insignificant that A.C.T.'s early board of trustees included two formidable women leaders, Edith Markson and Joan Sadler, whose torch was carried later by powerful and compassionate women chairs—Toni Rembe, Cheryl Sorokin, Kaatri Grigg, Mary Metz, and Nancy Livingston—and that the search committees that hired both Ellen Richard and me included strong female representation.

When Sheryl Sandberg, chief operating officer of Facebook, published her best-selling book on women's leadership, *Lean In*, I recognized much of the behavior she describes, from anxiety about asking for better compensation to women's propensity to assume they don't have a certain skill set if they haven't demonstrated it before, or to take responsibility for tough times or failure even if the conditions were adverse and the results beyond their control. Perhaps that's also what makes women good leaders, that sense of commitment to and responsibility for the whole. But it's also what makes female leadership a complex and often lonely proposition.

Over the years I've relished the chance to direct and write plays that have allowed me to wrestle with these contradictions theatrically. One such play was Schiller's *Mary Stuart*, which I staged at A.C.T. in 1998 and then took to the Huntington Theatre Company in Boston two years later. A fictional account of the tortured but obsessive relationship between Queen Elizabeth of England and her cousin Mary Stuart of Scotland, the play explores the near impossibility for a woman to achieve political power and romantic or maternal satisfaction simultaneously. While power seems to make men ever more desirable (I have always found it amazing that Henry Kissinger was repeatedly named one of the world's sexiest men), it tends to make women more vulnerable. Queen Elizabeth (played in my production by Caroline Lagerfelt) is in love with and longs to marry the dashing Earl of Leicester but is forced by political expediency to keep him at bay. Her rival, Mary Queen of Scots (Susan Gibney), on the other hand, forfeits her political power in order to pursue her heart's desire. It broke my heart, during rehearsals, to watch Caroline learn to mask her desires, fears, and vulnerabilities in service of the power Elizabeth needed to exercise to keep her fractious government from erupting. The actress, let alone the character, acutely experienced the price she was forced to pay: audiences thrilled to the romantic and sexual Mary and were critical of the brilliant but controlling Elizabeth, a situation that mirrors exactly how our society views those female choices today. Elizabeth holds on to her throne and ushers in an unprecedented period of prosperity and stability in England, at the personal price of solitude and childlessness. What a cautionary tale! The choices confronted by those two women onstage were choices I had confronted myself, on a smaller scale, again and again, and I loved that *Mary Stuart* triggered lively debate in our audience about what happens when personal and professional lines are blurred and a woman is in charge, a theme that reemerged when I directed Racine's *Phèdre* and one that I explored much later in my own play *Kinship*.

But in those early days, I wasn't always aware that my own struggles would enrich my work; I just felt exhausted by the fight. I had no idea that my introduction to San Francisco would be so fraught and contentious, and I suppose it was lucky that Lexie was only three when I began at A.C.T., so she didn't have to read the 750 hate letters I received during the course of my first season.

CHAPTER 6

Annus Terribilis

I decided to open the 1992–93 season with a rare Strindberg three-hander called *Creditors*, which I had directed to critical acclaim at CSC in a new translation by Paul Walsh, who would become our resident dramaturg at A.C.T. some years later. No one advised me that this taut little exercise in sexual warfare might not be the most celebratory way to begin one's tenure at a new theater ("A seemingly perverse choice," sniffed critic Dennis Harvey in the *San Francisco Chronicle*), but at least it was a gem (and an inexpensive one at that), and I figured that I knew the script well enough to direct it while trying to solve the endless cascade of problems that were bound to present themselves during my first months at A.C.T. But the problems were worse than I'd anticipated, and as soon as I went into production, I realized that I was at a theater without a full-time casting director, a literary department, or a dramaturg, nor was there a resident stage manager who was on my team. Navigating Strindberg's psychological complexity while learning to steer a rudderless institution was difficult at best. Nevertheless, *Creditors* opened on an incredibly hot evening in October 1992, and famed San Francisco columnist Herb Caen pronounced it "strong enough to keep the creditors from the door." The production's Pinteresque sexual tension, precise sculptural staging, and powerful cast (A.C.T. favorite Charles Lanyer along with newcomers Joan McMurtrey and William Converse-Roberts) intrigued our subscribers and introduced them to dramatic literature that was rich, resonant, and as yet unknown at A.C.T. *Creditors* was a gripping evening with vivid performances, and our audiences leaned forward and took notice.

Then the disasters began. It all started with Ken Ludwig's *Lend Me a Tenor*, a play I had selected in the fraught few months after being hired, before I knew anything about A.C.T.'s internal dynamics. I chose *Tenor* in my eagerness to find a light comedy to balance the rigors of *The Duchess of Malfi*, *Creditors*, and *Antigone*. The plot of Ludwig's play revolves around an ill-fated opera production that attempts to replace an ailing tenor with another singer disguised in blackface. On my first official day on the job, in June 1992, I began to hear rumbles from the conservatory about an M.F.A. acting class that had gone disastrously wrong. It was called Rock Stars, and its purpose was to train actors to work "from the outside in" by imitating in as precise a manner as possible the physical and vocal behavior of a chosen rock music performer. A well-intentioned but ultimately misguided white student, having decided to portray Grace Jones, appeared before her classmates in dark character makeup. This caused enormous upset in the school. At that time, there were few artists of color in positions of authority at A.C.T., and few safe avenues for the students to express discontent. Thus, in the wake of the Grace Jones episode, when the naïve new artistic director announced that for her first season she was programming a play that involved blackface, the place erupted. Benny Sato Ambush, the African American director who was associate artistic director at the time, explained to me that, in the context of the school, carrying on with *Lend Me a Tenor* was probably a very bad idea indeed.

To be honest, once I arrived at A.C.T. and had time to really consider the season, I was not sorry to replace Ludwig's slim comedy with a more interesting play. But I had no idea how myopic I was being when I chose instead a new Dario Fo farce titled *The Pope and the Witch*. Again, the choice happened for seemingly sensible reasons. In addition to Benny Ambush, I had made the decision to bring on board a second associate artistic director, Richard Seyd. Richard was a highly respected local director with whom I had collaborated in New York; he was the longtime associate producing director of Eureka Theatre Company, a beloved acting teacher, and a font of knowledge about Bay Area alternative theater. But in all his years as a Bay Area director, Richard had never played a role in A.C.T.'s work. So naturally there was a certain outsider status that he brought to the job, along with a desire to crack open the club that A.C.T. had become and introduce some new elements. Among his many local friends and colleagues was Joan Holden, a principal playwright of the San Francisco Mime Troupe, who had shared with him the untranslated *Pope and the Witch*, which depicts the upheavals caused when an eager Pope, in thrall to a drug-trafficking Witch, wakes up one morning suddenly believing in the right of women to obtain free abortions on demand. Richard and Joan were excited by the energy and invention of the piece and thought the role of the Pope would be a perfect fit for Geoff Hoyle, clown extraordinaire. Geoff was another Bay Area artist who had not been part of the A.C.T. circle; the Fo play offered a lively opportunity to introduce him to our audience, and his audience to ours. I knew how beloved Fo's work had been among Mime Troupe fans across the Bay Area and was interested in encouraging that audience to begin coming to A.C.T.

So, with little time to spare and lots of internal debate and agonizing, we decided to replace the previously announced *Lend Me a Tenor* with *The Pope and the Witch*. In New York, I was accustomed to season schedules changing all the time, so I was taken aback that the substitution of one play for another was considered amateurish and unacceptable in San Francisco, particularly in the first year of a new regime. But substitute I did, making the additional mistake of trying to explain the switch by being honest about the incident in the school. At that point, the howls of reproach began in earnest. It was bad enough, I was told, to bow to the politically correct pressure of a few students and displace a farce that had run so successfully in New York. But it was sheer idiocy to replace that farce with an Italian comedy about the pope's vision of free abortion, in a city as Catholic as

San Francisco. Within days, I was receiving outraged letters from religious subscribers, from churchgoers, and from the Catholic hierarchy itself, particularly from a group that called itself Catholics for Truth and Justice. (I longed to locate the Catholics who were *not* for truth and justice, who might be on my side.) Long before we even went into rehearsal with the Fo play, the city was up in arms. There were numerous articles in the *San Francisco Chronicle* and dismissive editorials abounded (and this was in the days before this kind of crisis could get tweeted and reposted across the cyber-universe). No one could understand why the controversy in the school had been permitted to engender this particular change in programming. Years later, with more artists of color in our midst and a clearly written appeals policy in place in our conservatory, we have other ways to respond to such internal issues, but at the time, it felt necessary to me, as the new head of an organization that prided itself on training and education, to respect the students' opinions and replace the Ludwig show. So it was devastating to be met with such derision and lack of comprehension. And it took me months to realize that tension between the Catholic and gay communities was particularly acute during that period, and that by my actions I had placed A.C.T. directly in a hostile crossfire.

Summoned to appear at the knees of one Monsignor Steven Otellini of St. Cecilia's Parish, I begged A.C.T.'s one Catholic trustee, Pat Flannery, to accompany me while I sat on a low stool and was castigated by the outraged priest, who had just written to the chair of the National Endowment for the Arts demanding that "the NEA should seriously reconsider future grants to A.C.T. in light of their callous treatment of a significant portion of the local population." In response to my letter of explanation, San Francisco Archbishop John Quinn replied, "It is ironic that you extol Dario Fo's concern about social welfare when the Popes of the twentieth century have been the most significant supporters of social justice among all the leaders of the world," and declared it totally unacceptable that we were "performing a play in which the Holy Father is portrayed assaulting homeless children and as supporting the drug trade." My attempts to contextualize the piece in the broader context of political satire, and to talk about the deep humanity of Dario Fo, failed miserably. Soon the *Wall Street Journal* decided to make a meal out of this naïve young artistic director who had tried to avoid offending blacks only to succeed in offending everybody else instead. There were threats by the Knights of Malta and the Order of the Holy Sepulchre to pressure donors with Catholic backgrounds and corporations with Catholic board members to withdraw funding from A.C.T.

When the production finally opened, it became clear that the play itself was rather pallid in comparison to the scale of outrage it had engendered. This minor piece of Italian political provocation couldn't begin to stand up to the scrutiny visited upon it by press and audience alike, despite brilliant central performances by the antic Hoyle and his sidekick, Sharon Lockwood. In the end, there were two silver linings to the *Pope and the Witch* debacle. One was the arrival on the scene of Alan Jones, the wise and gracious dean of Grace Cathedral, who descended from Cathedral Hill in his finest robes during the preview process and told the picketing crowds that, while dissent was honorable, censorship was not. Jones eventually moderated a town hall meeting in which those who were willing to show up (which didn't include most of the church protesters) got to have their say. He was passionate about the right and indeed the necessity of artists to freely articulate their world view, and he immediately became a treasured friend and later trustee of A.C.T., eventually presiding over a beautiful blessing on the reopening of The Geary.

The second silver lining came in 1997, when out of the blue Fo was awarded the Nobel Prize in Literature. In the statement accompanying the prize, the Nobel Committee described Fo as a visionary writer "who emulates the jesters of the Middle Ages in scourging authority and upholding the dignity of the downtrodden." When I was asked to appear on the *PBS NewsHour* with Jim Lehrer the evening the award was announced to comment on the significance of Fo's work, I felt a sweet moment of vindication.

But the *Pope* fracas was only the beginning. A couple of months later, as I began visiting rehearsals of *The Duchess of Malfi* (which were held in our scene shop due to the enormity of George

Tsypin's set), I slowly began to discover what it was that director Robert Woodruff loved so much about the play. He had been reading Camille Paglia and Susan Faludi at the time and wanted to put on-stage the graphic degradation of women that he felt was fundamental both to our own culture and to Jacobean drama. His was an eminently fair reading of the text, although there was nothing subtle about his conception: his brilliant set designer had created a giant metal scaffold filled with office cubicles and bisected by a huge tube through which viscous liquid could gush on demand. *San Francisco Chronicle* writer Steven Winn described the mise-en-scène (in an article written for the *New York Times* in June 1993 about my controversial first season) as follows:

> The Duchess stood centerstage in a punishing white light, bloodied, naked from the waist down, and bound in gray duct tape from knees to neck. Behind her, in a bank of cramped metal cells, images of masochism and misogyny formed a hellish living frieze. A woman squirmed inside a man's steel grip. Another sat in a glassy-eyed stupor, ropes of her long hair knotted to the cell's frame and clawlike pincers locked on her bare breasts.
>
> By the time the actress Randy Danson had endured her tortuous death, dozens of patrons had fled.

Indeed, Woodruff's production was a bold, graphic, shocking, rather heavy-handed reading of an admittedly violent and sexually aggressive play. And many A.C.T. subscribers, who had received no warning and were apparently used to their classics being somewhat more decorously presented, were appalled. One of my favorite trustees, an elegant and intelligent elderly gentleman who died shortly thereafter, said to me mournfully after witnessing *Malfi*, "And I thought you were such a nice girl." I will always regret his disappointment in me.

Their horror began at the first preview, when the intermission lasted a full forty-eight minutes because Woodruff had decided at the last moment to put the set on wheels, and the desperate stage crew risked hernias trying to move two tons of metal to a post-intermission position. The length of the interval gave the six-hundred-plus-person audience nearly an hour to line up and accost me with angry accusations about how I was rapidly desecrating the theater they knew and loved. *The Pope and the Witch* had been bad enough, but this "in-your-face" approach to a classic was the last straw. It didn't help that Woodruff's work needs a lot of rehearsal time to gel, and the four weeks allotted to stage this large and complex play was not remotely enough for him to refine his vision. The spectacle that greeted audiences during the preview and opening-night process was unfinished and still somewhat inchoate. By the time Woodruff led the Prologue (an audience discussion that happens on the Tuesday before opening night for each of A.C.T.'s subscription productions), he was mordantly predicting that the Little Man (a cartoon figure that accompanies every theater review in the *San Francisco Chronicle* and whose demeanor is meant to be a snapshot of the reviewer's reaction to the work) would have an axe in his back.

A quick sidebar about the Little Man, the icon that has tormented Bay Area theater artists for more than seventy years. There are few serious newspapers in America that apply a visual rating system to theater reviews, but the *Chronicle* has always found its Little Man illustration indispensable. he is seated in a theater chair beside every review, ready to dispense his verdict on the show by one of five positions: he is either 1) leaping out of his chair in ecstasy, 2) sitting and clapping politely, 3) sitting and staring straight ahead, 4) sleeping in disgust, or 5) most damningly, absent from the chair altogether, having fled the offending production. It is difficult to get past the icon long enough to read reviews in the *Chronicle*; typically, a potential audience member will simply ask, "What is the Little Man doing?" This is such a disservice to artists and critics alike that it hardly bears mentioning, except to say that Woodruff's fantasy of the Little Man with an axe in his back has remained with me for my entire tenure at A.C.T. Ironically, when the play was finally reviewed, the Little Man was actually applauding politely, an assessment that baffled the enraged crowds who couldn't wait to get home and write me hate letters about the production. I received 750 letters in all, which I preserved in two large black binders that I leave in a prominent place on my office bookshelf, as a reminder, I suppose, of those bitter early days.

Woodruff had to depart the day after opening, so I was left to respond to every complaint myself. This was in the days before email, so it was an arduous process, but, surprisingly, in the long run it was also somewhat rewarding. In preparation for writing this book, I re-read the entire collection of mail, and in spite of the pain of revisiting that tsunami of criticism, what strikes me twenty years down the road is the passion and intelligence expressed by A.C.T.'s audience. Despite the level of anger, it was clear that these were not philistines who were arguing for a season of easy listening; they were engaged theatergoers who desperately wanted to understand what was going on at a theater they had nurtured for years. I realized that I was no longer at the helm of a small organization in the vast cultural landscape of New York; I was running the flagship and everything I did was going to be highly visible and closely scrutinized. In responding one by one to all the charges against the casting, concept, and design of *Malfi*, I began to forge a relationship with an audience that I came to admire as one of the most open-minded and engaged theater audiences in the country. I tried as hard as I could to stay open to their criticism. Maybe because they saw my extreme vulnerability, they, too, became more open. Years later, in her brilliant essay "Whither (or Wither) Art?" Zelda Fichandler articulated better than I ever could why it is so important for artistic leadership to acknowledge mistakes, no matter how humiliating:

> The creative courage of the artistic director will inspire artists; they, in turn, will support the risks she takes on their behalf whether or not they succeed. The transparency she fosters so that information—whether good news or bad— is available to all, up and down and around the building, will deepen the sense of mutual respect and a communal destiny. And she will see to it that no one is made to feel

intimidated to speak up; in story and myth, the figure of Death is always silent. The artistic director's acknowledgement of ambiguity, relativism, second thoughts, and struggle that exist behind difficult decisions will draw the artists even closer to her, revealing her as worthy of having, using, and sharing power. The blinding glare of certainty always reduces intimacy and trust.

I wish I had had Ms. Fichandler there to remind me of this truth during the ordeal of my first season. It was a lonely time. The nadir came when I discovered that a telemarketer for a local theater was using the *Malfi* debacle as bait to lure our subscribers away at the same time that Lexie came down with scarlet fever.

Debacle Number Three came in the form of Sophocles' *Antigone*, which we produced after *Malfi* in a nearby smaller theater, The Stage Door (now a nightclub called Ruby Skye). Once again, best-laid plans went awry, and the subscribers were angry before they even walked into the theater. I had announced and fully intended to produce a new production of Euripides' *Hecuba* to feature my longtime colleague and mentor Olympia Dukakis in the title role. I commissioned the visionary playwright/translator Timberlake Wertenbaker to create a new version of *Hecuba*, and she agreed with alacrity, but by the time we dove into the project, we realized it was a massive undertaking, requiring extensive music and choral work that could best be developed in a workshop. Having been forced to announce the work long before it was ready to be presented, I had to take a deep breath and admit that to do it justice, the production needed time to develop. So we substituted *Antigone* for *Hecuba*, promising that the latter would emerge in a subsequent season. Indeed, when we finally produced *Hecuba* in 1995, with an original score by the now Pulitzer Prize–winning composer David Lang sung by Balkan-inspired Bay Area vocal group Kitka and starring a ferocious Olympia, it was one of the triumphs of my tenure at A.C.T.

But at the time, an already shaken audience felt betrayed. Where was Ms. Dukakis when they needed her? Why was *Antigone* being done instead? A.C.T. had rarely been in the business of commissioning new translations and adaptations of classics, a practice we had employed regularly at CSC, so the audience was less privy to the developmental steps it takes to ready a new version of a classical play for large-scale production and just assumed that we were simply too incompetent to complete the task. I began receiving more mail, this time with the comment, "We don't like Greek tragedy anyway and don't wish to see it at A.C.T." This truly baffled me, because, as far as I could tell, the theater had almost never produced a Greek play. How did our audiences know they would hate what they had rarely seen?

I suspected that their anxiety was tied to their expectation of seeing a declamatory drama performed by people dressed in white sheets, and I was sure that when they saw how immediate and visceral the Greeks could be they would change their minds. To lead my production I cast Elizabeth Peña, a Hispanic actress from Los Angeles, as Antigone; Wendell Pierce, a remarkable African American actor, as Haimon; and Ken Ruta, a powerful A.C.T. veteran, as Kreon. Lang scored the play for Rova Saxophone Quartet, who played it live from the balcony. I set the play in the rubble of a ruined theater and gathered real detritus from the damaged Geary to decorate the stage. One of the most poignant moments of rehearsal happened when Ruta bent down and picked up a piece of one of the gold rosettes that had broken off the damaged proscenium, and memories of all his years at The Geary came flooding back to him. Everything about the set was resonant for those of us who had grown accustomed to the tragic sight of that ruined playhouse: we even had a row of red seats onstage that were crumpled and bent like the seats that had buckled during the quake. We imagined that the chorus of old men, led by the inimitable Gerald Hiken, were aged subscribers whose primary hope was a desire to return to the status quo before the destruction.

Rehearsals for *Antigone* were a welcome escape from the horrors of the public relations machine that continued to spin out of control in the wake of the *Malfi* debacle. I relished the complexity of argument in *Antigone* and the passion of the characters to defend their conflicting views of history. I loved listening to Berkeley Law Professor Robert Post educate the cast and the audience about the difference between natural law (the law of kinship and family) and positive law (the law of government and the machine of justice) and felt that I was finally able to give to my audience something of myself, my own passions and predilections. But once again, when the production opened, a furor erupted. I had always practiced what was then called "nontraditional casting," and particularly with material as metaphorical as the Greeks, it seemed critical to cast the best talent regardless of race. In the early days, A.C.T.'s actors had been primarily white, but this was an area Ed Hastings worked hard to change, hiring actors of color such as Steven Anthony Jones, Judy Moreland, and Luis Oropeza. So it was with great surprise that I discovered that some of my audience did not seem eager to watch a multiracial cast perform *Antigone*. To be fair, if the *Lend Me a Tenor* debacle had not occurred, sensitivities might not have run so high. But in the wake of my decision about *Tenor*, the casting of *Antigone* smacked of political correctness to this bewildered and bruised audience, and the letters began to pour in again.

This time, the issue was "authenticity." It seemed that I was violating the authentic spirit of the play by forcing the audience to see it through the eyes of this very diverse cast. The response led to lengthy discussions about the nature of ancient Greek texts. I pulled out my dog-eared copy of Martin Bernal's *Black Athena* and argued that even if authenticity were a desirable requirement in the staging of ancient plays, there was nothing to say that the population of fifth-century BCE Athens was all blond and blue-eyed; I showed vase paintings and discussed the enslavement of Persians and the trade presence of Egyptians to bolster my case for an ancient Athens that looked something like the cast of my *Antigone*. But again, sadly, the production itself was overshadowed by a controversy it was never intended to incite. Years later, after seeing numerous productions of Greek tragedy produced to great success at A.C.T., our audience has come to enjoy them so much that many of them traveled to Los Angeles to see my production of Sophocles' *Elektra* (also with Olympia Dukakis) at the Getty Villa in the summer of 2010. But *Antigone* angered the audience at the time, and drove an even deeper wedge between them and the artists.

It was lucky that the spring of my first season brought some lighter comedies to the fore, or our subscribers would most likely have voted to abandon A.C.T. and leave The Geary ruined forever. March brought Albert Takazauckas's production of *Dinner at Eight*, a play I had been intrigued by for many years and thought would beautifully suit what was left of the A.C.T. company. To follow this particular leg of the journey, it is important to understand what had happened to the notion of company in the years following Bill Ball's demise. The band of forty-plus actors who had been lucky enough to receive seasonal contracts at A.C.T. had diminished over the years as actors left for Los Angeles and New York, and A.C.T.'s ability to sustain long-term contracts waned. By the time of the earthquake, none of the actors had guaranteed contracts anymore, although the attempt was still being made to give many of them as much work per season as possible. Associate Artistic Director Dennis Powers had endless sheets of graph paper on which he charted the needs of the repertoire and the availability of actors, but a strategic attempt to reimagine the company had not yet been made. A few of the truly great actors from A.C.T.'s early days, including Sydney Walker, William Paterson, and Ken Ruta, were still in town and prepared to do the occasional show, but, unsurprisingly, there was a paucity of leading men and women, along with a plethora of less-tested actors who lined up outside my office during my first months on the job to tell me they were ready to play Hamlet and Henry V. Meanwhile, many interesting Bay Area actors such as James Carpenter, Lorri Holt, and Charles Dean had not worked at A.C.T. and were eager to participate, and of course I had my own stable of favorites from New York whom I was interested in including in the mix.

I knew that A.C.T.'s audience had been weaned on great acting, and that it would mean a lot to them if some of their favorites were part of my programming. But I have to admit that in watching *Dinner at Eight* night after night, I began to feel that the prevailing style of A.C.T. acting was not always going to gel well with my own aesthetic, and I was anxious to inject new blood. The work of the great Sydney Walker, however, was an inspiration: by the time we got to Molière's *The Learned Ladies*, which mercifully closed the season, Sydney's astonishing comic timing and antic, openhearted collaboration with Jean Stapleton brought the house down and temporarily reassured the audience that I was not the violent iconoclast they had suspected. I will never forget Sydney standing at the lip of the stage after the show, exhorting the audience to resubscribe by promising them excitement "and just a little bit of controversy," with an enormous twinkle in his eye.

Toward the end of that first season, I went to Europe to fulfill an obligation I had entered into long before the A.C.T. job presented itself: I was directing the world premiere of a new Steve Reich–Beryl Korot opera titled *The Cave*. Steve and Beryl and I had been working on the piece for several years, and it remains one of the most fulfilling experiences of my life, watching it come to fruition at the Vienna Festival in the spring of 1993. *The Cave* was a multimedia opera in which the singers sang over the spoken texts of individuals from all walks of life who had been interviewed about the cave at Hebron, where Abraham and his descendants are believed to be buried. My job was to create a visual context for the singers on John Arnone's elegant set in juxtaposition to the video screens, and to conceive it in such a way that video and live performers melded into a unified image. Reich's music inspired me in the same manner Pinter's language did: it was spare, muscular, visceral, and filled with moments of surprising beauty. The third act of *The Cave*, which sings about the angels who come unannounced to Abraham's house and are taken in and fed, remains one of the most exquisite pieces of religious music I have ever encountered. As I traveled Europe on tour with *The Cave*, I realized to my great sadness that I felt more at home among that group of musicians, none of whom was known to me, than I had felt at my own theater for the past year. The attacks and frustrations had taken their toll: I was beaten up and discouraged. I was unsure whether the kind of theater I was interested in making would ever suit A.C.T.; I was homesick for the close downtown community of New York theater that had sustained and supported me at CSC; and I was in open warfare with my managing director.

The day before I left for Vienna I found, left in the fax machine, a letter John had sent to A.C.T.'s board of trustees, telling them that it was clear I was both incompetent and out of my depth and should be replaced. Indeed, although he himself denies it, I later heard from several key staff members that John had approached them to ask if they would support his efforts to have me removed. To be fair, we had lost over a million dollars on my first season, in part because the budget had never been realistically introduced to me, in part because of an economy in prolonged recession, and in part because of my lack of experience in running a theater of this size. In addition, we were already spending a considerable amount of money to launch our capital campaign to rebuild The Geary Theater and to cultivate major donors. Now we were faced with the need to renew subscribers who were clearly angry and disaffected and to try to raise capital dollars from donors who were not yet sure what the new A.C.T. was going to look like. Day after day during my first season, Alan Stein and I had valiantly appeared before every willing patron in town to share our vision of the future of A.C.T.; I had articulated the repertoire I wanted to pursue, I had attempted to wrap my head around the future of the training program, and I had talked personally to every audience member I could meet. I had even gone to Gap headquarters and sat on Don Fisher's famous baseball mitt chair at 7:30 AM to ask him to support our campaign, a challenging request given that I know nothing about baseball and Fisher told me as soon as I sat down that he liked to go to bed by 9:00 PM and thus had little interest in the theater.

Had only one of the litany of first-year controversies happened, or had they happened in the context of a stable artistic enterprise, each would have probably blown over quickly. But I was new, young, untested, female, and a New Yorker, and every move I made was read as an indicator of further dangers ahead. The economy remained weak throughout that extremely difficult first year, and the possibility of raising the millions required to rebuild The Geary seemed remote. I had a demoralized staff with limited experience in fundraising or marketing, and virtually no artistic team: Aside from Dennis Powers, there was no casting director, no literary manager, no line producer, no company manager. Benny Ambush and Richard Seyd were doing their best, but they, too, were outsiders and overwhelmed by the tide of events. One of my few allies in that lonely first season was the director of the Young Conservatory, Craig Slaight, who had kept his head down and done remarkable work with young artists throughout the darkest times at A.C.T. and continues to do so to this day.

And so, while I was in Vienna staging *The Cave*, I began hearing rumors that things were reaching a crisis point. Not only was our cash flow a disaster, but my producing partner had all but publicly declared that he had no confidence in my ability to right the ship. The day I got back from Europe, John and I met in my office. I remember the day vividly, because suddenly I felt extraordinarily clear about what the options were. I didn't want to come to work one more day with a colleague that so clearly doubted my capacity to do the job. I had no interest in internal politics and no desire to spend my energy guarding my back. I'm sure that John had only A.C.T.'s best interests in mind, and that supporting a maverick new artistic director like myself was a challenge he didn't believe would bear fruit. But the partnership had become impossible. I told John that I was aware of his desire to run the theater alone and that I thought it was most appropriate for him to go to the board and give them the choice. Either he would stay or I would, but I could no longer envision a scenario in which we stayed together. To my great surprise, when he went to the board and proposed that he be left in charge of the organization, the board demurred, indicating that that they had chosen to hire an artist and that they would stand by their decision.

I heard of this decision at a meeting at Alan Stein's stunning Russian Hill apartment on a sunny day in May. As had happened just over a year earlier when he asked me to come to his apartment in New York to invite me to take over A.C.T, he called and said he'd like a meeting, and off I went. I was almost certain that this would be the end of my tenure at A.C.T. Part of me longed to go back to New York, to a city and a community I felt I understood better, to friends and colleagues with whom I had made work for a decade, to the anonymity of a smaller theater, away from the wrath of the A.C.T. subscribers, the enormous fiscal challenges, the demoralized staff, the struggling school, and my antagonistic managing director. I felt like a stranger in a strange land, without friends, without instincts, overwhelmed and alone. When I got to Alan's apartment, we sat in the picture window of his living room, overlooking San Francisco Bay. I watched the sailboats pass by below and suddenly felt nostalgic for all that I would miss when I left the Bay Area. Alan came back with the coffee. He sat down, smiled, and said, "Look, Carey. It's been a hard year. Change is extremely difficult. We all understand that. But now that you've done the hard part, it's time to see it through."

It took me a moment to realize he was asking me to stay on. I couldn't fathom how this gentle, intelligent man had the courage to stick with a renegade choice who had caused so much pain and uproar over the past year. But Alan was unfazed. He seemed to take the long view. He liked much of the work he had seen. He liked my energy and enthusiasm. He liked my willingness to talk to the audience, my passion for writing about the work, my eagerness to ask anyone and everyone for support, my facility with public speaking. But most of all, I think he was banking on my spirit. A.C.T. had been through so many near-death experiences in its history, he believed that only a young person of indomitable spirit could keep it alive. We had no cash flow, no theater, no easy remedies. But somehow, he was willing to stick by me. And he was not alone. Many years later, I discovered that it was the women on the board who stood up and defended me, again and again, during that tumultuous first year when I was being attacked from all sides. It hadn't occurred to me how rare it was for a nonprofit theater board to have among its trustees the president emerita of a major women's college, an ex-nun who had started her own successful storage business, and a landscape architect with a strong personal aesthetic. These women saw in me an ally and a plausible colleague, and they fought for me when the going was tough.

I stress this because in recent years, as the economy has worsened and the risks of producing theater have increased, boards of directors are looking increasingly to short-term results and last-quarter returns to determine the fate of their artistic leaders. Artistic transitions are difficult and take time to manage; with a new leader comes a new aesthetic, a new energy, and a new way of working, and often that can take several years to come into focus. This requires a stalwart and flexible board that remains clear about the theater's mission and long-term goals and is patient about seeing them realized. It takes a great deal of skill to learn to successfully manage the intersection of art and business that is the job of the artistic director, and longevity can help. It helped that Joe Papp was at the helm of The Public Theater for forty years and could fight the long fight; it helped that Gordon Davidson cast a long shadow over the Mark Taper Forum for three decades. (As Thoreau famously said, "An institution is the long shadow of a man.") You learn from your mistakes, and if you are supple and lucky, and if you have a board of directors that has your back, you grow. This doesn't mean leadership shouldn't change and evolve with the needs of the organization, but a theater that switches artistic directors every three to five years is a theater at risk of eradication. The problem is that our attention spans are very short and our impatience with failure very great. It would have surprised no one if Alan Stein had fired me. The fact that he didn't was a minor miracle that I continue to wonder at to this day.

I walked out of Alan's apartment into the hot May sunshine in a daze, trying to understand what had just happened. Then I called Anthony, and we went out to dinner at our favorite Thai restaurant in Noe Valley, where the waiters charmed Lexie as she held court over the pad thai. Anthony was relieved—he was in the middle of law school at Berkeley, he was loving it, and he wanted to stay. I was exhausted but reconciled. I went into the office the next day to find a letter from John Sullivan pleading with me to let him stay on—he thought we would make good partners after all, and there was so much work to be done. But the die had been cast, and within a month he was gone. Although I promoted Development Director Tom Flynn to administrative director, I would now enter the next chapter of my life at A.C.T. as sole CEO, a position I have never relished and never sought again. The search for a new managing director began, and I dove into preparations for my second season.

As a fitting conclusion to that annus terribilis, we printed a subscription renewal brochure that was covered in quotes from the letters we had received over the course of the year. I leavened the most hostile ones with the occasional positive remark, but I let the criticism stand. The audience must have felt heard and therefore somewhat vindicated, because ironically a surprisingly large percentage resubscribed. Yale Repertory Theatre founder Robert Brustein, whom I had called in desperation during my darkest days, had wisely advised me to let the disgruntled audience go entirely and hope for a new audience to emerge (which he had done brilliantly in his early days both at Yale Rep and at the American Repertory Theater), and to some extent that happened. But at the end of that renewal campaign I learned a critical thing about the Bay Area: it is a community filled with opinions, ready to take umbrage at almost anything, but equally ready to go the distance when engaged. Those subscribers cared about A.C.T. Their outrage was a sign of their affection. They didn't want to see the theater go under, nor did they want to drive me out of town. They wanted to know that I was listening, that I heard their frustrations, that I would learn from my mistakes and do better. Certainly no one could say it had been a boring season, quipped the brilliant philanthropist Barbro Osher, who had supported the organization for many years. It was clear that this was no longer "your father's A.C.T." My first season had served, if nothing else, to expose the cracks in the infrastructure of the organization. I hadn't yet begun to take on the school, and the staff was only beginning to cohere into a reasonable force. But we had survived, and now, apparently, I had to stay and see it through.

CHAPTER 7

The Geary Campaign

If the struggle to rebuild the damaged Geary Theater were a play, its lead characters would be FEMA (Federal Emergency Management Authority) and SHPO (State Historic Preservation Authority), and the title would be *Waiting for Compromise.* When it is your fate to own a landmark building in the state of California, nothing is simple. Everything the federal government tells you to do to prepare for another earthquake is contradicted by the historic preservationists, who don't want a brick of the nondescript side wall of the theater to be touched, even in the name of seismic stability. Add to this the prerogatives of the donors, who rightly long to inject some new ideas and contemporary panache into the building, and you risk a constant state of stalemate.

The original vision for the rebuilt Geary was an entire campus of offices, classrooms, and studios wrapped around the historic façade of the 1910 building. This was a big idea, and unfortunately it came at a time when A.C.T. had no prayer of pulling it off. The board, having been kept at arm's length by management for many years, had little understanding of the day-to-day operations of the theater and had been unable to develop the long-term strategies necessary to move the organization forward. The internal atmosphere was too fraught to have safe discussions about how to imagine the future or where the priorities should lie. As soon as I arrived, I realized how limiting it was that A.C.T. had never had a dedicated second stage. (When Tom Stoppard first came to work with us, he asked in consternation, "But where is the Cottesloe?" in reference to the small studio space at the National Theatre in London. He couldn't understand how we could take risks or develop new work and new artists without a theater smaller than The Geary, and in many ways he was right.) But in the post–earthquake crisis period, contemplating a second stage or a new office and studio complex felt like a luxury. Nor was it politically permissible to truly analyze the cost to the organization of running an M.F.A. program without hurting everyone's feelings. Many assume that A.C.T.'s conservatory is a money-maker, despite the fact that by definition an M.F.A. program (as opposed to an undergraduate program) is small, elite, and expensive to run (while the Young Conservatory and Studio A.C.T. programs consistently contribute to the bottom line). Because actor training requires extensive facilities and faculty and is thus very costly, A.C.T.'s M.F.A. program in acting is one of the few such programs left housed in a free-standing theater rather than at a university. Yet, as I have said, rich synergies occur when training and production are linked, and during my tenure at A.C.T., Conservatory Director Melissa Smith and I have worked hard to make those synergies ever tighter and more effective. Of course, the more deeply training and performance are linked, the more desirable it has become to combine our rehearsal studios and classrooms with a smaller performance space and informal cabaret space, all under one roof in a single campus that is transparent, flexible, and accessible. But in the early nineties, when the campaign to rebuild The Geary was under way, the gorgeous designs of architect Joseph Esherick to create a single campus around the ruins of The Geary Theater were so beyond A.C.T.'s fundraising reach that they had to be scrapped before I even arrived.

Instead, the decision was made to rebuild the 1910 Beaux-Arts building in the most authentic way possible, while making considerable audience amenity changes and stagecraft improvements along the way. The first necessity was to create a shear wall of sliding steel that would protect the building and its inhabitants in case of a subsequent earthquake, and thus the decision was made to remove three hundred seats from the cavernous back of the house and create an eighteen-inch wall held together by sliding steel bolts. The beneficial consequence of dividing the space with this new wall was that we captured a considerable amount of new lobby space, both on the ground floor and on the mezzanine level. Before the quake, The Geary had about three square feet of amenity space per audience member; postquake it has ten, and that has made an enormous difference in the experience of attending an A.C.T. show. The renovation also created space for a new bar upstairs, as well as a garret that we now use for board meetings and cabaret performances, an expanded basement café, and a plethora of new bathrooms throughout the building. I like to say that my single most important legacy as the female artistic director of A.C.T. is the abundance of women's bathrooms, permitting "never more than a three-minute wait." I figured, if the plays were going to be challenging, at least the intermissions should be stress free.

FEMA is notoriously difficult to navigate. This was in the days before Hurricane Katrina made FEMA the infamous agency that it became in the wake of that disaster, but nonetheless, the paperwork and negotiations required to extract a single payment from FEMA were byzantine and time consuming, exacerbated by the fact that the state of California was in a financial crisis in 1992–93 and had not passed a budget for fiscal year 1993. Thus, even when our FEMA appropriation was finally approved in Washington, the funds couldn't be released through the state budget office, because Sacramento was in fiscal shutdown. One of my most vivid memories of the Geary rebuilding campaign was calling Congresswoman Nancy Pelosi, then a senior member of the House Appropriations Committee, on the floor of the Democratic Convention to beg her to intervene on our behalf to ensure that our FEMA funds came to us in time to begin demolition and reconstruction work. Pelosi, the consummate ward politician, worked her magic in such a way that the money was released on the day the cranes were set to be erected on Mason Street. Years later, after the project had been completed, we named the beautiful central windows of the newly rebuilt Geary after Pelosi and gave her an honorary M.F.A. degree in acting, in gratitude for her help.

Given that much of my career before A.C.T. had been spent at CSC, a renovated stable in lower Manhattan with three-quarter seating and a high tin ceiling, I was used to directing on a thrust stage. I had rarely worked in the kind of highly formal proscenium house that The Geary represented, yet I was called upon to make decisions on a daily basis about potential alterations to that remarkable space. Producing Director James Haire must have thought I was naïve beyond imagining, but he patiently walked me through each decision (where to put the stage management booth, whether to put in a hydraulic tilt stage, how big and deep to make the orchestra pit, and so on), and in the process I acquired a deep and abiding love for that unique historic building.

Because my primary training had been in classics and archaeology, the excavation of the building was resonant to me. As the interior was gutted before reconstruction, we uncovered twenty-six layers of paint en route to the base coat, discovering, for example, the psychedelic treatment that covered The Geary during the 1960s run of *Hair*. We removed the wood that boarded up the arched windows facing Geary Street, and reclaimed lobby space freed up by the removal of back rows of seats. We created a monumental new staircase dominated by a fanciful curved rail, and reimagined the color scheme of the auditorium to become what the designers at Gensler referred to as "dusty grape." Very slowly, the damaged structure began to return to life, its Dutch gold surfaces acquiring new sheen, its rotting hemp rope system replaced by mechanical counterweights, its plenum excavated to make way for beautifully appointed new dressing and wig rooms.

While all this was happening, I got pregnant with our second child. It didn't occur to me at the time how inappropriate this would seem to some of the trustees and supporters who were fighting to save A.C.T. and rebuild The Geary. And, once again, had I imagined what I was getting into, I would probably never have contemplated it. I hadn't stopped working for a moment during my first pregnancy; I actually liked being pregnant and barely showed, so when I finally told the board at six months that I would give birth at the end of May 1994, many of them were understandably flummoxed. Although we had survived my second season with far less chaos and animosity than the first, the rebuilding process was slow, the financial situation was perilous to say the least, The Geary capital campaign was an enormous challenge, and we still had no managing director. This was probably not the most fortuitous time to have a baby.

At the same time, the work had started to become highly pleasurable. For the 1993–94 season, I directed Paul Schmidt's new translation of *Uncle Vanya* and experienced that exquisite rush of recognition and emotional satisfaction that only Chekhov can provide. Interestingly, this production featured a cast as ethnically diverse as *Antigone*: Sharon Omi played Sonya, Vilma Silva played Yelena, and Wendell Pierce played Astrov, yet this time, no one in the audience complained. Perhaps they had begun to understand the thinking behind our casting choices, perhaps we were better at preparing them in advance for what they were going to see, and perhaps the production itself cohered more successfully than had *Antigone*, but *Vanya* turned out to be a major critical and audience success.

I didn't miss a day of work because of my pregnancy, but the board was understandably anxious about the future: How was I going to complete the fundraising and rebuilding of The Geary with a newborn? From where they sat, I must have seemed totally mad. Once again, I tried to convince them that fundraising while pregnant held certain advantages, a lesson I had learned at CSC. One of the last big donor events I did for the Geary campaign before giving birth was at the Fairmont Hotel, which sits atop Nob Hill, one of San Francisco's most challenging climbs; I remember walking up that ridiculously steep hill with my huge belly and high heels until I finally gave up the attempt to look elegant and professional, sat down on the sidewalk, took off my shoes, and began to hike the rest of the way up that urban mountain in bare feet. A generous donor saw me from her car, swept me into the front seat, and extracted my promise that I would never do such a stupid thing again if she made a final contribution to the campaign. Sweet, flaxen-haired Nicholas was born on May 23, 1994, and two weeks later he made his Geary Theater debut in a navy blue Chanel romper suit donated by the chair of the board. In early June, the groundbreaking commenced on the building, and I like to chart the phoenix-like rise of the ruined Geary to the growth of that little boy.

It is always dangerous to equate the fortunes of a theater company with the building that houses it. All too often in the American arts sector we have seen huge resources raised to create fancy new arts facilities that then prove unaffordable and unwieldy for the very companies they were supposed to save. Indeed, during the capital campaign, there was much discussion about whether reconstruction of The Geary was the most sensible move for A.C.T. Would it not be better, some donors opined, to raze the building to the ground and build a new space more suited to the twenty-first century and the needs of contemporary theatergoers?

There was a certain amount of sense in that argument. While it would have been heartbreaking to lose that historic playhouse, the discussion about space versus mission is an important one, and the issue must be reckoned with every day and every season. The Geary was originally built as a temple of culture by a city that had endured the 1906 earthquake and wanted the world to know that it was back with a vengeance and intent on being a major player on the national scene. The building is monumental, elegant, and filled with grandeur—high up on its gilded dome are delicate sculptures of fruits and flowers that can barely be seen by the naked eye, yet the architects believed that beauty had to fill every corner of this cathedral in order to lift the aspirations of the artists and audiences within. The historical preservation firm Page & Turnbull put it eloquently in a 1988 report on the state of The Geary:

> The exterior of the Geary Theatre, in a bejeweled, Neo-Classical style, still proclaims to passersby that it is a place of classical high culture, continuing ancient and respected traditions. . . .

Classical elements, such as the columns, hovering dome, coffered proscenium arch, relief ornaments, and wall pilasters, refer to palatial imagery as well as to the ancient origins of drama. . . . Like the theatrical drama unfolding on the stage, [its] theatrical architecture was intended to ennoble all those who experienced it.

Needless to say, The Geary Theater is not casual and user friendly; it was built to remind people that when they step into a theater they are entering a parallel universe, far removed from the banality of daily life. Under that golden proscenium, magical things will happen. Nearly every one of The Geary's thousand-plus seats has a perfect view and perfect acoustics: the architects made sure that the relationship of audience to stage is intimate and close in spite of its scale. It is a house for poetic language, large emotion, powerful acting, and great literature. If geography is destiny, it is clear why A.C.T. had never been home to the kind of television realism or intimate psychological drama beloved by many American theaters, nor to "star" performances by actors unable to fill The Geary vocally and kinesthetically. The Geary is the Wimbledon of theaters and demands true athletes to fill it well.

But in an era of austerity and media-driven appetites, this kind of magnificent playhouse, designed for large-scale classical work and major modern drama, poses significant challenges. Classical plays demand large casts, major design support, and an educated audience. All across America, these things are disappearing. Theater companies shy away from the classics, except for the two or three most recognizable titles, because they don't believe that they can sell them or that their audiences want to be challenged by three-hour, language-heavy plays. The gradual disappearance of permanent acting ensembles, one of the tragedies of late-twentieth-century American theater, and the rise of the dependence upon television and movie stars to sell tickets, has sounded a death knell for classical theater. When classics *are* produced, fiscal realities tend to dictate that they be done with hard-working ensembles of five or six, and while this can result in wonderful creativity, as the work of the New York–based collective Fiasco has shown, it means that the experience of seeing "the world onstage" is diminished considerably. Because we can't approximate the large and various acting companies for whom Shakespeare wrote his plays, we have made Shakespeare come to us, meaning we have cut and pared down his plays such that the rich crowd scenes and minor characters are excised in favor of intimate personal readings of the texts. Across the country, funders are willing to pay for more audience engagement but not for more actors onstage. It seems a bizarre priority. One particularly unfortunate result of this dearth of productions of classical theater is that many young writers may grow up without having seen major professional productions of Shakespeare, Euripides, Brecht, Lorca, Schiller, or Molière; thus the nearest influence is necessarily film and television. The kind of short, clipped scenes and mumblecore acting often characteristic of those media are difficult to sustain at a theater like The Geary.

We thus went through a period of profound soul-searching during the rebuilding of The Geary. There were many days when I wondered why we were undertaking such a project, and whether we would ever find a way to make The Geary relevant to a contemporary audience. I wrestled, and continue to wrestle, with what kind of work to put in that house and how to guarantee a standard of artistry that deserves such a gilded envelope. Several things became clear to me in the years that followed The Geary's reopening: it was crucial to nurture an acting company capable of taking on that house; it was valuable to insist upon work that was highly theatrical and that employed music and movement as strongly as language to penetrate that proscenium; it was imperative to sustain complex classical work by continuing to educate an audience about the literature they were about to see. At the same time, it would become increasingly necessary to provide alternatives for those people for whom a thousand-seat theater was never going to provide the intimate theater experience they craved.

In January 1996, The Geary officially reopened with my production of *The Tempest*, featuring David Strathairn as Prospero, Graham Beckel as Caliban, and David Patrick Kelly as Ariel, with shadow puppetry by Larry Reed and music by David Lang, performed live by Kronos Quartet. I will never forget standing in the back of the house for the first preview, listening to Lang's savage, pulsating storm music performed live in the newly renovated orchestra pit by David Harrington and the astonishing Kronos musicians. It truly felt as if a phoenix were rising from the ashes, shrieking and hollering about its new existence.

We had held numerous celebrations in the house to honor the donors, builders, designers, and so on, but during the run of *The Tempest* we realized that we had not held a private party just for ourselves, for the artists and staff people who had contributed to this renaissance. So on the final Sunday evening of the show, we decided to hold an ecumenical blessing onstage. Our friend and stalwart supporter Dean Alan Jones of Grace Cathedral agreed to officiate at this homemade resurrection ceremony, and artists and artisans turned out to participate. We started onstage and looked skyward as Eddie Raymond, head of the stage crew, shook incense over the new fly rail and intoned the names of all the flymen who had ever raised a sandbag at The Geary. We held hands as Kitka sang one of the group's choral chants of celebration, and listened to Olympia Dukakis read two poems: The first was by Brecht, written in 1954 on the occasion of the Berliner Ensemble's acquisition of a permanent home at the Schiffbauerdamm theater:

> You've acted theater in ruins here,
> Now act in this lovely house, not as a pastime.
> From you and us let arise the peaceful WE,
> So that this house and others too may stand.

The second piece was a Lorca poem that Olympia remembers copying from the wall of Arena Stage many years before, which she has treasured throughout her career; it became a touchstone for us, as well:

> the poem
> the song
> the picture

is only water
drawn from the well
of the people,
and it should be given back to them
in a cup of beauty
so that they may drink
and in drinking
understand themselves.

Up above in the new stage-management booth, actor Matthew Boston read Kostya's speech about the moon rising from Chekhov's *The Cherry Orchard*. Then we danced with Margaret Jenkins, gathered in the box office for Box Office Manager Richard Bernier's tribute to "St. Margarita," the patroness of box offices, and descended to the bar downstairs, newly christened Fred's Columbia Room after the doorman who had greeted Geary patrons for more than thirty years, where Development Associate Jerome Moskowitz read the Hebrew prayer for fertility over the fundraising wall. By the time the celebration was complete, we were like little dogs who had peed in every corner of the new space until we made it our own. In the end, it took years for us to believe that such a magnificent space truly belonged to us. We often felt like teenagers babysitting in a fancy house, waiting to be turned out at midnight when the parents came home. But slowly we have found a way to make the space our own. And this process began first and foremost with the artists who inhabited it.

CHAPTER 8

The Core Company

Central to those artists was Marco Barricelli, a powerful, Juilliard-trained West Coast actor who urged me to make the commitment to start an A.C.T. company again. This was not a decision to be taken lightly: an acting company is a complicated organism that demands tenacity to nurture and sustain. By the time I arrived at A.C.T. in the post-earthquake era, Bill Ball's legendary company had long been dissolved, but the idea of it still held sway. And I came to A.C.T. as a believer myself in the power of long-term collaboration, having worked repeatedly with many of the same actors in New York: Olympia Dukakis, David Strathairn, John Turturro, Julia Gibson, Joe Morton, Kathleen Widdoes, Jean Stapleton, Peter Riegert, Caroline Lagerfelt, and Pamela Reed among them. I have always treasured the shorthand and ease that can develop in rehearsal with actors who know each other well, along with the freedom to risk and to fail. When I arrived at A.C.T., there were actors who had been among the original A.C.T. company with whom I felt an immediate kinship, most notably the oldest among them, including Bill Paterson, Sydney Walker, Joy Carlin, and Ruth Kobart. With these performers in mind, I programmed (during my third A.C.T. season) an intimate David Storey play called *Home*, both to showcase their talents and to learn from them about the nature of company. Unfortunately, by the time we went into rehearsal, beloved Sydney was too ill to participate, but I was able to replace him with another A.C.T. veteran, Raye Birk, and those four actors were exquisite together as a collection of mentally fragile denizens of a nursing home who harbor endless fantasies, romantic and otherwise, as they live out their final days. Bill (who had been gruff and distant when I first arrived, and must have wondered why the board of trustees of his august theater had handed the reins over to a girl young enough to be his granddaughter) gave me a bottle of Tabasco sauce as an opening-night gift with a card that contained a scrawled quote from the play: "Turned out better." I still treasure that note.

It was palpably clear in watching those four actors collaborate that the benefits of a permanent acting company were important to reconsider, particularly in anticipation of returning to The Geary, a large theater that demanded very particular skills from its performers. In 1996, as part of our first full season in the new Geary, I decided to stage Tennessee Williams's *The Rose Tattoo*, featuring Kathleen Widdoes, a veteran of the Stratford Festival and the New York Shakespeare Festival and an actress possessed of extraordinary vocal and emotional power. The question was whom to pair her with as Mangiacavallo. Marco had just completed a successful *Richard III* at the Oregon Shakespeare Festival and was down at South Coast Repertory starring as Petruchio in *The Taming of the Shrew* when I contacted him about *The Rose Tattoo*. He replied in characteristic fashion that he wouldn't audition, "because auditioning is my tragic weak spot," but asked me to come see his *Shrew* and, if I were still interested, to stay and discuss our Williams project over drinks afterwards. I did. One drink led to another and another, as over the next decade we continued a rich and far-ranging conversation about company and the role of the actor in American theater.

Marco was committed to the notion that actors do their best work as part of a permanent ensemble that trains together and collaborates over long periods of time. As a student of the great teacher and director Michael Langham, he believed in transformation and in responsibility; he remains to this day an actor who takes charge of his rehearsal process from day one, who always brings power, intelligence, and surprise into the room, who demands the most from himself and his peers at every moment, and who is invested not only in his own performance but in the health and direction of the entire organization. (No wonder he went on to become artistic director of Shakespeare Santa Cruz.) In 1996, Marco committed to moving to San Francisco and joining A.C.T. full time; in exchange, I guaranteed him a fifty-two-week salary and a genuine role in season planning and in teaching and directing in the school.

Zelda Fichandler, again in "Whither (or Wither) Art?", put it best:

> Transient, temporary work sometimes feels as nothing but a high form of what the manufacturing industry calls "piece work"—you get paid for the number of "pieces of work" you turn out and how many you turn out is the measure of things, not you, yourself. On a rainy day, "jobbing-in"—our word for piece work—can make one feel devalued: a "gig" can only be followed by another "gig." You may be moving along but only from here to there—moving, but not evolving.
>
> If an actor is always cast because he's "right for the role" with no consideration for the development of his own range and versatility, if with each role he starts over again with a group of strangers who have no collective experience to draw upon, if he sometimes gets the sense of himself as a kind of commodity—paid to fill a need—and then "time's up and thanks," what is it we're saying to him? That "Theatre's a precarious profession, we always knew that, be glad you're working"? Is that okay? Is that enough? . . .
>
> Artists should be invited to become involved in the total life of the institution in order to provide it with their special knowledge and point-of-view and to have their say. I read that while Ingmar Bergman was heading the Swedish National Theatre, he established a five-member artists'

council that he consulted about repertory, company membership, casting, and the like. I don't know how this idea would play out in America, though I wish I'd tried it myself.

With A.C.T.'s burgeoning core company, this is what we tried. Once Marco was on board, the company grew. In casting a Stella to play across from Marco in *A Streetcar Named Desire*, we discovered an actress right out of Yale named René Augesen, who astonished us with her power, sexuality, and honesty even on videotape. Although she turned out to be unavailable for *Streetcar*, I subsequently cast René in the title role of *Mary Stuart* (in our co-production at the Huntington Theatre Company) and then asked her if she'd like to stay on at A.C.T. as a company member. René became our leading lady for over a decade, joining Marco and Gregory Wallace, who had come to A.C.T. to play Belize in *Angels in America* and impressed us with his remarkable wit, his expressive acting, and his deep experience teaching Chekhov. By the time *Angels* closed, we had persuaded Gregory to remain in San Francisco and to take a central role in reforming the curriculum of the M.F.A. Program. Another remarkable actor, Steven Anthony Jones, had been part of A.C.T.'s life for many seasons, ever since he fell in love with the Bay Area on a national tour of *A Soldier's Play*; Steven's broad understanding of Bay Area theater, and his range as an actor and mentor, made him a natural for the company. And while it was certainly never my intention to populate the company with so many men, I added the protean and beautifully trained Anthony Fusco to the mix (who already lived in San Francisco and had participated in much of our work), as well as Jack Willis, who came to town with Robert Wilson and Tom Waits's *The Black Rider* and stayed on, eventually playing everything from Big Daddy in *Cat on a Hot Tin Roof* to Max in *The Homecoming* with ferocity, wit, and compassion.

In those early years, the acting company was joined by resident designers Kate Edmunds and Peter Maradudin, and the whole artistic team met every week for two hours to plan the season and to evaluate our ongoing work. In the years since then, A.C.T.'s core company has evolved, grown, changed, and shrunk, following a trajectory that may have been a little too ad hoc for its own good, but we've learned as we've gone. Our philosophy for the core company began with the belief that each actor should be integrated into both the training and producing wings of the institution. Sometimes that has turned out to be a challenge; A.C.T. has been able to pay for the company by keeping actors employed both onstage and in the classroom, but teaching requires a very different set of skills from acting, and much coaching and patience has been necessary for that model to be successful. Furthermore, my idealistic view of actors as the perfect ambassadors to the funding and audience development world has also often collided with the reality that actors can be shy and introverted people who flourish when given a role to play but feel naked when asked to speak on their own or the theater's behalf. Finally, it might have been easier in retrospect if I had set official term limits for the acting company, since it's valuable for a pool of artists to replenish itself and to change over time. Shifts in personnel turned out to be painful and difficult. Nevertheless, the presence of an ensemble of actors with a long-term commitment to each other and to the organization radically changed the artistic life of A.C.T. and gave voice to a sector of our profession that often feels powerless and mute.

It saddens me that the issue of the actor's role in the American theater today is so rarely discussed in any sophisticated way. A few decades ago it was simply assumed that the mission of a major resident theater included the nurturing of a resident company of actors: Robert Brustein at the A.R.T. had Will LeBow, Karen MacDonald, and Tommie Derragh, among others; Garland Wright at the Guthrie had Isabell Monk, Sally Wingert, and a host of others; Seattle Rep had Jeff Steitzer, Larry Ballard, and Mariann Mayberry, to name a few; and Arena Stage, the theater I grew up with, nurtured such remarkable talents as Robert Prosky and Dianne Wiest. By the early nineties, these companies had all dissolved, with the exception of the A.R.T. company, which was let go with the arrival of Artistic Director Diane Paulus. While there are still important holdouts, such as the Oregon Shakespeare Festival, the Alley Theatre, and Trinity

Repertory Company, and some theaters with less formal long-term commitments, such as that of Brian Kulick at CSC or Michael Kahn at the Shakespeare Theatre Company, I have continued to be puzzled by our failure as a field to make a long-term commitment to actors. In the symphony world it would be considered ludicrous to expect a pickup band to play Mahler or Beethoven with the depth and breadth expected of a major orchestra. In ballet, it would be difficult to imagine major repertoire being performed by artists who had not trained and worked together for years. Only in the theater do we assume that a pickup group of artists with different levels of training and experience will be capable of creating a rich and unified production of a classical text, or providing the ongoing vision to develop a new play.

I suppose it is our fanatic free-market sensibility that says we want to be able to choose from anyone and everyone available to us, and that forcing directors to collaborate with acting companies is somehow restrictive. Yet I have never hired a director at A.C.T. who resented working with our company or who didn't have a positive experience in their highly capable hands. But the sensibility that says that it is worth programming and shaping the work in such a way as to sustain a group of actors over time has been all but lost. Theater is no longer "local" in that sense; whether in Seattle or Dallas or Hartford or Los Angeles, the actors in a given production are, for the most part, imported and thrown together for four weeks before being expected to deliver the goods on opening night. Sometimes that can be exhilarating and lead to success. But as Peter Brook noted so brilliantly in his seminal book *The Empty Space*, "Two hours is a short time and an eternity: to use two hours of public time is a fine art. Yet this art with its frightening exigencies is served largely by casual labour. In a deadly vacuum there are few places where we can properly learn the arts of the theatre—so we tend to drop in on the theatre offering love instead of science. This is what the unfortunate critic is nightly called to judge."

While the regional theater has largely abandoned the company model, there are certainly small New York theaters that have collaborated with a given pool of actors over a period of time, and important ensembles around the country such as The Civilians, Lookingglass Theatre Company, Pig Iron Theatre Company, and Tectonic Theater Project, that consistently create work together. But in conversations with funders, I have frequently raised the challenge of supporting an acting company, only to be told that this is no longer an imperative. Indeed, Diane Ragsdale, who served as program officer at The Andrew W. Mellon Foundation from 2004 to 2010, recently told me that I was the only artistic director she could remember who had asked Mellon to support an acting company. While we often talk about giving artists a home, at this moment "artist" usually means playwright, which I find somewhat odd, since an actor's work is by definition collaborative and needs to be associated with a group and with a production, whereas a playwright's work is in part solitary and can happen even if not attached to a given theater. The indifference to actors seems shortsighted to me for many reasons; surely our audiences would be more connected to our work if they made the kind of investment in actors over time that ballet audiences make to "their" dancers or jazz audiences to "their" players. Surely if audiences watched transformation rather than typecasting, they would better understand the art of making theater. Surely if actors were given a voice in the repertoire, they would respond with a stronger investment in the work they had helped to choose. And surely if playwrights had the opportunity to write plays for a given company of actors, their sense of having an artistic home would be greatly enhanced.

As I write this, I have to acknowledge that the fight to keep a company alive has all but defeated me recently; a combination of financial constraints, casting imperatives, personality clashes, and natural attrition has diminished our core company, while at the same time we have made a deeper investment in long-term collaborations with our actors in training as well as with core designers, core faculty members, and a broad cadre of like-minded actors such as David Strathairn, Bill Irwin, Michele Shay, Andrew Polk, Sab Shimono, Seana McKenna, Giles Havergal, and many more. Perhaps this is a natural evolution, as one is inspired and energized by different artists at different moments of one's career, and staying flexible and open to an evolving group of artists is important.

It is also true that, as the M.F.A. Program has grown in its richness and breadth and has become more deeply integrated into the overall creative life of the organization, we have come to view our M.F.A. students and alumni as the true "core company" of A.C.T., and have attempted to give at least one or two of them long-term contracts to keep them in San Francisco after they graduate. That way, the skill set and predilections of the young artists on our stage are well known to us before we go into rehearsal, and the M.F.A. core faculty can continue to coach and train them even as these artists become professionals. This practice feels consonant with the original dream of A.C.T. as a place of lifelong learning.

Indeed, one of the seminal experiences of my recent tenure at A.C.T. was watching alumnus and core company member Nick Gabriel play Clov to Bill Irwin's Hamm in Beckett's *Endgame* in April 2012. I had taught Nick during his three years at A.C.T. and was drawn to his physical expressivity, his mordant sense of humor, his precise use of language, his huge, innocent eyes, and his Michael Chekhov approach to gesture and character. Even when paired with a consummate artist like Bill, I knew he would hold his own. In reviewing the production, the *Wall Street Journal's* Terry Teachout wrote, "Mr. Gabriel's stiff-legged, sweetly patient, and unexpectedly youthful Clov (a nice touch) is one of the finest interpretations of a Beckett role that I've had the privilege to see." Perhaps if this confluence of training and performance were more common in the American theater, the hundreds of actors coming out of graduate school might feel that there was a home for them to keep learning and growing, and might find a reason to stay in the theater instead of gravitating primarily to film and television. A large part of the aesthetic of a theater revolves around the artists who are selected to create the work, so a serious look at what drives our choice of collaborators would seem to be in order.

Just as the students at A.C.T. remind us constantly that the goal of the organization is lifelong learning, there have been artists in my twenty-plus years at A.C.T. who have constituted my own form of continuing education. One of the hardest things about being an artistic director is figuring out how to keep growing and evolving as an artist within your own organization. Because the task is to support the successes and protect the failures of other artists, most of us have trouble understanding how to give ourselves that same permission to change, succeed, and fail. Who in our own organizations will tell us the truth, will challenge our assumptions, will open our eyes and keep us honest? In my tenure at A.C.T., one of the artists who has always had my back and has told me the truth, no matter what, is Olympia Dukakis. I have collaborated with Olympia numerous times as an actress; she has also taught extraordinary master classes in the school, talked to our audiences and raised funds from our donors, developed new plays, and introduced new ways of thinking, and she is currently a trustee of the organization. Because she had been an effective artistic director herself for nineteen years at the Whole Theater Company, she intuitively understood everything I was going through at A.C.T. And because I always knew she would be honest with me, I have turned to her for advice at every crisis and every new juncture. Knowing her has changed my life.

Interestingly, I first met Olympia over an argument about Sophocles. In 1987, I was visiting the home of James Laughlin (legendary editor and founder of New Directions Press) with my literary critic mother, who had collaborated with New Directions on many occasions. Knowing I was a classicist, Laughlin pulled an unpublished Ezra Pound manuscript out of his drawer and handed it to me. It was a brilliantly idiosyncratic version of Sophocles' *Elektra*, written while Pound was incarcerated at St. Elizabeths psychiatric hospital in Washington, D.C. I decided immediately that I wanted to direct the world premiere, whereupon I asked Olympia to play Clytemnestra. I had never met her and made the request through her agent, who called me back to say that Olympia had a thing or two to say on the subject of that particular interpretation of Clytemnestra, and would I like to talk about it. Next thing I knew, we were having lunch together in Midtown while she regaled me with stories about the history of the Goddess and why she (Olympia) found Sophocles' view of Clytemnestra unacceptable in light of this queen's ancient lineage and the justice of her claim against her husband (stemming from Agamemnon's murder of Clytemnestra's daughter Iphigenia). Surely, said Olympia, this was a woman whose desire for revenge was in fact a form of justice, and as such, she should not have been depicted as the harridan Sophocles assumed she was (notwithstanding Pound's hilariously trashy interpretation of the role). Our lunch was the beginning of a thirty-year conversation. Olympia encouraged me to dig deeper into ancient Greek culture, to question the assumptions made in the major tragedies, which were, after all, plays by men for male audiences, using women as tools for their own points of view. Yet Olympia is no ideologue; she's too funny, complicated, and self-questioning for that. She is an artist who revels in contradiction; in fact, she is more adept than any actor with whom I have worked at truly holding contradictory feelings onstage at the same time. When I accepted her resistance to playing Sophocles' Clytemnestra and asked her which Greek heroine she would be interested in exploring instead, she immediately said she wanted to take on the title role of Euripides' *Hecuba*. This is why, many years later at A.C.T., we joined together to explore the torment and vendetta of a dispossessed Trojan queen and the men who dared to take her on.

One incident in rehearsal with Olympia has always reminded me why long-term collaborations with truly curious artists are so key. We were working on the penultimate scene in *Hecuba*, in which the Trojan queen, having murdered the children of Polymestor and put out the eyes of the evil king in revenge for the destruction of her son, defends her actions to Agamemnon. Olympia was confounded by this defense; Hecuba had already accomplished the necessary deed, she reasoned, so why did she need to articulate her reasons to an enemy politician for whom she had no respect? It seemed counterintuitive, until our dramaturg, classical scholar Helene Foley, spoke up. "Don't you understand?" Helene asked. Up till this moment, she explained, the narrative had belonged to the Greeks. "This is your moment to rewrite history." Olympia stopped dead in her tracks. The nature of history is an essential theme of ancient Greek tragedy, and of course history belongs to those who write it. For Hecuba to achieve just redress for the murder of her son, she needed to proclaim her position not just to Agamemnon but in such a way that history would hear her and acknowledge the justice of her actions. This idea was electrifying for Olympia; she could be both inside the moment and at the same time outside of it, taking on the audience in an attempt to widen the lens and make her case for posterity. It was a vivid reminder that theater can serve both to reveal character and to stimulate a larger debate about human experience.

Olympia is rare in her ability to be inside and outside of a scene almost simultaneously (which is probably why she also excels at Brecht and made such a memorable Mother Courage). Her broad perspective also means that she always understands both the internal mechanism of making a theater run and the external pressures and suppositions that make the task so challenging. So on occasions when I emerged from a particularly bruising board meeting feeling in some way belittled or disrespected, she would exclaim, "It's not about you, it's about two thousand years of patriarchy!" and help me contextualize the situation. She reminded me how quick women are to take the blame when something goes wrong at their organizations, and she endlessly exhorted me to "stop banging your head against a brick wall and look for the open door." The idea of mentorship has become a common thread of contemporary success stories, and yet true mentorship happens in the American theater less often than one would think. This is a vast country, and each of us toils in her own corner, trying to reinvent the wheel and make the best decisions possible along the way. My multi-decade relationship with Olympia, and the way that at every step she has saved me from giving up and helped me to navigate the future, is something I will never take for granted.

Before leaving this reflection on Olympia and our collaboration, I want to return to the Lorca poem quoted earlier. What Olympia found so radical about the poem is its understanding that theater exists only in relationship to audience. As she told me the story of her journey as an artist, she recounted the stages of her own creative development, including a bleak period in her life in which acting had ceased to be meaningful to her. In her early career, she explained, she was obsessed with perfecting her craft. Then she went through a period in which she loved the thrill of the chase, the competition for roles, the desire to tackle larger and more difficult material and to beat out other similarly talented actors. And then she hit a wall, going through a period of intense burnout in which neither craft nor competition was enough, and she began to doubt whether acting mattered to her anymore. Obsessing about her own craft felt narcissistic; competing for roles felt wrongheaded. She was discouraged and uninspired, and considered leaving the field. What turned her thinking around was the audience. She began to understand that for her to stay current with herself, it was crucial that she stay current with the audience. Indeed, what shifted her perspective and has kept her energized about live theater to this day is her passion for involving audience members as directly as possible in the central issues of a play. She found nourishment in the notion that whatever script she is working on is indeed "water drawn from the well of the people," given back to them "in a cup of beauty." The mutual understanding that can happen when that exchange occurs in an authentic way in the theater is profound and unusual. Olympia constantly reminds me that with every rehearsal process, the goal is the same: to give something beautiful back to an audience so that, in experiencing it, they can "understand themselves."

Parents Marjorie and Joseph Perloff at the Grand Hotel in Cabourg, Normandy, early 1980s. PHOTO COURTESY CAREY PERLOFF

Carey (left) with her sister, Nancy Perloff, at Chatham, Massachusetts, 1963. PHOTO COURTESY CAREY PERLOFF

Carey Perloff as a teenage archaeologist in New Mexico, 1975. PHOTO COURTESY CAREY PERLOFF

Carey Perloff as a young ballerina in The Washington Ballet's Nutcracker, *1967.* PHOTO COURTESY CAREY PERLOFF

Carey Perloff and Harold Pinter during rehearsals of The Birthday Party *at New York's Classic Stage Company, 1989.* PHOTO BY TOM CHARGIN

Carey and baby Lexie with Lauren Bacall and Jean Stapleton at Classic Stage Company, 1989. PHOTO © TED KEENAN, 1989

Interior of *The Geary Theater* in ruins after the 1989 Loma Prieta earthquake. PHOTOS BY JOHN SUTTON

1992-93 SEASON OF DISCOVERY

Carey Perloff's appointment calendar for her first month as artistic director of A.C.T., 1992. PHOTO COURTESY

Anthony Giles and Carey Perloff with their daughter, Alexandra, in 1992, one week after arriving in San Francisco to begin the job at A.C.T. PHOTO COURTESY CAREY PERLOFF

Nicholas Perloff-Giles with Anika Noni Rose at the 2009 A.C.T. gala. PHOTO BY DREW ALTIZER PHOTOGRAPHY

Alexandra and Nicholas Perloff-Giles, 2006. PHOTO COURTESY CAREY PERLOFF

Renovated interior of The Geary Theater, 1996.
PHOTO COURTESY AMERICAN CONSERVATORY
THEATER

*Carey Perloff at the ribbon-cutting ceremony celebrating
the centennial of The Geary Theater, 2010.* PHOTO BY
TIMOTHY FAUST

Exterior of The Geary Theater, 1987. PHOTO COURTESY AMERICAN
CONSERVATORY THEATER

Carey Perloff with (left to right) Charles Lanyer, Scott Asti, Benton Greene, Claire Winters, and Chris Ferry in rehearsal of Pirandello's Enrico IV *at A.C.T., 2001.* PHOTO BY KEVIN BERNE

Carey Perloff with Joshua Roberts in an A.C.T. Master of Fine Arts Program workshop, 2010. PHOTO BY KEVIN BERNE

(Left to right) Anthony Fusco, Andrew Polk, Jack Willis, and Kenneth Welsh in The Homecoming *at A.C.T., 2011.* PHOTO BY KEVIN BERNE

Sabina Allemann and Jack Willis in The Tosca Project *at A.C.T., 2010.* PHOTO BY KEVIN BERNE

Gregory Wallace (left) and Peter Frechette in Waiting for Godot *at A.C.T., 2003.* PHOTO BY KEVIN BERNE

Tom Stoppard and Carey Perloff in rehearsal of The Real Thing *at A.C.T., 2004.* PHOTO COURTESY DAVIDALLENSTUDIO.COM

Carey Perloff with Alan Stein at the opening night of Travesties *at A.C.T., 2006.* PHOTO COURTESY AMERICAN CONSERVATORY THEATER

Carey Perloff and Olympia Dukakis, 2006. PHOTO COURTESY CAREY PERLOFF

Carey Perloff at A.C.T.'s 2007 fundraising gala. PHOTO BY DREW ALTIZER PHOTOGRAPHY

Rendering of the exterior of A.C.T.'s new Strand Theater. COURTESY SKIDMORE, OWINGS & MERRILL LLP

Carey Perloff with composer Byron Au Yong discussing the renovations of The Strand Theater. PHOTO BY DENYS BAKER

Renovation of The Strand Theater gets underway, 2014. PHOTO BY DENYS BAKER

CHAPTER 9

Who Are We Training and Why?

Along with tackling the question of company, I knew that my next big task was to consider the future of the conservatory, in particular, the M.F.A. program, which was called, at the time I arrived, the Advanced Training Program. While Bill Ball's notion of lifelong learning and of apprenticing young actors to master artists greatly appealed to me in theory, in practice the school had become oddly separated from the producing wing. Even before I arrived, the ATP was going through an identity crisis: In the post-earthquake years, A.C.T. no longer had a full-time company to provide employment for the actors whom it was training or to provide teachers for their education, so it was necessary to ask what the purpose was of having a graduate school under those circumstances. Was it to altruistically prepare young artists for American theater as a whole? Or was it intended to provide talent for A.C.T. in particular? If the answer was the former, could an organization as strapped as A.C.T. continue to provide that service to the field? But if the students training at A.C.T. were not being trained specifically for work at The Geary, what were they being trained to do? What were the priorities, the skill sets, the aesthetic choices that we were attempting to inculcate? Of course, when Ball first conceived of A.C.T.'s conservatory, things had been much clearer:

91

A.C.T. was a classical theater whose repertoire was most noted for works such as *Cyrano de Bergerac* and *The Taming of the Shrew*, which required an acting company possessed of an athletic grace, a sense of period behavior, and enormous verbal panache. The A.C.T. training, which supported the company, thus built up physical stamina, taught scansion and speaking in verse, opened up the voice, and built an ensemble. It was the perfect preparation for the work of that particular acting company on the Geary stage. Naturally, as A.C.T.'s mainstage work evolved over time, questions about the nature and purpose of the actor training continued to arise as well. In her thoughtful book *Ecologies of Theater*, scholar Bonnie Marranca asks, "How can schools hope to train artists, when they give so little thought to the cultivation of artistic values? How can students know against which standards they are to be measured if they lack knowledge of the wonder and variousness of theatrical life? Students might become more passionate about their art, and learn what it means to be part of an artistic heritage, if they could be made to appreciate the great world achievements in theatrical thought of more than two thousand years."

Of course, there are as many theories about how to teach acting as there are schools to do it. The famous Stanislavsky training of Harold Clurman, Stella Adler, and Lee Strasberg introduced a generation of American actors to their own complex interior landscape, and the actors who succeeded best were those who had access to their emotional lives in a way that was transparent enough for film and natural enough to seem unrehearsed. When Zelda Fichandler began teaching at New York University, her dream was to train actors to join repertory companies, so transformation and a facility with heightened theatrical styles were at the top of her list of priorities. Fichandler's actors had to have the imagination to enter into a variety of roles, to lose themselves believably in the Spanish Golden Age, in Arthur Miller's small-town America, or in rural Russia; she sought out actors who could handle everything from William Shakespeare and George Bernard Shaw to August Wilson and Tennessee Williams and could move from one kind of material to another with facility and appetite. This is not to pit authenticity against transformation—both are critical tools of the flexible actor—but merely to say that the focus of actor training depends upon the context for which actors are being trained. Each acting program has to interrogate its own methods and determine its own measures of success.

When I arrived at A.C.T. in 1992, I tried to understand the values that were guiding its form of actor training. On a fairly regular basis there were large student critiques in which the faculty was invited to judge the work being presented. At the first critique I attended, a young woman was trying to explore Lady Anne's behavior in the wooing scene in *Richard III*, and from all corners of the room, commentary was being thrown out in a highly public way, while the student became tearful and tried to make adjustments on the spot. The one thing I could gather from watching this exercise was that A.C.T. prized the ego of the director/teacher and expected its students to be prepared to be thrown into public situations in which they would have to sink or swim.

At the same time, a revival of *Cyrano* was going on at The Geary in which nearly the entire second-year class was being used as non-speaking cannon fodder onstage, which didn't seem to me the best use of their precious tuition dollars and was reportedly causing much unhappiness among the student body. Given that the ATP was only a two-year program, every second counted; by the middle of the second year, the students were already thinking about how to graduate and enter the profession. Overall, the instruction seemed somewhat fraught to me and without a coherent aesthetic. The speech training was based on Edith Skinner's work, which I had always admired, but many of the students had that strange British inflection characteristic of the mid-Atlantic tonality beloved by Skinner disciples. I realized that as much as I prize good speech, I value the authenticity of an individual voice even more, and I was curious about a form of training that asked students to substitute other sounds for their own native sounds, in a way that often came out sounding formulaic.

I was also surprised that the movement training included ballet and period dance but little in the way of physical characterization or clown work. While I adore ballet, and studied it myself for years, it's not clear that its formal alignment and tight muscle requirements are very helpful in releasing the actor physically. It seemed to me that the school had taken on the tension of the rest of the organization in those years, which posed a formidable challenge: actor training is based on trust and on the freedom to fail, and these seemed to be in short supply in the early nineties at A.C.T.

While it seemed to make sense that the majority of classes in the ATP curriculum were taught by actors and directors working with the theater at the time, I was concerned that when vocal coach Judy Moreland was cast as the lead in *Miss Evers' Boys*, the result was that the students lost their regular voice class. The question of the faculty's relationship to the producing wing of the organization seemed crucial to address, but it was dangerous territory; I felt that I was challenging doctrine every time I asked a question or visited a class.

On my very first day on the job, a large WASC (Western Association of Schools and Colleges) accreditation team arrived to assess A.C.T.'s training program and determine whether to continue providing accreditation. WASC had indicated grave concerns both about the institution's financial ability to run a graduate school and about the lack of transparency and commonly held goals among faculty and students. It was a tense visit. The students were allowed to communicate with the WASC team by posting remarks on an anonymous open forum at the end of the formal study; a number of their comments were damaging and despairing. Clearly, if A.C.T. was going to continue in the business of actor education, major changes would have to be made in how we ran the ATP, but the anxious atmosphere that prevailed made serious change hard to imagine. The fact that Richard Seyd had joined the artistic team and had his own distinctive philosophy of teaching acting made things even more complicated.

We had big issues to solve if we were going to keep the graduate school alive. We had to understand what teaching acting actually meant in the late twentieth century. What profession were we preparing these actors for? Was the kind of verbal dexterity necessary to perform Stoppard in a thousand-seat house really going to be useful for most American actors, who might never have that opportunity? In a culture in which so many theaters had begun to use microphones on a regular basis, was vocal strength still an asset? Was the collaborative effort of blending into a larger ensemble and becoming one with a family of other actors valuable in a culture that prizes celebrity and individual personality above all else? Was fulfilling a director's vision the most central goal, when the dwindling amount of work available meant that actors were increasingly required to become their own producers and creators? With so many actors of color among the student body, was the dramatic literature we were exposing them to broad and culturally diverse enough?

That first year, A.C.T. Alexander Technique instructor Frank Ottiwell handed me a quote to hang over my desk: "The only thing harder than moving a cemetery is changing a curriculum." And even harder than changing a curriculum is paying for it. Actor training is expensive, complicated, and ever changing. It requires a great deal of space, a problem exacerbated at A.C.T. by the fact that the Bay Area is among the most expensive real estate markets in America. Furthermore, because it is experiential, actor training requires small classes taught by a dedicated faculty. A.C.T.'s top competitors (Yale, Juilliard, UC San Diego, and NYU) fund their elite graduate education by having large undergraduate programs to support them. At some universities, graduate students teach undergraduates in exchange for scholarship support, and the faculty is supported by both undergraduate and graduate teaching and by university endowments. Free-standing M.F.A. programs like A.C.T.'s, without undergraduate schools to support them, are rapidly disappearing from this country; in 2012, the Denver Center Theatre Company abruptly terminated its M.F.A. program, deeming it too expensive to sustain. We often say that "conservatory is our middle name," but it was clear that if the organization was going to continue to invest time and resources in that endeavor, we had to define how the M.F.A. Program served the mission of the larger institution.

Logic would indicate that the value of training young actors within the bosom of a producing theater is that they can perform the young roles in that theater's repertoire. But not at A.C.T. One of our many challenges has always been our LORT (League of Resident Theatres) designation: Because of our large house and historic position in the American theater, we are, for collective bargaining purposes, a LORT A theater, a category we share with only four other theaters in the country. We are the only LORT A theater with an accredited school, and our LORT A status puts us at an enormous competitive disadvantage because, under the terms of our union contract, we are forbidden to use nonprofessionals onstage without putting them on a paid Actors' Equity Association contract. Of course, this makes it difficult to compete with, say, Yale School of Drama, which can put its students into its mainstage shows at Yale Rep (a LORT B theater) with greater frequency. I have wrestled with this problem since the day I arrived at A.C.T., because the conditions seemed so palpably unfair to me; here we were losing nearly a million dollars a year on our graduate school, yet we were forbidden to take advantage of the fact that we had talented young actors in our midst by including them in our shows without Equity-level pay. After years of discussion, Equity finally gave us a concession by which five young actors a year were allowed on the Geary stage without being put on a paid contract.

The issue of young actors collaborating on mainstage work is obviously crucial, because one of the joys and benefits of an in-house education is that we can develop a young company of artists whom we have selected and trained in a shared way of working. This ancient tradition goes back to theaters like the Comédie Française or more recently to Ingmar Bergman's Royal Dramatic Theatre, which regularly replenishes its acting pool with young talent trained from within. At its best, I knew that the A.C.T. training could yield a seamless company of young and mature actors who would be capable of working in perfect unison. But figuring out a mechanism for getting our students on our stage has been a challenging part of our ongoing agenda.

In 1994, with the departure of John Sullivan, A.C.T.'s conservatory went through a period of transition. Conservatory Director Susan Stauter, at the urging of A.C.T. trustee and arts education champion Ruth Asawa, moved on to do groundbreaking work in San Francisco's public schools, helping to establish the district's first Arts Education Master Plan. We began a year-long national search for a new conservatory director, using that opportunity to study best practices in the field by inviting a handful of exceptional teachers to come lead a series of master classes for the rest of us to observe and learn from. The person who impressed us the most was a Yale-trained actress who had been running the theater program at Princeton and seemed to have a remarkable mix of erudition and experimentation in her blood. This was Melissa Smith, whom we hired in 1995 and who has run A.C.T.'s M.F.A. Program ever since. I knew that Melissa was as enamored of Mac Wellman as of *Macbeth*, and would help our students learn to tackle contemporary dramaturgy with the same gusto they had used for Shakespeare. Her love of Sanford Meisner's teachings meant she prized immediacy and interaction over rhetoric and analysis, which was exactly the jolt the school needed. It was clear that she was flexible and fearless enough to be open to creating an entirely new program for A.C.T.

As soon as Melissa arrived at A.C.T., she said that we should aspire to be one of the top five acting programs in the country. Then she set about making it happen. Her courage and tough-mindedness astounded me; in the quest for professionalism, she let anyone go who seemed amateur or unable to rise to the challenge. She set very high standards, hired a remarkable core faculty, championed the use of company actors to inspire and mentor the students, and insisted upon public performances so that her young actors understood their relationship to an audience from the get-go. We didn't even have a small theater for the students to perform in for the public, a ridiculous situation for an acting school, so we began to rent spaces all over town to accommodate student productions. Interestingly, this was the beginning of a very fertile cross-pollination between A.C.T. and the local theater community. Our students performed at the Magic Theatre, New Langton Arts, New College, and ultimately The Theater at the Children's Creativity Museum (previously known as Zeum). Slowly, the community began to realize that a group of incredibly talented young artists was growing and evolving right in their midst, and that for about ten dollars audiences could attend their shows and watch them work. One result of this is that more and more of our best graduates have chosen to stay in San Francisco after graduation, because there are now multiple theaters that will hire them.

Melissa also took up the ongoing battle to make the ATP (a two-year training program with an additional independent study project) a three-year M.F.A. program. Up to this point, students could only earn an M.F.A. degree at A.C.T. by doing a post-graduation thesis project that involved performing at A.C.T. or another institution or creating their own performance project, and then writing an extended essay about the experience. This meant that A.C.T. had no control over the quality of the endeavor and also that we were judging young actors in no small part by their ability to write a thesis, a skill they would most likely rarely use again in their careers. So, by the turn of the millennium, an entirely new structure was created, and we admitted our first three-year class, with a comprehensive curriculum that used the entire three years of training to achieve specific goals.

As the renamed A.C.T. Master of Fine Arts Program became more tightly stitched with the producing wing of the organization, we developed a metric called "Geary readiness," by which all training had to be measured. By their third year of training, every M.F.A. student was expected to have the kinesthetic, vocal, verbal, imaginative, and professional skills to succeed on the Geary stage. This, of course, implied that our actor training program was intended first and foremost to serve A.C.T.'s own producing needs, the only goal that made sense to me given the overall needs of the organization. With the recalcitrance of Equity to permit our students to work on our stage except on a paid contract, we have tried a variety of creative solutions to the student-actor problem, including guaranteeing each student two paid contracts in exchange for tuition. Such are the gymnastics we have gone through to employ our own young artists. But the goal of Geary readiness was key to defining our training and our expectations.

Aiming for The Geary is like preparing for the World Series—its scale is daunting, and many actors are defeated by the skills it necessitates. We came to realize that, because of the Geary-readiness standard, there was no point accepting students or putting them through a training process if they couldn't ultimately succeed on our own mainstage. This has meant, over the years, that we have forgone the chance to accept some extremely talented actors whose instruments were not compatible with the Geary stage. But that was the barometer. Step by step, we itemized those skills most central to success at The Geary and began recruiting actors who had the appetite and potential to achieve those goals. We made the class size smaller and smaller until we had a fighting chance of including the majority of students in our mainstage work.

We introduced the students to the process of new-play development and began to use them as our company when listening to new work or collaborating with writers. And, most important, we began to teach our students how to be total theater animals. In this economy, it is no longer enough to graduate with an excellent degree from a good school, get an agent, and wait for the phone to ring. Survival as an actor today means being able to find or generate one's own work, and often that includes devising and/or producing it oneself.

The current curriculum at A.C.T. thus blends rigorous movement and physical improvisation, language and text work, acting class and script analysis, the rehearsal process, and collaboration on new plays, along with the tools to create work from scratch, to use social media to promote the work and find an audience, to perform in non-traditional spaces, and to understand theater budgets and producing protocols. With the arrival of our head of movement, Stephen Buescher, we began to start every teaching year with The Leap, a two-day exploration in which faculty, students, staff, guest artists, and anyone else we can rope in join together to make collective work throughout the building, and to share it with each other in a celebratory way. Each January we host the Sky Festival, born out of whatever work the students have the greatest passion for, produced, directed, and performed predominantly by them. In these ways, over time, the M.F.A. Program has again become the artistic engine of the organization, establishing expectations for the creative process that are followed throughout the institution.

The questions about what field we are training actors for have not disappeared. But from an institutional point of view, the presence of talented, hungry young artists at the heart of A.C.T. means we can rarely get smug or complacent about what we're doing, because a twenty-something is always on hand to question the choices we make. Our school mitigates against allegiance to the status quo. This can be exhilarating or harrowing, depending upon the occasion.

One of the most traumatic events in my A.C.T. tenure occurred in 1998 when an African American female student, who had brought pepper spray into a project rehearsal as a character prop, used it on a white male fellow cast member in a moment of tension in a scene. The incident caused enormous upset among the student body and she was suspended, whereupon she contacted the press and a number of A.C.T.'s donors, accusing us of racism. This incident forced us to articulate much more clearly our standards of safety within both the classroom and the rehearsal room, and also reopened many of the fault lines about race and gender that had been exposed during my first season at A.C.T.

Graduate school tends to be a tinderbox, as the search for self and identity is made all the more fraught by the vulnerability of being young and in a radically new environment. Issues of sexual preference, body image, race, gender, and personal voice cause ongoing debate, sometimes healthy and sometimes less so. Whenever there has been an incident or conflict, we have tried to learn how to keep the dialogue open while encouraging our students see the bigger picture and the long history of the organization of which they have become a part.

Recently we underwent a terribly difficult controversy when I asked the students to join me in revisiting Mac Wellman and David Lang's *The Difficulty of Crossing a Field*, the music-theater piece we had commissioned for Kronos Quartet and eleven performers, and had produced to great acclaim in 2002 at Theater Artaud. I was eager to return to the piece precisely because we had such a large African

American contingent in the school and I was looking for exciting material for them to work on. But in examining the piece, this group of students was deeply resentful of being asked to play slaves, in part because some felt their casting up to this point had not given them broad enough opportunities. Despite my argument that the slaves in *Difficulty* had knowledge and justice on their side and were the agents of change in the piece, and despite the fact that *Difficulty* was based on a short story by abolitionist Ambrose Bierce, whose career had been committed to the end of slavery, many students remained adamantly opposed to the project. When we convened a schoolwide meeting to discuss the situation, it erupted into tearful name-calling and harsh words, reminding all of us how hard it is to have an objective conversation about representation. Once again, it took months to move past the recriminations. Once again, we had to keep reminding ourselves that if we didn't all love this organization, we wouldn't be fighting so hard to make it better. It was excruciating to be the target of rage and accusation, since I felt I had devoted so much energy to trying to create a more inclusive and open theater. But I also know that by trying to create an environment in which students feel free to express themselves, we have become a more supple and vigorous institution. No matter what, our constant aspiration is to truly become one artistic community.

The financial side of the M.F.A. equation continues to present endless challenges, which leads me back to my initial quandary. Can an individual producing organization afford to invest so significantly in the future of the art form? Perhaps not. But if not us, then who? Teaching acting is like teaching medicine; it is a hands-on activity in which professionals and students work side by side to grow. Actors learn best in the bosom of a theater, just as doctors learn in the bosom of a hospital; otherwise the work risks becoming academic and obsolete. But while the last decade has seen an explosion in the funding opportunities for new plays, it has seen virtually no support for training new actors. Major foundations routinely support the commissioning and development of scripts, but I have been unable to interest any of them in the development of actors, nor have I have interested them in the support of a core company, and this has made the choice to sustain a graduate school at A.C.T. an ongoing struggle. It seems we are loath to invest in the long-term training of an artistic labor force in America, perhaps because we fail to value the contribution that performing artists make to our society as a whole. Actor training is considered elitist and not worth funding, while we spend millions training young athletes. To my mind, this represents a decidedly short-sighted lack of investment in our own cultural future.

In the absence of discrete funding for the M.F.A. Program, new ideas have begun percolating. In 2010, A.C.T. completed a strategic plan that helped us pick our heads up and make a commitment to aspects of our work we had previously taken for granted. Although A.C.T. had one of the oldest student matinee programs in America (which we call SMATs), we had never made a major investment in arts education in the schools, assuming that that lay outside our own mission as creators of the work. But with educational funding drying up and pedagogical priorities shifting from learning to testing, the presence of an arts curriculum in the public schools has become severely endangered. Time after time, studies have shown that children who participate in the arts at school display better concentration, greater empathy, richer imaginations, and less truancy than their peers, yet in many public schools today, the arts are all but absent. And without arts education, there are no future audiences, since without a gateway experience to teach them the pleasures and benefits of interacting with the dramatic arts, young people aren't likely to seek out theater on their own later in life.

Several years ago, A.C.T. decided it was time to leap into this void; we began hiring teaching artists to develop curricula and collaborate with public schools, reviving a summer learning program called Back to the Source (initiated in a different form by Craig Slaight in the nineties) that focuses on the teachers themselves, collaborating with the school district to create ongoing arts-rich professional development opportunities for principals as well as teachers, and sponsoring two programs for students of continuation high schools serving socioeconomically disadvantaged communities. This has radically shifted our relationship to our own neighborhood and to our broader city, but it has also presented new avenues for our M.F.A. students, whom we are training to become "citizen artists." Many of them have instinctively gravitated toward our education programs, volunteering to work in after-school programs, in senior centers, and in schools. This has complemented the mentorship our M.F.A. students have received from our Young Conservatory for years, as they learn to become proficient teachers and pass on what they know to children and teenagers. All of these efforts have led us to create a broader curriculum encompassing teaching and community building, with the goal of leveraging actor training not only in the service of performance but in the service of mentorship, educational outreach, and deep engagement with the community in which they practice their craft.

As I've noted, most M.F.A. programs in America are housed within the confines of universities and have little relationship to their surrounding communities: the students are transient and usually invest scant time and energy in the cities in which they study. A.C.T. is different, embedded as it is in the center of San Francisco and adjacent to the Tenderloin and Central Market districts, where issues of poverty, class, and race loom large. If the American theater could figure out a way to link the best young actors to the best in their communities, think of the energy that could be released. The rationale for an acting program inside a producing organization becomes clearer when we realize that we are training our citizen artists specifically to engage with audiences who might otherwise never encounter the art form.

No matter how complicated, the presence of a school at the heartbeat of A.C.T. has kept me artistically energized. It is often true that you find out what you know and what you value by teaching it, and this has certainly been the case for me. With each newly matriculated class, I have tried to understand more deeply what I value in actors and how to help nurture that. Even before we had a formal company, I came across students whom I knew I would work with as professionals once they finished their training; I could feel an affinity and a mutual excitement that held the promise of successful collaboration in the future.

Interestingly, some of our most exciting students have pursued areas tangential to acting: Ryan Rilette became a director and producing/executive/artistic director, first at New York's Rude Mechanicals Theatre Company, then at Southern Rep in New Orleans, at Marin Theatre Company (where we collaborated very happily with him), and now at Round House Theatre in Maryland. Hal Brooks developed a talent for new-play development and now helms the Cape Cod Theatre Project. Others, such as Daniel Cantor and Ray Dooley carry the teaching torch and help run acting programs across the country; Peter Friedrich established a revolutionary theater department at The American University of Iraq-Sulaimani. And some have become very visible as actors.

Of the latter group, one of my favorite alums is Anika Noni Rose, who, among many distinguished credits, went on to earn a Tony Award and to voice the first animated African American princess in Disney film history. I had taught a scene study class to Anika during her first year at A.C.T., but I really got to know her the day she marched into my office after performing the title role in a student production of *Hedda Gabler*. She sat down beside my desk and said, "Well that was bad, wasn't it?!" While her work was anything but bad, her candid and openhearted question deserved an answer in kind. We spent hours that afternoon talking about Hedda and about how an actress such as Anika might approach that elusive role. In watching the production, Anika felt constrained to me, as if she were playing some idea of correct "Ibsen behavior" rather than bringing all of her feisty, complicated, African American self to the role. The merging of self with character is one of the greatest challenges an actor can face, especially when the character is seemingly so far away from the performer's own experience, ethnicity, or class background. But Anika hadn't gone to graduate school to bury her own history and persona in a cliché. She had to learn to find the historic authenticity of repressed nineteenth-century middle-class Norway and at the same time tap into the rebellious impulses of a contemporary black woman. The fact that she dared to walk into my office and ask the right questions was so much more important than whether she had conquered the role.

From that day forward, Anika and I sought out every opportunity to work together.

Anika came to epitomize much of what we strive to accomplish in A.C.T.'s M.F.A. Program: she is a consummate self-starter who has the skills and imagination to transform into a wide variety of roles, the discipline to keep working and learning, and the breadth to seek out opportunities and create her own projects when necessary. She helped develop *The Difficulty of Crossing a Field* and played a leading role in its premiere. She created a hilarious Dorine in Charles Randolph-Wright's all-black *Tartuffe* at The Geary, and then returned in triumph to sing Polly Peachum in my production of *The Threepenny Opera*. On that occasion, a well-known actor involved with the production insisted on taking the final bow in that show despite the fact that young Anika was carrying the largest role. I remember reassuring Anika that she herself was going to be a big star one day and could easily sacrifice this bow. She behaved with incredible grace and took the lesser bow, and my prediction about her glorious future eventually turned out to be true.

CHAPTER 10

The Question of Aesthetic

Peculiarly enough, I discovered early in my career in the nonprofit American theater that "aesthetic" is for the most part a dirty word. Or, rather, a nonexistent one. It is equated with taste, and taste is considered a limitation for artistic directors. Indeed, while the word aesthetic is rarely evoked, an artistic director will be quickly accused of having an agenda if certain kinds of works, themes, or forms seem to dominate his or her programming. How odd. We are artists, not bureaucrats—of course we have an agenda, just as religious leaders have beliefs! But beliefs are considered polarizing. Artistic directors are exhorted to be objective and catholic (with a small c) in their predilections, to select a season of work in which there is, to quote theater brochures since time immemorial, "something for everyone." I have heard the refrain often in my directing career: that to survive and flourish as an artistic director I need to broaden my taste, and that the most important ingredients in a season are balance and breadth. Certainly, when you are as vulnerable as the current American theater is to the vicissitudes of the box office, it is dangerous to paint yourself into a corner by programming too narrowly or too eccentrically, and breadth can be refreshing and invigorating. But if you think about a theatrical season as a kind of meal, it makes sense that in some way the ingredients have something in common. Or at least that it is possible for the ingredients to harmonize. And that happens by exerting taste. It doesn't help to put *Camelot* next to *Hamlet* and then say the season is balanced. But if, for example, the actor playing King Arthur also plays the ghost of Hamlet's father, one could argue that a theatrical window is being opened for the audience that is potentially illuminating. One has to consider what the journey is throughout the season. This doesn't mean one must assume that all audience members are seeing all plays, but rather that if an audience member chooses to see a given production, he or she will understand from the artistic experience of that work what kind of theater this is and what role it is trying to play in the community.

Of the theaters I have most admired over the years, none ranks higher than the Glasgow Citizens Theatre under the direction of Giles Havergal, Philip Prowse, and Robert David MacDonald; from Giles, who became a close friend and colleague following his delightful *Travels with My Aunt*, which we produced at A.C.T. in 1996, I learned the power a clear and forcefully articulated aesthetic can have in developing a community-based theater with a passionate national and international following.

I have attended many theater conferences in my lifetime and been part of countless discussions about marketing, branding, diversity, mentorship, audience outreach, and other issues crucial to our field. But I can't remember having a conversation anywhere about aesthetic. This has always surprised me. To return to the food metaphor, there are many restaurants that serve chicken, so in evaluating which to patronize, it becomes important to know how that chicken is being prepared: Where is the chef from? What are his or her predilections? Is the kitchen open or closed? Can you eat with your hands? What aspect of world cuisine might one find in this restaurant? And so on. The same applies to theater. For better or for worse, the artistic temperature of a theater reflects that of its artistic leadership. One hopes it is not anodyne and interchangeable with theater seasons around the country: if an artist has a true aesthetic, every play in the season will be a reflection of that vision. And indeed, if we were being honest, the mission statement of a theater would be "This theater produces plays that its artistic director values," just as a restaurant serves food that a given chef wants to prepare and promote. But one is rarely encouraged to say that—mission statements of nonprofit theaters tend to be uplifting, general, audience directed, and moral ("We seek to celebrate the truth of the American experience") and never divisive in the way that a real aesthetic can be. (Next to the quote about curriculum on my bulletin board is a *New Yorker* cartoon in which a husband says to his wife, "No, dear, I don't think our marriage would benefit from a mission statement.")

In part this may go back to the question of the longevity of tenure of artistic leadership: if you assume your artistic director will only be around a short time or until the quarterly profits really tank, you avoid creating a mission statement for your theater that reflects the taste of that individual, since he or she may be gone by next season. It would be unthinkable, by contrast, in discussing Théâtre du Soleil not to focus on the aesthetic of Ariane Mnouchkine, or to fail to equate the work of Complicite with the aesthetic of Simon McBurney. I remember Moisés Kaufman, founder and artistic director of Tectonic Theater Project, telling me that funders were sometimes hesitant to support his company because nearly all the productions were directed by him. But the Mark Morris Dance Group receives support precisely because the work is mostly created by Morris himself. Why the difference in theater? Is it because American theater will always be burdened by having a commercial correlate that exists purely to sell tickets and provide entertainment, and thus the notion of a strong and evolving aesthetic practiced by a given artist over time is less valuable or relevant? Is this why the gap between institutional and ensemble-based or experimental theater continues to grow, as the institutional theater becomes more and more invested in keeping the institution alive at all costs, long after the originating impulse has been forgotten? This is an issue being hotly debated in the American theater, now that many nonprofit theaters in the country are nearing their fifty-year mark and are having to measure themselves against the founding missions of their organizations.

I think back to the Garland Wright days at the Guthrie Theater in the late eighties and early nineties. Wright had incredibly eclectic taste, but everything that I saw there during those years reflected his abiding passion for lively theatricality, for complex ideas, for transformative acting as embodied in a company, for bittersweet and challenging stories and magical visuals. In a tenure that included *The Screens*, *Home*, and *The Play's the Thing*, there was a unified aesthetic that was dictated in part by the acting company that shared the roles, in part by the thrust stage of the Guthrie, which dictated a certain kind of design, and in part by the elegance and wit of Wright's direction, intelligence, and oversight. There was no mistaking the Guthrie seasons for those of another theater.

But this has become something of an exception in the American theater, in part because iconoclastic artists either don't want, or don't get chosen, to run institutions, and in part because artists are discouraged from trumpeting their own tastes or predilections too loudly for fear of alienating an audience. Of course, the sign of a great artist is an ability to evolve, and few of us are interested in directing at age fifty the same plays we wanted to explore at age twenty-five, or at least not in the same way—that's the beauty of growing up in the theater. However, I have learned the hard way that it is valuable and indeed critical to be honest about one's own predilections and tastes. So I want to make a detour here and try to better understand how my own particular aesthetic evolved, and how that aesthetic shapes, for better or for worse, the choices I continue to make as a director, a writer, and a producer.

One of the quests one undergoes in reading new plays is the search for a kind of authentic or idiosyncratic voice that leaps out, that proclaims its particularity and its own often messy specificity. Finding one's voice, and then observing as it changes and develops over time, is one of the most challenging things an artist must undergo, and in the piecework landscape of the American theater it is often nearly impossible to listen to one's own heartbeat or to see one's own work grow and change over time, because each project starts from the beginning, with a new audience, a new set of artists, a new geography.

I had a true epiphany about this in the summer of 2002 when, wearing my playwriting hat, I was invited by James Houghton (artistic director at the time) to be part of the Eugene O'Neill Theater Center's National Playwrights Conference. Under Houghton's regime (as had been the case with Lloyd Richards before him), it was the practice to open the conference by having each writer read his or her play aloud for the other assembled artists. Knowing this put me into a state of total panic; my play, *The Colossus of Rhodes*, was an epic with vaudeville songs about a fanatic British imperialist who falls in love with a young man in South Africa and ends up creating the Rhodes Scholarship as a kind of warped tribute to the memory of this passion. I am not an actor and certainly not a singer, and I couldn't fathom why anyone would find it useful to hear me read my play aloud. Fortunately, I was among the last of the writers to read, so I had the opportunity first to listen to Lee Blessing, Romulus Linney, Julia Jarcho, and several others present their work. As I did, the brilliance of the method revealed itself. Precisely because the writers were not performers, what came through with remarkable clarity was the singularity of personal obsession, predilection, sense of humor, and verbal pattern of each writer; listening to them, I could hear the rhythm of their lives as it found its way into their plays.

It has been said that every great writer writes the same work over and over again from different angles, and certainly I have found that if you can once get truly inside the heartbeat of a play, you will understand that playwright's entire universe. This goes back to a belief in a body of work: a director who finds a congenial writer with whom to collaborate (either a contemporary writer or one who is long dead) will find it deeply satisfying to go on repeated journeys with that writer; she will know what questions to ask, what pitfalls to avoid, what secrets to look for, what rhythms to listen for, what luggage to pack. One of the privileges of running your own theater is having the opportunity for a deep and repeated exploration of those writers with whom you have a particular affinity. As my friend Liz Perle once said to me, "You are holding a thousand people hostage every night with a given play—you'd better be clear about why you chose it and what you hope to say with it!"

For me, it began with the Greeks. I was not a theater kid growing up; while I had performed in high school plays upon occasion, I spent far more time in the world of dance than theater (having done ballet, jazz, tap, and modern dance all through school). I had barely seen a Broadway show or listened to a Broadway soundtrack by the time I went to college (the only one I can remember is *A Chorus Line*), and my imagination was more occupied with the excavation of ancient worlds than with the analysis of plays.

My love affair with the theater began in the autumn of 1976 during a first-year Greek class at Stanford, which I enrolled in to further my archaeological ambitions. My professor, Helene Foley (who continues to be a close friend and advisor thirty-plus years later), used a decidedly theatrical method for teaching ancient Greek. Naturally, our first task was to learn the alphabet. Armed with that crucial knowledge, we were introduced to the famous central Chorus of Aristophanes' *The Frogs*, "Brekekekexkoaxkoax," and suddenly we were reading ancient drama in the original.

I will never forget that moment, staring at the mysterious unfamiliar letters and imagining a group of actors on the Athenian stage, leaping ahead in glorious unison as antic frogs while reciting these words to defy the god Dionysus on his journey into the underworld. I was immediately hooked. Not only could we understand those simple words after a single Greek lesson, but through them we were introduced to a universe in which drama was a subject of momentous importance. In *The Frogs*, Dionysus is in despair over his war-torn city and over the paucity of interesting plays being produced to energize the citizens, so he decides to descend into the underworld, hoping to bring back one of the great playwrights of the past to ameliorate the situation. Imagine our own political leadership deciding to stage a debate between Bertolt Brecht and Arthur Miller in order to trigger a dialogue about our current political quagmire, and you get the gist of *The Frogs*. The play's central debate, or *agon*, is a contest between Euripides and Aeschylus to determine which writer offers the greatest hope for the city of Athens; each writer quotes extensively from his own oeuvre, throwing whole phrases and lines of verse onto a vast scale to be weighed for value. Dionysus eventually chooses Aeschylus, as the more elevated and less melodramatic of the two writers, and he is brought back to earth with the charge of revitalizing tragedy, leaving Sophocles to take his seat in the afterlife.

My head was spinning when I walked out of that first Greek class into the hot sunshine of the Stanford Quad in the fall of 1976. Not only was I delighted with my newly found ability to read an ancient play (or at least five words of it) in the original, but I had encountered a universe in which the answer to a population struggling with war and political chaos was *better drama*. Those of us who make theater in America today are constantly depressed by our own marginalization; it is difficult to believe that what we do matters, or that anyone in the culture would really notice if we just folded up shop and stopped doing it. We desperately seek relevance and look for ways to engage audiences in the art form we love, so that it will seem more meaningful, more central to the cultural discourse. The current obsession with audience engagement and audience participation is the latest attempt to fend off what we perceive as theater's obsolescence by getting everyone in on the game. We eschew classics in favor of contemporary plays that presumably speak more closely to the current climate. And when we encourage an audience to react vocally during or after a show, we think that we are inventing something new.

But in fact, twenty-five hundred years ago, Greek tragedians were struggling to find a way to tell the complex stories of their own time to an audience wary of political jingoism and weary from the toll of the Peloponnesian War. Sitting in broad daylight during performances, Athenian citizens served as a kind of ongoing jury for the arguments of the plays: undoubtedly, like the audiences of Shakespeare, they were loud, opinionated, and engaged. The Greeks understood that the most potent way to criticize public policy was to find in an ancient myth a parallel that the whole audience would know and share, and then exploit that parallel for all it was worth. After all, one could never be censored for merely resetting the Elektra story. Euripides didn't directly criticize Athens's ruthlessness in the Peloponnesian War, he wrote *The Trojan Women* and let his audiences draw their own inferences. Metaphor and myth have always been the theater's most useful tools: At the height of the Cold War, when it was forbidden to write anything critical of Soviet policy, Poland was filled with productions of *Richard III*, whose title character was seen through Polish eyes as an Elizabethan Stalin. The remarkable thing about classical plays is how they change, in the eyes of the beholder, from generation to generation; we need to connect ourselves to things past in order to have a context for things present. The interpretation of great drama is a kind of code that can serve to unify a population in a common and subversive reading of a current political moment.

It distresses me that in many quarters we consider classical theater to be obsolete today, and that we spend so much time and energy trying to invent ways for an audience to be more than a passive spectator of theater, because for both the Greeks and for Shakespeare, theater invited a level of audience participation that was inherently muscular and democratic. Audience engagement is not a new idea—it was Brecht who famously said that for theater to matter it had to be as good as boxing, and when a play is truly alive and well written, it demands an audience's active attention in the same manner as a great sporting event. The deeper I went into the world of Greek tragedy, the more I was seduced by this astonishing art form that managed to be at the same time metaphoric and immediate, poetic and specific, linguistic and physical, political without being didactic. I ended up spending much of my undergraduate life working on classical drama, staging outdoor productions of Greek plays in Frost Amphitheater or in the backyard of my professor's Palo Alto home, delighted to have to find a visceral means of telling a story in a language most of the audience did not know.

Eventually, of course, I also found my way over to the drama department, following a Canadian graduate student with whom I had fallen in love and a new roommate who was a costume designer. The first professor I encountered was Martin Esslin, whose passion for the work of Samuel Beckett and Harold Pinter was infectious. From the epic poetic dance-drama landscape of the Greeks, it was something of a shock to arrive at the rarefied minimalist air of these two brilliant twentieth-century writers. But I was equally seduced.

Here is another puzzling sidebar. I have a long-standing love-hate relationship with all things British. Having spent a fair amount of my life overseas, I am at home in many environments, but England has never felt particularly congenial to me. Whenever I'm there, I feel too loud, too confessional, too physical, too Jewish, too emotional, too much. During my year as a Fulbright Fellow at Oxford, I was often lonely and conflicted, to say nothing of freezing, since the English don't have much truck with central heating and seem to believe there's nothing that an extra layer of clothes can't solve. Yet when I look back on both my creative life and my personal life, England has loomed large: I married a remarkable British man (whom I met that lonely and cold year at Oxford) and have devoted a great deal of my professional life to the work of such writers as Pinter, Stoppard, and Beckett (interestingly, all writers from the British Isles who are in some way outsiders owing to their status as Jews, immigrants, or Irishmen) as well as Timberlake Wertenbaker (a transplanted American), James Fenton, Tony Harrison, Ursula Rani Sarma, Colm Tóibín, and many more. Somehow the language of those writers captivated me more intensely than that of their American counterparts.

Although I am more Mediterranean in my passions, I am perhaps more English than I'd care to admit in my love of verbal dexterity and my fascination with the linguistic code the British employ to keep from exposing their inner lives too transparently. I am a firm believer in the Stoppardian premise that ideas can be sexy and that great plays should make us think as well as feel, while waking us up to the clichés of our own quotidian language. Perhaps this is why, to be honest, I have never been drawn to classic American drama. Most notably (or most egregiously), I feel scant affinity for the work of Arthur Miller. It's hard to put my finger on why. I distrust confession in drama the way I often distrust therapy in life, I find earnestness somewhat embarrassing, and I tend to find transparent theatrical language uninteresting and often false. I don't actually believe any real woman in speaking of her husband's near-suicidal nervous breakdown would use the locution "Attention must be paid." I understand that people are often deeply moved by *Death of a Salesman*; it has just never called out to me as a play I would wish to direct. I like contradiction, I like characters who employ irony, who speak more nimbly than I speak—perhaps because I revere virtuosity, or perhaps because I have always been careful to subsume my personal feelings in the envelope of something larger than myself, on the assumption that my own instincts, problems, and contradictions are, unmediated, not that compelling.

At any rate, a vivid and insistent bell went off the moment I walked into Esslin's class on Beckett and Pinter. The first surprise was that, despite being labeled abstract and absurdist, the work of both writers springs from a profoundly real and specific universe, mediated by a mordant wit. Both Beckett and Pinter were deeply shaped by World War II. Beckett not only lived through but actively resisted the Nazi occupation of France, serving as a code runner and then, after the war, as an ambulance driver in Saint-Lô; much of the imagery of his great plays *Waiting for Godot* and *Endgame* is derived from the terror and physical pain of those experiences. Pinter, a quintessentially Jewish writer, lived in London during the height of the Blitz, before being evacuated first to Reading and then to rural Norfolk. In Michael Billington's *The Life and Work of Harold Pinter*, Pinter is quoted as saying, "For a young boy, there was a great sense of the dramatic. Sporadic but pretty intense bombardment. Air-raid warnings all the time. A real sense of an extreme and perilous life. The blackout left a sharp memory. . . . It was also a world that was highly sexual . . . there was a sexual desperation about the place. People really felt their lives could end tomorrow." The violent menace of his play *The Homecoming* surely derives from the hideous memories of war (so poignantly reflected in Sam's silence after Max's aggressive taunt, "Who did you kill?") and the fear of being displaced from one's home. I was fascinated by this dramaturgy that was both highly specific and decidedly metaphoric; as with the Greeks, these are plays that live in the physical, guttural reality of their characters and yet breathe a wider poetic air that rescues them from didacticism or literalness.

Maybe I also loved the work because it is unapologetically literate and literary; it reminded me of the ideas-obsessed, word-besotted world of my own family. I come from people whose religion is culture. My mother, a distinguished literary critic and author, is a Viennese refugee whose family members were so devoted to Goethe and Schiller that the antagonism of the Nazis seemed to fill them with surprise: How could German culture have turned against *them*, the ultimate keepers of the German cultural flame? When they mercifully escaped Vienna in 1938 after the Anschluss, my mother's relatives carried their culture with them to Riverdale and never let it go, in spite of their relative poverty and the trauma of immigration. I remember that my Grandpa Max could call to mind every single painting in the Kunsthistorisches Museum in Vienna thirty years after he emigrated, and that my beautiful and sad Grandma Ilse, who looked like a painting herself, would hold court in her small living room on Sundays at 3:00 PM while listening to Metropolitan Opera radio broadcasts and eating Sacher torte. My mother's intellectual universe in America became the surprising world of contemporary poetics and the avant garde.

A passion for ideas and for beauty reigned supreme in this fierce Viennese family, and when my physician father from New Orleans married into it, he adopted the prevailing gestalt and became more culturally literate than any of them. As little Jewish girls growing up in Washington, D.C., my sister and I were rarely taken to synagogue (none of us could keep quiet for that long), but we did go religiously to the Smithsonian and other local museums: one of my first childhood memories is of sitting in my stroller at the bottom of the grand staircase of The Phillips Collection, looking up at Renoir's *Luncheon with the Boating Party* while my father explained what impressionism was. After college, when I suddenly announced my theatrical aspirations, my parents were dubious, regarding theater as a lesser art form not necessarily worthy of lifelong devotion. It was only when I directed the premiere of Ezra Pound's *Elektra* at CSC (with the inspired Pamela Reed) that they began to believe that this might involve serious culture after all.

So I was drawn to the passionate cultural appetites of Beckett and Pinter, both of whom were extraordinary autodidacts. Beckett at least had the benefit of a university education, which Pinter did not, but the literary echoes in their work were the result of a lifetime of reading. Beckett spent a great deal of his early career studying that most artificial and rigorous of French classical writers, Racine, and indeed Beckett's long monologues owe a great deal to the tense, sexually charged arias of Racinian heroes and heroines. Pinter was a Shakespearean; during the early fifties, he acted in a Shakespearean repertory company that performed across Ireland, and his work is deeply informed by that experience. Max in *The Homecoming* divides, or refuses to divide, his kingdom just as Lear does, with language resonant of that great and irascible ruler.

This brings me back to the question of voice and aesthetic in theatrical work. Again and again, Beckett explores the liminal ends of existence, the necessity of silence, the biblical pain of existing without purpose or meaning. Yet he is also mordantly funny, almost clownish at times, and the collision of despair and hope that characterizes all of Beckett's work is the voice that a director must strive to find in production. As with the Greeks, Beckett and Pinter's work is profoundly physical. It is about bodies in space. The language is crystalline and particular; it is not, as Beckett famously said about Joyce's writing, "about the thing, it is the thing itself." Beckett's stage directions are like choreography; the plays are all about stillness and movement. Perhaps because of my dance background, the physicality of the plays makes intuitive sense to me, and I try as soon as I get into a rehearsal room with Beckett's work to free the actors from overly intellectualizing the material and encourage them to jump in with both feet. The most important thing is what is happening to their bodies in real time as they speak that language and live through the plays.

Performing Beckett always involves pain. Poor Gregory Wallace, who played Estragon in *Waiting for Godot* at A.C.T., had such a sore ass from sitting for so long on that jagged rock that he begged us to pad either the set or his bottom, but nothing helped (his stiff clown shoes were even worse!). One could argue that Beckett's work is not about the experience, it is the experience itself; inevitably that experience involves claustrophobia, physical compression, and bodily aches of all kinds, as Beckett traps his characters in ash cans (*Endgame*), sand piles (*Happy Days*), funeral urns (*Play*), rope lassos (*Godot*), and more.

Having lived through extreme physical privation himself, he knew exactly how to represent it onstage. The more you work on his plays, the more you come to accept that performing them is like walking a gauntlet: eventually you stop acting and just live through them. Thank god they also make you laugh.

Pinter takes Beckett's physical and verbal tension and adds a huge dose of sex and power. Many years after my college encounters with his work, I had several opportunities to work with Pinter himself in the rehearsal room, and those encounters transformed me as an artist. Pinter's huge physical presence, his bass and resonant voice, his unwillingness to ever make small talk, his lively sexuality, his fascination with women, his wicked sense of humor, and the quick blade of his temper all became instantly clear the day he first walked into CSC to watch us rehearse *The Birthday Party*, which we were presenting on a double bill with the American premiere of *Mountain Language* in the fall of 1989. To listen to Pinter talk was akin to reading our plays aloud at the O'Neill Playwrights Conference—all at once, the tone of his plays became absolutely clear. My first encounter with that famous voice was on the phone: His agent had asked me to ring him that spring with my thoughts about whether to adapt the language of *Mountain Language* to suit an American audience. When I dialed his number in London with some degree of trepidation, I took a deep breath, and waited. Somewhat to my relief, the answering machine picked up. A sonorous voice was heard to utter, almost as an accusation, the existential statement "I'M NOT HERE." Whereupon I waited for what seemed like an eternity (note the power of the Pinter pause) until finally a terse command was pronounced: "Leave a message." Only six words, pregnant with meaning and menace. I hung up, terrified.

In Pinter's view, there is nothing symbolic about his plays; contrary to the moniker "theater of the absurd," which irritated him, his work represents a highly distilled version of a very specific reality. "I've never started a play from any kind of abstract idea or theory and never envisioned my characters as messengers of death, doom, heaven, or the milky way," he insisted in his famous essay "Writing for the Theatre." Everything in Pinter is relational, because the work is about power; as critic Austin Quigley eloquently argues in *The Pinter Problem*, none of his characters exists except in relation to the other characters onstage, locked in a kind of dangerous game in which the loser is whoever drops the mask first. If Brecht's stage was a boxing ring and Sophocles' a jury box, Pinter's was a platform for predator to meet prey, for human beings to fight for survival wielding wit, sexual dominance, latent violence, and the power of suggestion. Pinter's scenic requirements are like Brecht's in the extreme selectivity required on the part of the designer: it is not that the real world is absent from the plays, merely that only very particular elements of the real world are allowed in. Less is more in Pinter—the language must bounce off a stripped-away world or it will get mired in irrelevant details. The more mysterious the world outside the play, the better.

As an artist and as a woman, I am often too quick to compromise. I tend to avoid conflict; I want my casts and my co-workers to be happy. The lesson from years of exposure to Pinter has been the huge role that conviction plays in creating a piece of art. It's not that Pinter resisted collaboration in the room nor that he refused to change things when a better idea came along. (He was so fascinated by seeing his play *The Birthday Party* on a three-quarter thrust stage rather than on a proscenium that he added a new line for the CSC production: As Peter Riegert, playing Goldberg, ascended our very visible staircase, Pinter asked him to pause, turn to Meg, and quip, "What a lovely flight of stairs!") But he was unapologetic about the idiosyncrasies and challenges of his work. Despite years of criticism, he did nothing to water the plays down, make them clearer, reduce their menace, or widen their appeal. The work is ferocious, specific, and true, and as an artist Pinter had the blazing and blessed self-confidence to keep it that way. Billington describes the Boston tryout of *The Homecoming*: "The producer Alexander Cohen asked Pinter 'to fix the second act'. . . . As Peter Hall recalls, 'Harold took his glasses off, his eyes glinting. "What exactly did you have in mind?" he said. It was one of the few times I have ever seen a Broadway producer at a loss for words.'" Every time I direct one of Pinter's plays, I am struck by that courage. I am made aware of my own tendency, as a director, as a writer, as an administrator, to want to please, to accommodate, to compromise. Exposure to Pinter's work makes me fiercer. His writing is like a laser. No cant, no sentiment, no apology. He has always made me feel supremely *alive*.

In 2011, to commemorate Pinter's life and memorialize his death, we staged *The Homecoming* with our core company and two brilliant Canadian actors (Ken Welsh and Adam O'Byrne), surrounding the production with readings of Pinter's major plays, as well as M.F.A. performances of several of his one-acts. With Pinter, the rehearsal process is an event in itself, a daily round of boxing and slicing. In attempting to create the kind of highly charged physical atmosphere in rehearsal that I thought the play required, and because *The Homecoming* is a thriller about territory that opens with a break-in during the night, I decided to board up the windows in the rehearsal studio and work on the play in the semidarkness. Only when a practical light was used in the play did we illuminate the room. Not only did this make the actors learn their lines exceptionally fast (since they couldn't see to read their scripts), it also raised the stakes throughout. As Ruth and Lenny sat tensely across from each other in their first encounter, for example, the sole light in the room was on the table between them, illuminating Ruth's sexually charged hand as she slowly toyed with a glass ("If you take the glass, I'll take you") and finally lifted it toward Lenny's throat. The move was terrifying. Later, as Teddy sat below on the couch with his bags packed, a shaft of light on the long threatening staircase created a dangerous path leading to the upper bedroom where hidden transgressions were occurring (or not occurring) between his wife, Ruth, and the men of the household. The person who controlled that stair light controlled the universe, at least for a brief moment. Having rehearsed the play as a film noir in the studio, we had a glorious time when we got into the theater, because the strangely menacing atmosphere and the precise choreography with which the actors navigated the light and dark zones of that frightening room had already been achieved.

From Pinter I learned to relish healthy competition among actors. An accomplished cricketer, Pinter adored games and encouraged his actors to play to win. Sitting in on our *Birthday Party* rehearsals, he roared with appreciation when, during the first preview, Peter Riegert forgot his lines and kept repeating the only noun he could remember in the rapid-fire series of lines in which Goldberg and McCann torment Stanley: "We'll provide the skipping rope. . . . The baby powder / The back scratcher / The spare tyre" is how the sequence was meant to go, but Riegert went blank and kept repeating, "The baby powder! The baby powder! The baby powder!" like a broken record, until Richard Riehle as McCann finally rescued him with, "That's it!" Pinter reassured Riegert that when he played that scene with the great Irish actor Patrick Magee, he too forgot the threats he was supposed to hurl and looked desperately to Magee for help; Magee apparently grinned victoriously, as if to say, "You wrote the damn thing, you come up with the lines!" and left Pinter to suffer alone.

When probed, Pinter was always less interested in some specific biographical reality ("Was Stanley Jewish?" we asked. "Possibly," he replied) than in the physical power of language to decimate and in the precise reality of the encounter happening in the room. Conflict is a zero-sum game in Pinter's plays—someone wins, and someone loses. That's what matters. If you accuse a person of enough crimes, Pinter liked to say, one of them might just turn out to be true. Like Beckett, he refused to view his characters as representatives of anything metaphorical; they were as real to him as his own family, and just as needy, violent, and mysterious. "Beware of the writer who puts forward his concern for you to embrace, who leaves you in no doubt of his worthiness, his usefulness, his altruism, who declares that his heart is in the right place, and ensures that it can be seen in full view, a pulsating mass where his characters ought to be," he admonished, again in "Writing for the Theatre." It is both the formal beauty and the unmistakable specificity of characterization and dialectic that has kept the work of Beckett and Pinter from dating in the manner of other writers of that period.

Pinter's notes to actors were always supremely precise, a lesson I absorbed again and again; the work was not intellectual or philosophical, but always about action, circumstance, and real observed behavior.

("Why does Meg keep asking Petey to read the newspaper to her?" we inquired, seeking a psychological clue to this strange marriage. "I think she has forgotten how to read," he replied, a note that Jean Stapleton found invaluable and played to the hilt.) He never explicated the text or delivered a meaning, but often he told anecdotes about his own life that made you realize how real those Pinteresque situations actually were.

One story stands out in my mind as being especially representative of Pinter and his particular sense of humor: In his 2000 one-act *Celebration* there is a loquacious waiter (played at A.C.T. by Gregory Wallace) who is fond of interrupting the clientele at a moment's notice to make bizarre observations. "I say, do you mind if I make an interjection?" he would ask. "It's just that I heard you talking about T.S. Eliot a little bit earlier this evening. . . . And I thought you might be interested to know that my grandfather knew T.S. Eliot quite well. . . . I'm not claiming that he was a close friend of his. But he was a damn sight more than a nodding acquaintance." I had lunch with Pinter at Le Caprice in London, in preparation for directing the play, and laughingly told him what a bad waitress I had been in my day. "I'll bet you were a damn good waitress," he replied, and then proceeded to ask, "You know what happened to me when I was a waiter? I was out of work, you know, as an actor, so I did a bit of waiting at the National Liberal Club. I actually heard two men having lunch and talking about Kafka and the publication date of *The Trial* or *The Castle*. I stopped at the table and said, 'No, no, *The Trial* was published in 1922,' and they said, 'Really, was it? We thought it was later,' and I said, 'No, you'll find out that it was.' I went back into the kitchen and was fired on the spot for talking to the customers. That was my experience as a waiter." I loved that story because it took the seemingly surreal Waiter and put him firmly in the land of the living. He was Pinter's alter ego, and we relished him.

We were performing Pinter at A.C.T. when the tragedy of 9/11 occurred. On September 13, 2001, two days after the twin towers were hit, we were slated to perform our first preview of a double bill that included Pinter's new comedy *Celebration* alongside his very first performed play, the 1957 one-act *The Room*. The latter is a play about terror, in which a very ordinary bedsit is invaded by strangers who seem bent on destroying the life of the frightened woman who inhabits it. *Celebration* is a raucous and rather outrageous farce about masters of the universe and the brutal way they treat their wives, their colleagues, and their own lives. We wondered in our collective numbness whether we should even be doing theater on such an occasion, let alone theater that our audience might find upsetting. Again, I was confronted by Pinter's ferocious courage—his one-acts are not easy, feel-good plays, they are tough, elliptical, trenchant, and uncompromising. As it turned out, this was one of those moments in which theater actually *mattered*. Peter Riegert later said that performing the two plays that night was the most memorable experience of his acting career. During *The Room*, the spectators at The Geary sat spellbound and terrified as Diane Venora, playing Rose, paced in her cell-like room, fried bacon for her huge, silent husband, and then leapt up in horror when strangers knocked on the door. They didn't ask who these strangers were or why they were invading the home of this woman, they just took in the event in all its power; the code was clear. They felt empathy with Rose's plight, and a strong emotional connection with each other, as audience members and as Americans witnessing a story about terror at that confusing and frightening time. After the intermission, *Celebration* gave everyone the collective release they had been waiting for—the laughter was instantaneous and enormous. Watching nine hundred people packed into The Geary Theater to experience Pinter on the night of September 13, 2001, reminded me why we had rebuilt that theater in the first place. To be able to gather the community together in the shared experience of theater at that moment was vital and satisfying. It made me think of Winnie, buried up to her neck in sand in *Happy Days*, desperately holding on to the poems and songs she remembers from her youth in order to keep present despair at bay. "One loses one's classics!" she laments. And then she takes a deep breath and assures herself, "Oh, not all. A part remains. That is what I find so wonderful. A part remains, of one's classics, to help one through the day."

The plays of Beckett and Pinter, along with the Greeks, have become signatures of A.C.T.'s aesthetic during my tenure and have consistently given shape to my own artistic life. Another writer in my pantheon, Tom Stoppard, only came into my life when I arrived in San Francisco and staged *Arcadia* in 1995. Stoppard had been a favorite A.C.T. playwright from the theater's early days in San Francisco, and since I've been artistic director, we have produced *Arcadia* (twice), *Indian Ink* (American premiere and again in 2015), *The Invention of Love* (American premiere), *Rosencrantz and Guildenstern Are Dead*, *Night and Day*, *The Real Thing*, *Travesties*, and *Rock 'n' Roll*. My friendship and collaboration with Stoppard began in 1995 when I sent him a letter begging him to intervene with Lincoln Center Theater, which held the rights to *Arcadia* and was reluctant to release them for a San Francisco production. (This is standard practice in the theater but it has always infuriated me.) In late May, we still had no assurance about whether we were going to be permitted to open our fall season with Stoppard's gorgeous new play. I knew *Arcadia* would resonate with A.C.T.'s audiences, and my instinct told me that directing it would be a turning point in my creative life. So I kept at it, calling both Lincoln Center's executive producer, Bernie Gersten, and Stoppard's London agent on a weekly basis, while also writing Stoppard letter after letter, which he always answered with great warmth and generosity. Just when I had given up, I got a phone call from London and a terse message: "The rights are yours." And off we went. Before the production opened, Stoppard gave an interview to *SF Weekly* in which he said with amusement, "Carey made a special appeal, asking if I would throw the weight of my good will on her side, which I was more than happy to do. . . . Her personality is irresistible; her sincerity and enthusiasm are something. And she writes a good letter." We were still in post-earthquake diaspora in 1995, so we produced *Arcadia* at the Stage Door Theatre, a smaller venue we rented near The Geary. The production was extended and launched one of the happiest collaborations of my career.

From *Arcadia* onward, Stoppard became a regular presence at A.C.T., first via letters and then in person and in the rehearsal room, where I found him to be a very different theater animal from Pinter. While Pinter, an actor at heart, was always ready to step into a role and demonstrate how it should best be played (he particularly liked to demonstrate the power of acting with one's back to the audience), Stoppard revels in the intricacies of the making of theater without desiring to act it out himself. Pinter's notes tended to be terse, declarative, and actable; Stoppard's are loquacious, funny, and filled with ideas that have to be translated into action. Where Pinter's best work comes from a deep and close observation of that which lies closest to him, Stoppard's imagination is triggered by ideas, arguments, and universes far removed in time and place from his own. As he once said in an interview, "I don't think of my life as a well into which I drop my bucket with a sense of going deeply into myself. . . . The area in which I feed off myself is really much more to do with thoughts I have had rather than days I have lived." Any idea can provide a fertile touchstone for Stoppard: Heisenberg's uncertainty principle (*Hapgood*); landscape architecture, chaos theory, and Byronic poetry (*Arcadia*); A.E. Housman and Latin lyric (*The Invention of Love*); Dubček, Husák, and the Rolling Stones (*Rock 'n' Roll*); Tristan Tzara, James Joyce, and Lenin in Zürich (*Travesties*); and so on. The dramaturgical preparation for work on one of Stoppard's plays is like a graduate seminar. This is clearly part of what Stoppard loves about writing: He who never attended university is the most erudite of playwrights, traveling with a spectacular little trunk that opens to become a library shelf on which is contained source material for a given play. His endlessly curious mind is always searching for more. After all, as Hannah assures Valentine in *Arcadia*, "It's wanting to know that makes us matter."

I was told that Stoppard could be fierce in rehearsal but have never witnessed that myself; in my experience, he has always been solicitous of actors, fascinated by designers, and gracious to the audience. "It goes through me like a spear," he lamented when he heard the sound of seats closing as some tired audience members left early during previews of *The Invention of Love* in 2000. He knows his plays can be difficult and long, but he always hopes that they will be entertaining enough to keep restless subscribers in their seats, and when that does not prove to be the case, he is as distraught as a jilted lover. He commented once in *Harper's Bazaar*, "You have to bow down before the true god of theater, who is merciless and is saying, 'This is not a text, this is an event happening in this room at this time in front of people who are under no obligation to remain.'" Stoppard is also wonderfully self-deprecating about his own tendency to show off verbally or to include arcane references most audiences will never follow; actor Max complains to playwright Henry in *The Real Thing*: "They *did* say—I mean, it's a tiny thing but I thought I'd pass it on because I do feel rather the same way. . . . I mean all that stuff about the Japanese and digital watches—they suddenly have no idea what I'm talking about, you see, and I thought if we could just try it one night without—" at which point Henry stops him cold and asks how big the audience was that night.

Over the years, his answers to my queries about the plays have been priceless and often bemused. For example, asked about Valentine's underestimation of Thomasina's equations in *Arcadia*, Stoppard wrote: "Valentine's 'I don't know' answers [Hannah's] question about marginalia; the rest of his speech slides into accommodating the equations, too. It's not *tidy*; it's more like life or incompetent playwriting, which resemble each other, luckily." Or when I asked, "Why is Hannah's comment 'April the tenth' so particularly outrageous to Bernard?" Stoppard replied, "Bad news. It's a pun on date rape. Perhaps it's less stupid in England."

Among other things, *Arcadia* introduced A.C.T.'s audience to the important aspect of having an acting program embedded in a producing organization; if you don't have terrific young actors to play Thomasina, Septimus, and Chloë, you can't do the play. Among the many joys of that first *Arcadia* cast (which included the hilarious Graham Beckel as Bernard and elegant, intelligent Katherine Borowitz as Hannah), our young M.F.A. students truly shone in their roles and reminded our audience of the breadth of A.C.T.'s endeavor. Indeed, in preparing for my twentieth-anniversary season, bringing *Arcadia* to The Geary was at the top of my agenda, and we were blessed with a young actress in the M.F.A. Program named Rebekah Brockman who was born to play Thomasina, just in time for this revival. *Arcadia* also put on the map A.C.T.'s famous *Words on Plays*, a book-length publication we create for each mainstage subscription production that details the production history, creative concept, historical context, and other relevant insights about a given play. Stoppard was very taken with editor Elizabeth Brodersen's work on *Arcadia*; indeed, he quipped that by reading *Words on Plays*, he finally understood his play. He also grew to realize that the A.C.T. audience was ideal for his work: engaged, intelligent lovers of language who would devour their dramaturgy in advance and come fully armed for the exhilarating and complex journey ahead.

Unlike many playwrights, Stoppard actually thrives in the collaborative nature of the rehearsal process; the craft of making theater interests him, and he gives a great deal of thought to how technical problems can be solved amid his intricate storytelling. (In the preface to *Rock 'n' Roll* there is a note that begins, "MEN'S HAIR . . . is a problem," in which he describes the necessary changes in hair length over the course of this time-travel play, and how to effect them.) Each time we've produced one of his plays, we've remarked upon the evident pleasure he has taken in our midnight tech notes sessions in the basement bar of The Geary, the process whereby the entire design team works through the show, seeking solutions to troublesome moments.

He was particularly delighted when lighting designer James Ingalls solved the very last moment of *The Invention of Love*. Stoppard had written a speech for the elder Housman that ended, "But now I really do have to go. How lucky to find myself standing on this empty shore, with the indifferent waters at my feet," followed by the stage description, "Fade out." But as we watched the ending in previews, it became clear that what was wanted was a sense of continuum, a sort of "dot-dot-dot" ending that would keep the mystery of Housman's ambivalent feelings in the air, like water flowing in the river. We experimented with many solutions, none of them wholly satisfying, until at about 5:00 PM on the eve of opening night, Ingalls added moving lights (which became known in A.C.T. lore as "the famous twin spinners") to the last cue. Suddenly, without the actor having to telegraph it, everything kept subtly moving throughout Housman's last rumination, as if the inquiring spirit of the poet were continuing to swirl overhead. Stoppard was enchanted. "It's the equivalent of the potter and the clay," he once said to theater critic Mel Gussow. "I just love getting my hands in it. Clearly there are many writers who can mail the play in. . . . It stays the way they write it, I am told. I think they miss all the fun. I change things to accommodate something in the scenery, or something in the lighting. Happily. I love being part of the equation. I don't want it to be what happens to my text. I like the text to be part of the clay which is being molded."

Yet the text is a piece of music that Stoppard hears clearly in his mind, and the ability to articulate language is what Stoppard values most about actors. On his first visit to A.C.T. he held a Conservatory Hour for our M.F.A. students, who were immersed in Chekhov at the time. During the question period, one student asked Stoppard what he most values in an actor, hoping that he would expound upon interior landscape and psychological complexity. "Clarity of utterance," Stoppard immediately replied. As Henry argues in *The Real Thing*, words are "innocent, neutral, precise, standing for this, describing that, meaning the other, so if you look after them you can build bridges across incomprehension and chaos." And while he marvels at the transformational ability of actors and gives them great latitude of interpretation, he is not a writer of confession and is always alert to actors who try to make his tight British line a soppy American one filled with pauses and sentiment. There was a telling moment during the rehearsals for *Indian Ink*, in which the young actor playing David Durance wanted to make sure the audience understood the emotional weight of his proposal to Flora. The lines read:

DURANCE: Flora.
FLORA: No.
DURANCE: Would you marry me?
FLORA: No.
DURANCE: Would you think about it?

FLORA: No. Thank you.
DURANCE: Love at first sight, you see. Forgive me.
FLORA: Oh, David.
DURANCE: Knees together.
FLORA: 'Fraid so.

Stoppard wanted this terse and beautifully written little proposal scene to be played with no pauses, believing that the enormity of this Englishman's feelings could best be expressed with the least possible emotional betrayal. The actor, thinking he knew better, spent most of the preview period building as many pauses and freighted moments into the text as possible, while Stoppard stood in the back of the theater shaking his head and occasionally shooting him with an imaginary gun.

During each rehearsal process I have experienced with him, Stoppard has been assiduous about giving the actors tips on how to lift his language and make it sing; for example, it is crucial to him that in a conditional sentence, the word "if" at the top of the sentence has to be hit hard no matter how interesting the subsequent information, so that the proposition never loses its setup. He is fond of urging the actors to "look after" key words or actions that help land the punch lines of his famously pun-laden texts and to assist the audience in recalling crucial images and sounds. Early on in *Indian Ink*, the painter Nirad Das tells Flora that the *rasa* of erotic love is aroused by "the moon, the scent of sandalwood, or being in an empty house." Much later in the play, a weeping Flora takes Das's handkerchief and comments, "Your handkerchief smells faintly of . . . something nice." We must remember the specific reference to sandalwood to understand the hidden desire in Flora's remark; Das has to lift that image successfully in act 1 for it to pay off in act 2. Because his plays move very quickly, that sculpting of verbal and visual attention is key. Recently, during a rehearsal of our revival of *Indian Ink*, Stoppard somewhat apologetically remarked that performing his language is like driving a car with a clutch: you have to change gears very precisely and abruptly, or you risk going off the road. Little words like "oh" and "yes," which seem innocuous and which actors often ignore, actually function as markers alerting the speaker to shift gears. "Oh, I see. Yes, yes . . . I did look," says Flora when Das accuses her of having looked at his painting behind his back. Flora's one-line speech travels from discovery to acknowledgment to confession, one word at a time.

The precise structure of Stoppard's language ensures that an actor can't race blindly forward or make a sudden left turn, but has a degree of control over the sometimes dizzyingly complex speeches he or she is asked to utter. Indeed, in a world of mumbled and inarticulate speech, Stoppard is unapologetic about the level of articulation and verbal dexterity his scripts demand. He once told Mel Gussow that he is simply more drawn to people who speak well, and that if he were to write a dustman, it would have to be a highly articulate and well-spoken dustman. That is his passion and his mode. It's what makes his plays so sexy and vibrant. Early in his career he told Gussow, "All my people. . . speak as I do. When I write an African president into a play, I have to contrive to have him [be] the only African president who speaks like me."

Many landmarks in my own life have run on parallel tracks to my collaborations with Stoppard. For example, when Stoppard met Lexie, he decided that my preternaturally verbal daughter reminded him of the endlessly curious Thomasina. Perhaps that is why I find the character so moving, because I know what it is to be the mother of a bright little girl who has to navigate a world in which female intelligence is often regarded as off-putting and inappropriate. I turned forty during *Indian Ink*, and Stoppard won an Oscar for *Shakespeare in Love* on the final Sunday of *Indian Ink*'s run; I seem to remember that we were all together the night after he won and everything was celebrated simultaneously and joyfully. Events surrounding *The Invention of Love* were appropriately apocalyptic and millennial; it was during rehearsals for the American premiere of that play that my house nearly burned down. We had had a New Year's Eve party with the entire *Invention* company; ashes left in the fireplace that night found their way into a paper bag in the basement that, the following day, began to smolder and then to burn. In the middle of technical rehearsals for *Invention* (a play, ironically, that is filled with references to fire and burning), an assistant came running into the auditorium to tell me that my house was surrounded by fire trucks. When I finally got home, we were greeted by the sight of a heavily damaged house, the windows and doors of which had been smashed in to let the smoke escape. Although my calm English husband, Anthony, said, "Well, I think we can still sleep here tonight," we in fact couldn't live in the house for six months, while it was being restored. So A.C.T.'s production of *The Invention of Love* was completed by a homeless director who wore the same clothes to rehearsal every day and slept with the family on borrowed beds at her managing director's house, a feat that prompted Stoppard to write in his opening-night card, "When I think of the fire and trauma you have endured just to get my play on the stage, I feel I must drop my English reserve and thank you profoundly and from the bottom of my heart."

It was on the brink of the new millennium that Stoppard began to explore his Czech Jewish background, something he had studiously avoided previously (owing primarily to his mother's reticence and his stepfather's insistence). By the time I first met him, I had been corresponding with him for some time, but when we finally connected in person in 1996 at a coffee bar in London's National Theatre, I was understandably nervous. I needn't have been, because as soon as we sat down, I had an instant rush of recognition: as British as the man seemed on the surface, underneath he immediately reminded me of my own European Jewish ancestry. Which was not surprising. As a six-year-old, Stoppard (born July 3, 1937, as Tomáš Straussler) had been evacuated from his hometown of Zlín, Czechoslovakia, with the families of other Jewish doctors employed by the Bata shoe factory. His father, Eugen, a popular young surgeon at the factory hospital, took the family to Singapore (which initially seemed safe during the war), where eventually he was killed by a Japanese gunboat, whereupon young Tomáš's mother, Martha, married an English major named Kenneth Stoppard, who promised to take the boys back to England and raise them as British citizens on the assumption that they would abandon all things Czech. Many years later, when

Stoppard finally began to explore his own Jewish heritage in greater depth, he wrote a remarkable essay (published in the 1999 inaugural issue of *Talk* magazine) titled "On Turning Out to Be Jewish," in which he explained, "My stepfather, formerly Major Kenneth Stoppard of the British army in India, believed with Cecil Rhodes that to be born an Englishman was to have drawn first prize in the lottery of life, and I doubt that even Rhodes . . . believed it as utterly as Ken."

By the time I read that piece, I knew of Stoppard's famous distaste for biography (he has always said he hoped any biography of him would turn out to be "as inaccurate as possible" and has delighted in making biographers, such as Eldon Pike in *Indian Ink* and Bernard Nightingale in *Arcadia*, objects of amusement if not derision). "I'll get him a reporter doll for Christmas," says Ruth to her husband in *Night and Day*, "Wind it up and it gets it wrong." Nevertheless, it fascinated me, as the daughter of a Viennese refugee who knew a great deal about her family's past, to meet this extraordinary man who seemed to know so little about his own. It feels clichéd to say that the antic absurdism and formal invention of Stoppard's early work seem to share DNA with his Czech counterparts Sławomir Mrożek and Witold Gombrowicz, but I do believe that, for all the meticulous British veneer, Stoppard's Eastern European origins have clearly shaped his work and his worldview even as he has steadfastly avoided self-discovery of this kind. As generous as he was to Charter 77 and as outspoken as he has been about artistic suppression under Soviet Communism, it wasn't until his mother's death and a subsequent encounter with newly found relatives that Stoppard understood the depth of his Jewish roots, including the awful reality that both his maternal and paternal grandparents died in Nazi concentration camps. In his play *Rock 'n' Roll*, there is a frightening interrogation scene in which a Polish Communist bureaucrat interrogates the young intellectual Jan (called Tomas in the first draft of the play) in the following exchange:

INTERROGATOR: You left Czechoslovakia just before the
    Occupation.

JAN: No, in April, for the summer term.

INTERROGATOR: The Occupation. The Nazis. Hitler.

JAN: Oh! Yes. Yes. The Occupation. Sorry.

INTERROGATOR: Because you were Jewish.

JAN: So it seemed.

INTERROGATOR: Well, are you or aren't you?

JAN: Yes.

INTERROGATOR: Right. I don't know why you make such a thing about it.

Throughout the play, one can watch Stoppard imagining what would have happened to someone like him if he had returned to Prague after the war and lived through the Communist terror, instead of living safely and happily in England.

Here we come back to the voice, to that moment when you hear the playwright speak and you know the world of the play. By the time I directed *Rock 'n' Roll*, in the fall of 2008 at A.C.T. and then at Boston's Huntington Theatre Company, I had known Stoppard for over ten years. I knew about his fascination with the fragments of Sappho (embedded in the Cambridge sections of the play), I knew about his love for sixties English pop music, and I knew that the Jewish/Czech question in regard to his personal identity was percolating in his mind. My mother, Marjorie, had just published her own memoir of escape and emigration, *The Vienna Paradox*, which Stoppard admired very much. In rehearsal with Manoel Felciano, who played Jan, I thought a great deal about Stoppard's own personal history and about how much more autobiographical that play is than almost anything else he had written. Critics have often accused Stoppard of verbal pyrotechnics at the expense of "heart," but once you know him, you realize that the verbal pyrotechnics are a necessary part of the protective tissue that maintains the playwright's private world; hidden behind that tissue are layers and layers of feeling, memory, and regret. As he has gotten older, he seems to have felt less compelled to hide, and the plays have become more transparent in their sense of longing and loss, culminating in *The Coast of Utopia*, which is a fervent exploration of the process and pain of exile.

134

During rehearsals of *Rock 'n' Roll*, Stoppard wrote me copious explanatory notes about parts of the play that seemed opaque or contradictory at first blush. I remember getting a call from him on my cell phone while I was in the men's department at Macy's, trying to find a last-minute birthday present for my husband. I sat on the floor amid dress shirts and ties while Stoppard walked me through the complicated emotional argument that led to Jan returning files from the secret police to Max (a scene that apparently flummoxed director Trevor Nunn, as well), while I scribbled notes on the back of the Macy's receipt. At the same time, Stoppard has always been solicitous about my own writing, giving me brilliant dramaturgical notes on my plays before they went into production. There can be few things more intimidating and indeed humiliating than showing Tom Stoppard early drafts of one's own plays. But it was always worth it. Over the past twenty years, he has kept my intellect sharp, my mind alert to new ways of thinking, my heart open to the subtle worlds of feelings evoked in his plays. His endless appetite for new ideas, new ways of making theater, new countries to explore, has kept me energized and invigorated. On my fifteenth anniversary at A.C.T., he wrote, "I think Carey and I must have been born on the same wavelength. Not every playwright is as lucky as I to have a director who is usually slightly ahead of him instead of slightly behind. . . . She is a theater animal— she behaves towards the writer as if the writer is in charge, the master, but really she is taking the master for a walk." I have never had a dog, but ever since I became a playwright, I have remembered that image and hoped to find a director willing to take me on a walk.

I couldn't end this section about collaboration without a quick note about David Mamet, a writer who has played a strong role in A.C.T.'s signature voice. Interestingly, working with Mamet has little to do with taking a writer on a walk; it's more like buying stock. Unlike Pinter and Stoppard, I have not yet found in Mamet (in my brief encounters with him) a particularly kindred spirit with whom to share the work, but a tough negotiator for whom collaboration is a transaction to be accomplished. I have always admired Mamet's ferocity, wit, and linguistic prowess and have produced many of his plays, but I had never directed his work myself. I did end up collaborating with him, however, on one occasion, when he offered to create an adaptation for me of Harley Granville-Barker's *The Voysey Inheritance*. The idea emerged in 2004 in the wake of the Enron scandal, when we were searching for a play that tackled greed, philanthropy, and community culpability. Mamet admired Granville-Barker's story of a wealthy patriarch who spends his career skimming profits off the trusts he has been hired to manage, only to mask his illegal dealings in a benevolent philanthropy that wins the hearts of everyone in his village. In the play, Voysey's son turns out to be a morally upright prig who decides, after his father's death, to clean up the family business in the name of justice, but in doing so ends up bankrupting his clients and ruining their lives. The elder Voysey, like Tom DeLay and the Enron barons, was so woven into the fabric of his society that the revelation of his criminal behavior not only stunned his community but laid bare the collective greed of everyone in town who had been complicit in profiting from his illegal speculations.

The "always be selling" credo of plays like *Glengarry Glen Ross* matched *The Voysey Inheritance* perfectly, and Mamet had an immediate sense of how to adapt the long nineteenth-century work so as to render it visceral for a contemporary audience. He took Granville-Barker's multi-set play and shaped it so that all the action took place within the Voysey living room (obviating the need for expensive and time-consuming set changes), he reduced the cast size to eleven, and he trimmed the running time to two hours, without removing any of the real meat of the play. It was masterful. Mamet is fond of comparing playwriting to flying a plane—what's important is to jettison excess baggage so that the play has no drag and can fly unencumbered. He was thus relentless about cutting, making mostly judicious choices with the exception of the main female character, Beatrice, who ended up being reduced perhaps too considerably. But once he'd set his mind on it, there was no arguing, or even discussing other options.

He delivered his first draft with perfect punctuality, and we arranged a reading on an afternoon when Mamet said he would already be in San Francisco. We spent exactly three and a half hours working through the play, Mamet making notes and adjustments with great efficiency, after which we had a collegial dinner, thanked him for his work, and got his promise of a final draft within the month. Mamet's work helped reanimate a remarkable piece of writing, and *Voysey* hit exactly the nerve we hoped it would with our audience. But the *Voysey* collaboration was not the beginning of a beautiful relationship with a playwright. It was, like Granville-Barker's searing play, mostly about business.

CHAPTER 11

The International Connection

So many things go into finding one's own aesthetic; for me it was a background in dance, a passion for archaeology and hidden clues, an obsession with the infinite variety of the English language. Mixed in with all of this was my appetite for foreign work, for ways of creating a theatrical event that had nothing to do with the conventions of American realism. While many theater artists spend their young years in New York second-acting (sneaking into the second acts of Broadway shows without paying), I spent mine as a secretary on the Upper West Side at the International Theatre Institute, a theater-service organization devoted to an exploration of global theater. The U.S. Center of the International Theatre Institute (ITI/U.S.) in the eighties was headed by Martha Coigney, a six-foot-tall American visionary who was married to an urbane Frenchman and was a tireless champion of international theater. She hired me on a whim when I was twenty-two, rescuing me after a series of humiliating interviews at employment agencies that had culminated in a particularly painful appointment on the hottest day of the summer, at which the grim interviewer declared: "Ms. Perloff, you have no skills. And you'll never get a job in New York if you don't wear pantyhose." Martha didn't care about the pantyhose; she liked it that I was multilingual and had an appetite for global adventure. So she deposited me at the front desk of her office on West 63rd Street, where I sat surrounded by priceless books and magazines from around the world, as the glitterati of the international theater scene paraded through. One day the office would be full of Indonesian puppeteers; the next it was Meredith Monk and her cadre of a capella singers. Peter Brook showed up to take Martha to lunch and talk about the Théâtre des Bouffes du Nord and his African adventures, and the great Russian director Lev Dodin of the Maly Drama Theatre in St. Petersburg would arrive bearing vodka and toasting everyone in the room, including the lowly secretary who would become one of his most devoted fans. On slow days, Martha let me wander through the stacks of the library, beautifully organized by a librarian called Birdie, where I learned about *Shakuntala* and Persian theater, Khatakali and Indian dance, Mnouchkine's Théâtre du Soleil and Giorgio Strehler's Piccolo Teatro di Milano, and the extraordinary flowering of Romanian directors (Andrei Şerban and Liviu Ciulei made frequent appearances at ITI).

It was like a graduate seminar: I kept notes on everything I learned, I went to see the work whenever I was invited, and every day brought a new actor, singer, director, or puppeteer into my consciousness. I met artists for whom the making of theater was an incendiary political act, and artists for whom theater was a spiritual practice. Martha didn't discriminate; she recognized passion when she saw it, and she made sure her international brood felt welcome in the United States, at least on 63rd Street.

When I left ITI after a year to begin my internship at The Public Theater, I was surprised to discover just how parochial much of the rest of the American theater really was. It seemed then, and still seems to me now, that we are not interested enough in what is happening beyond our borders, particularly if it isn't happening in English. We keep forgetting that it was international events—such as the visit of Stanislavsky and the Moscow Art Theatre to New York in 1922 (with its unprecedented impact upon idealistic young theater artists of the time) and that of Jerzy Grotowski's Teatr

Laboratorium in 1969—that helped crack open the modern American theater. (The same fertile aesthetic collision happened to Brecht when he first saw Chinese theater and began incorporating Eastern techniques into his own practice of theatrical gesture.) I remember hearing about Grotowski for the first time in the late seventies; without having been to Wrocław or seen the work firsthand, we began reading *Towards a Poor Theatre* and imagining a theater of extreme physical and spiritual expressivity far removed from American realism. Grotowski's vision was born out of the specific landscape of twentieth-century Polish suffering and transgression, but it touched a nerve in the American avant garde, introducing a potent imagery and rigorous physicality to our work that in turn influenced world theater in the decades to come. The more local or specific a theatrical universe is, the more power it has to transcend its origins, which is why, I suppose, the flip side of my fascination with locavore theater is my appetite for international theater practices that are intensely local to someone else.

This brings me to an aspect of American theater that may merit discussion. As a field, we talk passionately about multiculturalism or, to use the terms in currency today, diversity and inclusion, and rightly embrace that concept as being central to our work. Yet "multicultural" in our context usually means American. When I teach, I find again and again that as Americans, we know far too little about the cultures of our ancestry: we know Nilo Cruz but not Lorca or Lope de Vega; we know David Henry Hwang but nothing about Chinese dramatic traditions, we want to encourage African American work but ignore Wole Soyinka or Derek Walcott. Many Americans tend to believe the rest of the world speaks English and that proficiency in a foreign language is an unattainable or unimportant skill. We also tend to believe that psychological realism is the only acceptable mode of making theater, which limits our cultural pluralism considerably. When A.C.T. produced the remarkable Chinese epic *The Orphan of Zhao* in 2014, our local critic was mystified by (and dismissive of) its formal structure and its intensely realized moral code that prized collective need over individual feeling; he seemed unprepared for a dramaturgy that didn't follow the familiar conventions of American realism. But it is when one produces work that is formally and culturally completely "other" that one can really learn how many ways there are to tell a story, and how brilliantly the tools of theater have been exploited in cultures different from our own. It is humbling and important to remember that our myopic American worldview is not the only plausible way to experience reality.

Alas, only those lucky enough to get to festivals such as Under the Radar or the Next Wave Festival in New York or Fusebox in Austin get to experience world theater in any significant and recurring way. Our lack of knowledge about foreign theater and about dramatic literature from languages other than English is a shame, in that it limits the scope of our own theatrical explorations. While the British have developed a cottage industry of commissioning their own playwrights to translate and adapt foreign plays (which not only creates strong new versions of foreign work but earns the English writers a royalty), the issue of translation has stymied the American theater for much of its history, with the result that we often do Russian or German plays with British accents.

The art of translation is something I began investing in very intensely while at CSC (Lincoln Center Theater dramaturg Anne Cattaneo and I created an innovative but short-lived National Theatre Translation Fund, sponsored by The Pew Charitable Trusts), and I brought my passion for commissioning and developing new translations with me to A.C.T. Over the years, I have worked on Russian plays with Paul Schmidt, Greek and French plays with Timberlake Wertenbaker, German plays (Brecht and Schiller) with Michael Feingold, Scandinavian plays with Paul Walsh, Molière and Gorky with Constance Congdon, Pirandello with Richard Nelson, French Canadian plays with Linda Gaboriau, and Chinese epic with James Fenton. Some of these projects involved translations by writers with access to the original language, some were adaptations by writers working with a native speaker, but in every case the process was akin to developing a new work in English, and the goal was to create a vital piece of contemporary theater based on or inspired by a foreign work.

When one creates a new translation for the stage, the process ultimately involves not just reimagining the words but the whole gestalt of a play: body language, spatial demands, relationship to the audience, all this must be translated from one culture to another. Great translation is a work of cultural anthropology, a way of much more deeply understanding human behavior from parts of the world unlike our own. I'll never forget working with Paul Walsh on Strindberg's *Creditors* and bumping into a strange phrase about "dipping one's hand into the bowl." The image seemed to evoke fondue, but Paul understood its sexual connotations and was able to find a translated equivalent that suggested intimacy and transgression perfectly without the literal food imagery. Every act of translation is an act of the imagination.

Our cultural isolationism is exacerbated by the fact that most theaters in America operate under contract with Actors' Equity Association, which is a protectionist union. Foreign nationals are rarely permitted to perform on our stages without considerable amounts of bargaining and concession wringing, although the restrictions have been noticeably diminished as of the 2013 contract. This may seem bizarre in an age of globalism, but anti-immigrant policies prevail in difficult economic times, and the American theater always seems to be in difficult economic times. Yet exposure to global theater is life-changing. I learned again and again, first at ITI and then through the Center for International Theatre Development's intrepid Philip Arnoult, that theater is one of the strongest bridges one can build between cultures. I think about the Israeli-Palestinian issues that have been explored through theatrical exchange at Theater J in Washington, D.C., Russian-American conversations that began when George White invited artists of the then Soviet Union to be part of the O'Neill playwrights' conference, recent meditations on contemporary torture and terrorism in the wake of performances by the Belarus Free Theatre at La MaMa in New York, and vivid collaborations between East Africans and Americans at the Sundance Institute Theatre Program. Americans should be regularly participating on the global stage by exchanging artists and scripts with other cultures, but for that to happen, we need to keep picking our heads up to discover what is out there. Over the past decade, A.C.T. has done a great deal of work with Canadian artists, for example, as we are permitted to exchange work freely across that border; the Canadian theatrical culture is fertile and accessible and has immeasurably deepened our own work.

We learned the challenges of international exchange the hard way at A.C.T. when we brought Robert Wilson and Tom Waits's visionary music-theater piece *The Black Rider* to A.C.T. in 2004. This landmark production came into being through the tenacity of independent producer Michael Morris, with whom I had gone to Oxford; he called me out of the blue one day and asked if A.C.T. would team up with the Barbican in London and the Sydney Opera House in Australia to create an English-language version of the famed Hamburg production of *The Black Rider*, a story about making a pact with the Devil and about what people will do when they want something too badly. Having seen the original German production at BAM (Brooklyn Academy of Music) many years before, I jumped at the chance—this was exactly what A.C.T. was meant to be doing.

Watching Robert Wilson in rehearsal had been a lifelong desire of mine. Like many people, I was first introduced to his unique theatrical world through *Einstein on the Beach* in 1984, and I remember stumbling out of the opera house at BAM after six hours of hallucinatory images and endlessly pulsing music and wondering how he (and Lucinda Childs, Philip Glass, and the rest of the team) had managed to bend time in that way. From the *Einstein* days forward, it was easier to see Wilson's work in Singapore, Berlin, or Tokyo than in the United States, so I was thrilled when, twenty years later at The Geary, I got to witness the process firsthand.

Of the many lessons learned from months of preproduction, rehearsals, and tech with Wilson, two things stand out. The first is that there is a whole other universe operating underneath our quotidian lives that becomes accessible if you figure out a way to literally slow down time. That's Wilson's gift. The rules he creates onstage are his own. The time it takes a human being to walk across the stage or to lift up a glass of water is infinite. So the experience of watching his shows is like entering a parallel world where everything is heightened, surreal, *more*. Because time is altered, the imagination of the audience can be unleashed—Wilson's images trigger emotional and mental responses that linger and slowly bloom, unfettered by plot or pace.

Lesson number two was that, while the result was utterly mesmerizing, the process of getting there is anything but pretty. Wilson will not move forward until every single aspect of what he sees onstage meets with his approval. Light is his religion, and color his magic pill. If the cobalt blue on the scrim is not absolutely evenly distributed and a perfect match for the perfect blue in his mind's eye, rehearsal grinds to a halt until the color problem is solved. The great Czech actress and opera singer Soňa Červená, a legendary Carmen who was a regular at San Francisco Opera for many years, was a key member of *The Black Rider* ensemble and, at almost eighty, a Robert Wilson veteran. She warned us that his tech rehearsals could be grueling, and over drinks when she arrived told us the story of her last outing on a Wilson piece, in which she had been required to stand with one foot atop a large rubber ball for what seemed like an eternity, as Bob adjusted the lighting. The heat finally overcame her and she fainted to the ground. Any other director would have picked her up, settled for whatever lighting had been achieved, and moved on. Not Robert Wilson. He came onto the stage, asked in a loud voice, "Is there an understudy available?" and kept working, never breaking his fierce concentration. Soňa didn't seem the least bit resentful of this behavior, and although I found her story somewhat shocking, it was also a wake-up call.

Like many of my peers, I have become so used to the poverty and penny-pinching of the American nonprofit theater that compromise is my middle name. Watching Wilson in tech rehearsals, I couldn't remember when I had last held my ground and insisted on perfection (if such a thing were even possible); instead, I was used to working as quickly and efficiently as possible under the circumstances and trying to keep everyone happy while doing so. Wilson didn't care if people were happy, or how long and over-budget the process was, nor was he interested in compromise. He had a dream in his mind and he tried with all his power to conjure that dream on-stage. Anything less was not worth his time. I certainly don't possess the depth and genius of Wilson's vision, but as I watched him work, I found myself wishing I had a little more of his fanaticism.

Producing *The Black Rider* took every ounce of patience and expertise we could muster. It began with the question of casting. *The Black Rider* is the story (based on an old German folktale) of an ordinary clerk named Wilhelm who falls in love with a young maid named Käthchen. Her father, Bertram, objects to the match because Wilhelm is not an accomplished hunter. One day, Wilhelm encounters the Devil in the forest and makes a pact to acquire magic bullets that miraculously hit every target. When William Burroughs was asked to adapt the story, those magic bullets became like drugs to which the hapless Wilhelm was soon addicted. "Before long, he can't hit anything without 'em," explained Burroughs. "He is completely dependent on the bullets. . . . The moral is, the devil's bargain is always a fool's bargain, because you're trying to get something for nothing, and you end up giving everything for nothing." Given the cast of characters, we had to find actors to play everything from an innocent maiden to a sardonic Devil, and from the surreal old ancestor, Kuno, to the braggart rival, Robert; each actor had to have a powerful and highly articulated physicality and be able to carry the vocal demands of Waits's score. Wilson wanted to keep several of the German actors from the previous production, with whom he worked so well. We wanted to make sure that the piece, scripted by iconic Beat writer Burroughs, included enough Americans to make the language sound authentic, and the Barbican producers felt the same about incorporating British performers. Through a complex negotiation with Equity, A.C.T. Producing Director James Haire managed to carve out an exemption whereby, of the twelve performers, we had permission for four to be European, four British, and four American.

This then meant a complex process of visa acquisition for the European artists, fraught with near disasters. If Equity is suspicious of foreign artists, Homeland Security is even worse. Half a week before rehearsals were set to begin, we were notified that three of our petitions (for Soňa, the wig master, and the musical director) had been refused. In desperation we turned to our immigration attorney, who told us that he had close personal connections to the American embassy in Paris and that if we could get the three artists there at the same time, ASAP, he could pull some strings and have the ruling overturned. Octogenarian Soňa took an overnight train from the south of France to Paris and met up with the other two artists on a street corner across from the embassy, where they were told to proceed down a side street to a small, unmarked door behind which an embassy authority would meet them. When they got there and knocked, the door was locked. They stood on the street as the clock ticked, desperately trying to figure out a solution. With Jim Haire working two phones at once, the intrepid three entered the embassy and said they had an appointment with the head of visa disbursals, but no one would see them and they were told to take a number and wait. By the slenderest stroke of luck, when Soňa's turn finally came and she went to the next available authority, minutes before the embassy was to close for the night, she discovered a mad opera fan who revered her work and was only too happy to help. Only in this way did the company arrive together in London for their first rehearsal of *The Black Rider*.

Meanwhile, trying to get Waits and Wilson in the same room at the same time to cast was almost as impossible as procuring European visas. Robert Wilson leads a peripatetic life that exhausts one just to think about it; Tom Waits lives fairly hermetically with his wife and co-songwriter, Kathleen Brennan, in Petaluma, California. There were funny days when my casting director, Meryl Shaw, and I would get phone calls from Waits and Brennan saying they'd heard an amazing gypsy singing on the street in Sebastopol, or seen a busker juggling in Petaluma, and could we consider hiring them for *The Black Rider*? Wilson, on the other hand, was fond of asking every celebrity he met during his many projects around the world if they wanted to be in the show, regardless of whether they could sing or carry eight shows a week. It was the most complicated jigsaw puzzle imaginable.

While casting was going on, a great deal of work needed to be done on the script, which led to a surreal day during which Wilson and Waits were both in San Francisco and we arranged to meet at A.C.T.'s studios to hear the revisions. It happened that San Francisco's enormous Pride Parade was going on down Market Street that afternoon, and for many hours it looked as if Waits was going to retreat back into the Four Seasons Hotel rather than try to cross through the crowds. When we finally all arrived in the studio, we listened to members of A.C.T.'s core company read the script, which was a series of short scenes punctuated by songs. Knowing little about Wilson's aesthetic, they had no idea how to approach the material, and they read it as naturalistic dialogue, whereupon Wilson pronounced this the "*A Streetcar Named Black Rider* reading" and launched into a two-hour disquisition about the kind of performers he actually needed for his work. He loves to talk about "the space behind" the actor and longs for actors who are always aware of the vastness surrounding them, so that the work cannot become "conversational," which is anathema to him. (As Burroughs wrote approvingly, Wilson is able to "circumvent the crippling conventions of dramatic presentation: what he calls 'ping-pong dialogue' and soap opera plots.") Instead, Wilson aims for a highly controlled, formalized performance. He does not believe that the inner life of a character is his purview, any more than the psychological makeup of his collaborators is his purview. His job is to create a magical envelope without emotional signals, and let the audience feel what it will. "Usually the theater is happening so quickly that we don't have time for interior reflection," he said in an interview with Jonathan Marks at the American Repertory Theater in 1985. "In my theater, you do. . . . I think it has to be cold before it can be warm, and it has to have distance from the emotions in order for us to feel it. If we press the emotions on the audience then we're forcing the situation."

Wilson's theater might be more easily understood in connection to Asian theater traditions like Kabuki or Khatakali, but he insists that he is fundamentally an American artist and he longs to have his work produced in America. That this rarely happens, particularly in the American regional theater, is a source of great sorrow to Wilson, and has to do with both the lack of funding for this kind of work in the United States and the inflexibility of our rehearsal structures. There was a remarkable period in the 1980s when the American Repertory Theater under the direction of Robert Brustein staged five consecutive productions of Wilson's work, including his first exploration of a classic text. But the A.R.T. was the exception.

Most contemporary American theaters follow a highly predictable path in producing a play: once the script is deemed ready, a play gets cast; it gets designed in roughly a three-month period before the first rehearsal; it gets four weeks of rehearsal in the studio, a few long days of technical rehearsals in the theater, and a small number of preview performances, at which point it is "frozen" and opens to the press. Wilson works in an entirely different way. His productions always start with a fully staged workshop (often at The Watermill Center, his developmental space on Long Island), in which a group of performers comes together to help Wilson imagine the entire visual landscape of a new piece, working with complete lighting, costumes, and makeup, usually before there is even a script or music. Once he figures out the visual world, the songs or text can be fitted in, but it is not they that are driving the piece. Wilson sketches every scene in gorgeous free-form drawings that are works of art in and of themselves; he creates production books in elaborate detail before the staging even begins. While his process may be at the extreme end, it is indisputable that American theater works faster and in more circumscribed ways than theater in other parts of the world, with the result that fitting foreign artists into our cookie-cutter producing model is extremely difficult. A Russian director such as Kama Ginkas is used to six months of slow, painstaking work to arrive at his seemingly simple and resonant productions, and that is time we can never seem to find in the American theater.

For Wilson, the rehearsal process is one of extreme precision and rigor. "My work can't be over-rehearsed," he has said. "It's difficult to keep it alive and interesting, but the more it's rehearsed the better. The more it's repeated. When I did *A Letter for Queen Victoria*, I staged it in two weeks, but we rehearsed it for six months. Run-throughs. We just kept repeating it over and over and over." This is, of course, a far cry from the kind of free-form exploratory rehearsals most American actors are accustomed to, and many of the actors we auditioned for *The Black Rider* bristled at being treated like automatons. But the longer I watched Wilson work, the more fascinated I became with his process. As with all automatic actions, the more routine the behavior, the freer the imagination. It is when one walks the same route to work every day that the mind is free to wander, to take off, to explode. When one has to think about the route each time, the imagination takes a backseat. One needed to find actors who would trust that, through the rigorous collaboration with Wilson, a freedom would emerge at the other end. This was hard to describe to actors in advance, and the international casting process was complex and filled with misunderstandings. In the end, we had four European actors, including the aforementioned Soňa (whose patience and concentration were legendary), and four British actors, including the aptly named Richard Strange, who had his own band, his own way of being, and an ability to create a catalogue of outrageous creatures. From North America, we had the irascible and brilliant Jack Willis, who later joined A.C.T.'s core company, the wondrous Matt McGrath, who played Wilhelm as he journeyed from innocence to madness, Mary Margaret O'Hara of the luminous voice, and Marianne Faithfull.

Therein lies a tale. The role of Pegleg the Devil was originally conceived as a man, but having searched high and low, we could find no one suitably demonic and charismatic enough to fit Waits's and Wilson's vision of the character. One day Wilson called me and said he had seen Faithfull in Paris and thought she'd make a fine Devil. This worried me, since I wasn't sure that she could either sing or act the role, but he was adamant. The Marianne Faithfull decision turned out to be a difficult one: Wilson's work is meticulous, and Waits, for all his seeming bad-boy rule-breaking, had extremely clear notions of exactly how the music should sound. When I went to London to see a preview at the Barbican, the piece had not yet gelled. I was concerned about the sound mix, about how under-rehearsed the singers seemed to be, and about the fact that Faithfull had not yet succeeded at driving the show, as Pegleg had to do. Waits had been unavailable for the London rehearsals, so the music was not integrated well into the overall vision, and Faithfull was struggling to understand Wilson's unique way of working. In those early days in London, the outlines of the piece were visible, but the kind of extraordinary luminosity it eventually acquired was not yet in evidence. The chair of A.C.T.'s board, having gone to the Barbican to see the production, came back to San Francisco extremely upset and told me that she thought we had a potential debacle on our hands.

This was, of course, terrifying news for Managing Director Heather Kitchen and me, since we had staked a great deal on the piece, both with our board and with the community at large. Having required that we raise over a million dollars to produce our portion of this international collaboration, *The Black Rider* needed to be a major hit to recoup our investment and sustain the board's trust. However, knowing the potential magic of Wilson's work, I firmly believed that if we could finish the rehearsal period properly in San Francisco, the piece would come together and the result would be memorable. The first thing I did when I returned from London was to beg Waits and Brennan to come to San Francisco and be an integral part of the process. They agreed; when rehearsals began at A.C.T., they dove in and worked absolute miracles in a very short amount of time.

Unlike Wilson, who is huge, aristocratic, Texan, and intimidating, Waits is small, wild, shy, and extremely kind. He watched the first preview from one of the side boxes in The Geary, and afterwards he gave one of the greatest notes I have ever heard. The show opens with a black box out of which, in classic burlesque style, the entire cast of characters emerges, while Pegleg invites the audience to "come on along with the black rider," promising "a gay old time." The problem was that, from the first note, the band and Marianne were never together. She wasn't a singer who liked to count, and she had a hard time figuring out when her entrances should be. The opening number needed the bold feeling of a carnival in which a surreal barker introduces the frightening world of the play, but on that first preview, it felt labored and effortful. After the show, the cast gathered onstage.

Tom sat with his porkpie hat on the edge of the orchestra pit railing and thought for a moment. Then he leaned down into the pit, and said to the band, "Listen. She's the Devil. You're the band. She's a scary lady. You have to follow her. Wherever she goes, whatever she does, you follow her no matter what. 'Cuz she's the Devil." Rather than insisting that his lead singer begin to count bars and make the right entrance, Waits gave Faithfull the freedom and confidence to walk onstage and dominate the proceedings while the more musically adept band figured out how to compensate. From that moment on, the opening number began to cohere, and the rest of the show followed suit.

If Tom Stoppard inculcated our students in the value of "clarity of utterance," Robert Wilson was equally adamant about clarity of gesture. Even in auditions, Wilson would leap to his feet, explain that he wasn't in any way a dancer, and then proceed to show the nervous auditioner exactly how the scene ought to move and feel. His lanky and imposing body allowed for a kind of riveting physical presence that was difficult but inspiring for his actors to approximate. While *The Black Rider* was in rehearsals, I brought our M.F.A. students over to the theater to observe, wondering what they would make of the process. They watched Kansas-born Jack Willis wrestle with Wilson's insistence that he deliver his long monologue about magic bullets with one arm lifted over his head, and Matt McGrath attempt to fly incredibly slowly across the stage in white makeup without tangling wires with Mary Margaret O'Hara while singing the highly romantic ballad "The Briar and the Rose." There was little discussion about what Wilhelm felt or Pegleg's "obstacle" was. Yet at its best *The Black Rider* was full of inner life. It was clear that those actors who could hold on to their own rich emotional beings within the envelope of Wilson's staging achieved something potent through this arduous collaboration. Others adhered to the physical envelope perfectly but never truly filled it. It was up to the individual actor. That was the magical freedom of Wilson's aesthetic.

The Black Rider was different in San Francisco in part because Waits is a local artist and we know his music extremely well. The task of creating his distinctive rhythms and timbres night after night in an authentic way was a thrilling challenge for the musicians. As the show's associate musical director, David Coulter (who played the saw and didgeridoo and many other instruments in the show) explained, "There are certain things you need to play his music. . . . There's upright bass of course, and pump organ and drunken piano; lots of things that are slightly out of tune with each other, or 'sour,' to use Waits's own word." In an article in *The Guardian* in 2004, critic John Walters noted that "the musicians' pit looks like a downtown pawn-shop, packed with arcane and/or beautiful instruments." Waits spent the San Francisco rehearsals experimenting with how to tighten the sound, sharpen the rhythms, and wake up the room, which was crucial, because in this particular Wilson/Waits collaboration, it was Waits who brought rough edges, sexuality, longing, and wit into the world of *The Black Rider*. Wilson was brilliant enough to shape the piece so that the songs could work their own magic in the pristine landscape of the visual world, but it was up to Waits to make the music swing and wail. On the first Saturday matinee, a jeep pulled up outside the stage door a half hour before curtain; there was Waits with a huge box full of percussion instruments of all sizes and shapes, which he proceeded to hand down to the band in the pit right before the show was to begin. Our audience waited in delight as Tom demonstrated the new ideas he wanted his intrepid band to try, and then we all got to watch the results in action. Waits is an actor himself and a natural storyteller, and he seemed to intuit where he could enrich the overall piece, and how he could hold on to the idiosyncrasies of his own unique sound while sticking to the dramatic cues of the extremely demanding production. The music had a joy and a naïveté that was infectious and accessible, seducing even those who initially thought they would be put off by the oblique storytelling of the production.

It amazed me that the sophisticated audience of the Bay Area had rarely had the opportunity to see Wilson's work, despite the heroic efforts of Robert Cole at Cal Performances. Again and again I was reminded of the huge gap between the universe of the American regional theater and the larger trends in world performance. Our need to fill our houses with name brands, television stars, and recognizable properties has led us further and further from the large-scale experiments of Yukio Ninigawa or Ariane Mnouchkine, of Kazuo Ono or Tadeusz Kantor. I worried that the two worlds would not find a meeting point at The Geary. But watching the show unfold on opening night, I remembered what Burroughs had said when he first encountered Wilson's work: "Robert Wilson is primarily concerned with beauty—which implies, in certain quarters, escapism. And why should escapism carry an opprobrious connotation? Are lifeboats and fire escapes to be shunned as Escapist? Recent dream research has demonstrated that dreams are a *biological necessity*. . . . Robert Wilson is presenting beautiful life-saving dream images on stage." To our board's infinite relief, *The Black Rider*'s dreamscape landed perfectly at The Geary: its blend of visual shimmer, performance muscle, choreographic beauty, and musical joy finally came together in a coherent way, and the audience was overwhelmed. "Theater, like design, has to be about one thing first, and then it can be about a million other things," Wilson has said. The international endeavor of *The Black Rider* made me feel both bigger and smaller: bigger for having figured out how to pull it off, smaller for rarely daring to think and behave as enormously as the *Black Rider* team during the creation of the piece. The show went on to the Ahmanson Theatre in Los Angeles and then on to the Sydney Festival in Australia, but nowhere was it as complete and outrageously full as at The Geary.

Ever since *The Black Rider*, we have tried to launch another Waits/Wilson collaboration, spending several years researching the Hans Christian Andersen story "The Shadow" and seeking a writer to adapt it for the stage. But the miraculous confluence of time, energy, and money that brought *The Black Rider* to fruition has not materialized again. Wilson's form of theater doesn't easily fit the gestalt of the American institutional theater: it will never go to Broadway, it is profoundly uncommercial, it takes years to develop, and it needs large venues with dedicated shops and artisans to realize the vision. In this constricted and anxious moment in our culture, these qualities are in short supply. The legacy of Robert Wilson at A.C.T. was the appetite to make nonlinear, multidisciplinary work a regular presence on the Geary stage, and to learn to create this kind of work ourselves. In the wake of *The Black Rider*, we began devoting considerable time and energy to devising and presenting our own large-scale collaborative works, which ultimately led us to *The Tosca Project*, *Stuck Elevator*, *The Orphan of Zhao*, and many others.

CHAPTER 12

The Yale Detour

The Greeks, Beckett, Pinter, Stoppard, dance-theater—these are among the sources of my own personal aesthetic. Much has changed in my work and in my theatrical voice as I have gotten older, but much has remained the same: I am a lover of language, of irony, of poetry, of theatricality, of physical theater, of coded theater, of mystery, of music, of international theater and foreign dramatic genres. It was supremely good luck that the theater that chose me was housed in a city that matches my personal predilections fairly neatly, a city that introduced me to the Far East, has given me access to extraordinary music and dance collaborators, that is passionate about ideas and literate enough to adore three-hour Stoppard dramas, and that doesn't seem any more invested in realism than I am.

So I felt a certain degree of consternation when, in the winter of 2001, Yale President Rick Levin approached me about becoming the new dean of Yale School of Drama and artistic director of Yale Repertory Theatre. Oddly, this was history repeating itself: A decade earlier, I had been approached by then President Benno Schmidt about the Yale job, just before I became artistic director of A.C.T., and I went through a long interview process before losing out in the final round to Stan Wojewodski. Now President Levin had put his head together with Gerhard Casper, who was then president of Stanford University, and who sat on the A.C.T. board at the time but was also a Yale trustee; the two of them took me to breakfast at the Stanford Court Hotel in January 2001 to discuss my future in New Haven.

By this time, I had been at A.C.T. for nine years. The trauma of my first few seasons had slowly faded in the collective memory as our Geary campaign successfully resulted in a magnificently rebuilt theater and the fortunes of A.C.T. began to rebound. The first tech wave had flooded the Bay Area with money just as the millennium hit, and our 2000–01 season was notable for the expensive large-scale shows we were able to undertake, including a thirty-person *Threepenny Opera* with full band and the American premiere of Stoppard's *The Invention of Love*. *Invention* was our second American premiere of a Stoppard play and a remarkably satisfying experience. For a brief period, we had the resources to be ambitious and an audience to match. But the bursting of the tech bubble hit San Francisco very hard in 2001. The explosive potential of a new industry suddenly seemed like a vanishing mirage, and the money supply constricted, just when we were beginning to spread our wings. Once again, A.C.T.'s ambitious plans seemed to be in jeopardy.

It had become absolutely clear, even before the 2001 recession, that without a permanent endowment for A.C.T., this vulnerability would be perpetual. By the time I was being wooed by Yale, I could see that building such an endowment was going to be far harder than I had imagined (and ultimately, it never would have happened without the indefatigable duo of Alan Stein and Nancy Livingston, who refused to countenance the words "tech bust" and raised $31 million for A.C.T.'s first-ever endowment through sheer grit and determination). I began to wonder whether I wouldn't be more at home in an academic institution that was protected from the vagaries of the marketplace, inside a school that was well established and well supported by a robust undergraduate program. It had been nearly a decade, and I was restless. So I agreed to go to Yale to take a look. I remember vividly that I left San Francisco for New Haven in the middle of April on Easter Sunday. Despite my deep Jewish roots,

I have always been partial to Easter egg hunts and the pleasures of chocolate bunnies. My family gathered on top of Diamond Heights early that Easter morning while I hid eggs and made up games, and Lexie and Nicholas rushed around the grass in the hot sun screaming with delight whenever another sweet was discovered. And then, without much discussion about where I was going or why, they went with me to the airport and I got on the plane. Anthony was depressed about the whole idea: he had already followed me across the country once, he loved San Francisco, and he had no desire to relocate to New Haven. But, remarkable gentleman that he is, he was willing to let me go figure it out for myself. I truly don't know what he would have done if I'd decided that Yale was the answer, and I can only imagine how he felt as he held the children's hands and waved goodbye to me that Easter morning.

My time at Yale was fascinating. I remember what Robert Brustein said when he agreed to go to Yale during the Kingman Brewster years but tried to resist the title of dean, which he felt ill suited him. I felt the same way. When I got to New Haven, I had lunch with the other deans, toured the architecture school with Robert Stern, who had designed many of the mansions in the Napa Valley in which I had spent the last ten years fundraising, and spent time with the faculty, many of whom were already friends. There was much to admire. The students were lively and engaged, the school and the theater were fairly well integrated, and I saw some strong work at Yale Rep. But as I walked around New Haven at the end of the day, two things gnawed at me. One was that, in spite of his intelligence and his obvious commitment to sustaining a professional theater within the bosom of the university, it was President Levin's profound wish for the theater to break even and lessen its cost to the university. In other words, my dream of a university theater that could engage in truly challenging and risk-taking work because it was supported by the largesse of the university as a whole was, in fact, just that—a dream, without much basis in reality. While there was clearly appetite for an extraordinary law school and a first-class art museum at Yale, both of which cost a great deal of money, there did not seem to be commensurate appetite for a money-losing theater. And a theater embedded in a wealthy university represents a particular challenge, because outside donors usually assume the university is paying for it all, while within the fundraising wing of the university, the theater is often asked to wait in line for funding opportunities until other more important initiatives have been addressed. Thus, it became clear to me that, as difficult as it was going to be to keep A.C.T. solvent in the wake of the tech bust, there were perhaps more opportunities for me to experiment and grow in the brave new world of San Francisco.

But the second factor was even more important. I suddenly realized, from a distance of three thousand miles, that the biggest draw for me at A.C.T. was the Bay Area audience. Even with our relatively arcane repertoire, we'd been able to fill a theater The Geary's size on a regular basis with a surprisingly diverse and highly engaged audience that seemed to really care about the work. We had weaned them so thoroughly on high-quality writing about our productions that when we were trying to cut costs one year and decided not to publish dramaturgy in the performance program for *American Buffalo*, there was virtually a riot in the lobby and we had to reinstate it. Where else would that happen? And why was I considering walking away just when I had finally laid the tracks? The gestation of an aesthetic doesn't happen overnight—it is a long, slow process of building trust, of conversation and debate, of trial and error, of becoming a citizen in a new town and learning to reflect that town back to itself. By now, my audience and I had been through many battles together, and we knew each other. They were willing to give me room to grow, because I had been willing to listen to their opinions and to acknowledge their feelings. I realized that if I went to New Haven, I would miss my collaboration with this unique audience. There was more that we could do together. I had promised them a second stage, a larger core company, more new work, visionary directors, and international repertoire, and I was only just beginning to deliver on those promises.

So I thanked Levin profusely, flew back to San Francisco, and told the board that I had decided to turn down the Yale job and stay in San Francisco. It was a nerve-wracking but important moment, because in deciding to stay I renewed my commitment to the big dreams that had brought me to A.C.T. and embarked for the first time on a strategic planning process with the board and senior staff. It was also after this decision that I stopped worrying so much about what my New York colleagues might think and whether they were interested in what I was doing or not. This is a constant source of tension. The hegemony of the New York theater industry is a difficult strangle-hold to escape: while we pretend to be making theater for our own regions and cities, most of us spend a great deal of time looking over our shoulders, terrified that we will be forgotten by the all-powerful industry in New York. It was in the wake of the Yale offer that I started to let go of that anxiety. I was increasingly interested in the alternative ways of thinking and making work that the West Coast provided. I wanted to take Trustee Sue Yung Li up on her offer to travel to China with her on my sabbatical. I wanted to spend more energy articulating what it was I valued and what I longed to see happen at A.C.T.

The decision to remain also meant that Anthony and I could commit to putting our children through school in San Francisco. We were ready to dig in. We bought a house by Golden Gate Park, and I began riding my bike to work. Pedaling down the Panhandle and through the Lower Haight every day to Market Street, I finally began to feel for the first time that I was becoming a San Franciscan. As charming as San Francisco is on the surface, for me it was stubbornly hard to get to know, and it took me years to feel as if I belonged. Of course, this is one of the occupational hazards of being the Boss—it's difficult to get too close to colleagues within one's own organization, and for me it was equally difficult to befriend my peers at the other major arts organizations—they were mostly older men, and while they were very welcoming (San Francisco Opera General Director Lotfi Mansouri and San Francisco Symphony Maestro Michael Tilson Thomas, in particular) I was just at too different a moment in my life at that time to have that much in common with them. So with my daughter in high school and my house right beside Golden Gate Park, I began to connect in other ways to the city around me. I had worked so hard for ten years that I had barely picked my head up long enough to look around and notice my surroundings. Now that I did, I found a city I wanted to be part of. I started to get to know smaller theater and dance companies, from Campo Santo, Intersection for the Arts, and Shotgun Players to Zaccho Dance Theatre and Joe Goode's company; I met Bay Area novelists like Andrew Sean Greer, Michael Chabon, and Yiyun Li; my foodie daughter introduced me to the creativity of San Francisco chefs; and I began to hike in the hills around the Marin Headlands. I found surprising new worlds waiting to be discovered. But perhaps most important for me, I started writing again, after having left playwriting for many years.

CHAPTER 13

Telling My Own Stories

In my first decade at A.C.T., my task was to marry the very public demands of producing, public speaking, and fundraising with the much more private rehearsal-room explorations I was engaged in as a director. But that truly private act, which is writing, found no place in my early life at A.C.T. There were not enough hours in the day, it seemed, and the frenetic pace of my life as an artistic director and a parent left little time for introspection. But fate intervenes in strange ways, and just as I was beginning to yearn for the opportunity to tell my own stories again, an invitation presented itself.

In my early twenties, long before I started to direct professionally, I had written my first full-length play, *The Colossus of Rhodes*. It was an epic with songs that juxtaposed the secret love affair of mining mogul Cecil Rhodes (who created the famed Rhodes Scholarships) and the young Englishman Neville Pickering in South Africa in the 1860s with the music-hall antics of Jewish vaudevillian-turned-diamond-magnate Barney Barnato, who became Rhodes's nemesis. An early draft of the play had found its way into the hands of the late, great producer Lucille Lortel, after I made my directorial debut at her White Barn Theatre in 1983. At the age of eighty she hosted a reading of *Colossus* in the heady atmosphere of her Sherry-Netherland apartment on Fifth Avenue before an audience of one. Lortel's own story was a fascinating one: A successful young actress who trained briefly in Berlin under the legendary Max Reinhardt, Lortel (née Wadler) married a man who refused to permit her to continue her life as an actress; after spending fifteen years trying to find an alternative theatrical pursuit that would be acceptable to her husband, Lortel opened the White Barn Theatre on his estate in Westport, Connecticut, and began a career of supporting new and experimental work both in Westport and in New York, which included her landmark production of Marc Blitzstein's version of *The Threepenny Opera* at the Theater de Lys in 1955. This visionary theatrical maverick was one of my earliest and fiercest champions; she inspired a kind of artistic courage and idealism in everyone who met her, especially me. Not only did she engage me numerous times to direct at her theater, but she championed my writing and committed to producing *The Colossus of Rhodes* at the White Barn, believing that it perfectly suited her sense of theatrical adventure. Alas, Ms. Lortel passed away before that could happen, and shortly thereafter, I was hired to run CSC. Once I took up my post at CSC, I put the play and my playwriting ambitions aside for quite a long time.

I'm not sure why this happened. Perhaps proximity to geniuses like Harold Pinter made me wonder why I would want to add to the store of mediocre plays in the world when there were such extraordinary writers in my midst. Or perhaps the stories I wanted to tell weren't urgent or insistent enough yet to demand realization. Perhaps at the time I wasn't brave or tenacious enough to buck the odds. And perhaps this was a "female" reaction: it was clear that getting a play produced in the American theater was difficult enough, but for women it was triply difficult. (The sad statistics still prevail. It has been widely reported that only 17 percent of the plays produced in the United States are written by women, and if those plays have female protagonists, that number is cut in half.) Whatever the reason, I stopped writing and focused my energies on directing and on learning how to be a nimble producer, first at CSC and then at A.C.T.

It was over a decade later when Vincent Curcio, general manager of the White Barn Theatre, set about to reanimate the legacy of Ms. Lortel by producing a series of new plays at the White Barn, and one of the first projects he wanted to do was the premiere of *The Colossus of Rhodes*. He called me out of the blue in the spring of 2001, shortly after I had turned down the Yale job. Thus it happened that in August 2001 I went to Westport for Loy Arcenas's beautiful production of my first play. By then, I had been leading A.C.T. for almost exactly a decade. Naturally I was pleased when *Variety* critic Markland Taylor wrote, "With *The Colossus of Rhodes*, a bold theatrical exploration of Victorian England's Cecil Rhodes, Carey Perloff can add playwright to her résumé without blushing"—but of course, I *was* blushing! By this time, I was not the twenty-something emerging theater artist who had written the play, I was an executive and a leader of a major American theater and I had no idea how to fit this very private part of my personal expression into the larger public context of my life. So I all but hid the fact that I had had a play produced from my colleagues and trustees at A.C.T.

When I was invited to the O'Neill National Playwrights Conference the following summer to further develop the play (adding a crucial female character), I became acutely aware of my bifurcated self. I wanted to be seen purely as one of the O'Neill writers in residence for the summer, but I knew that to the other playwrights I was an artistic director who had the power to produce their plays. It was an awkward balance to maintain, but Jim Houghton (then the O'Neill's artistic director) did everything he could to help give me permission to be a playwright. That experience with *Rhodes* changed my life.

Once I dove back in, I became addicted to writing. I realized to my surprise how much of myself had ended up in this epic tale about nineteenth-century diamond mining. Despite his manifold flaws, Rhodes was a character for whom I had intense empathy: he was an outsider looking in, a restless soul who could never remain still, a complicated striver with antagonists on all sides. No wonder I identified with him! At the same time, of course, I identified equally with Barney Barnato, whose music-hall patter, Jewish jokes, and self-deprecating humor erupted onto the page with manic energy.

Having directed Brecht and the Greeks for so many years, I felt free to interrupt scenes with a song or dance directly addressed to the audience, before diving back into the emotional and moral tug of the play, enlarging the personal lives of those conflicted men by setting them against the epic landscape of British colonialism in Africa. *The Colossus of Rhodes* was a young effort filled with all the usual first-time mistakes: I had done so much research on 1860s South Africa that I had a hard time letting go of my favorite details, and the late-breaking addition of an African woman as Barnato's lover was not as well integrated as it might have been. But the gradual and ultimately painful love relationship between Pickering and Rhodes was specific and compelling enough to draw audiences into this unusual and un-familiar world and to stimulate some interesting comparisons with our own.

And so began my somewhat-secret other life as a playwright. Stories began emerging, in the quiet of my study after midnight, or on the weekends when I could steal time or my family was otherwise engaged. The next play, *Luminescence Dating*, began with a single line that came to me without any explanation. It was a woman emphati-cally saying to a man she loved, "I'd rather be right than be desirable." That slightly disturbing thought launched a thriller of sorts, set in the world of classical archaeology. The title (a natural metaphor for a certain kind of courtship), refers to the scientific practice of dating an ancient object by analyzing the radiation given off by the dirt in which the object has been buried. *Luminescence Dating* takes place in a museum basement much like the one at University of Pennsylvania where I had spent my teenage years engaged in the piecing together of broken pots. The seed of the play had been with me since child-hood; during one of our Sunday visits to the Smithsonian, my father and I heard a speech by Iris Cornelia Love about her famous excava-tions of the temple of Aphrodite at Knidos. I was captivated by that sexy female archaeologist in fishnet stockings whose name was Love and whose passion was to find a lost statue of the goddess of love in the Turkish ruins. This particular statue, sculpted by the great Prax-iteles and memorialized in the poetry and travel literature of the day, was said to be so lifelike and erotic that grown men had been seen trying to make love to its cold stone body. Praxiteles' Aphrodite disappeared without a trace, and despite heroic efforts on Love's part it had never been found. I was haunted by the story of a massive missing sculpture and the woman who longed to find it, and *Luminescence Dating* was my way of solving the puzzle, getting inside the competitive male world of archaeology, and watching a female practitioner pursue an obsession that nearly destroyed her.

Perhaps because the name of the inspirational figure was Love and the search involved a statue of Aphrodite, the play naturally evolved into a love story, as well—or, rather, multiple love stories. As always, I was fascinated by what happens when professional and personal lines become blurred and it seems a choice has to be made between love and success. In addition to the warring archaeologists in the play (Nigel and Angela), I created a character called Victor (written specifically for A.C.T. core company member Gregory Wallace), who is an African American queer theorist looking for evidence of male-to-male love in burial practices in ancient Greece; Victor carries a torch for a young scholar who in turn only has eyes for Nigel. In the midst of this romantic chaos and professional struggle, the goddess Aphrodite tries desperately to right the ship and to bring the lovers and their professional theories to a successful conclusion. "Nothing is more exhausting than being the world's oldest love object," she sighs.

Luminescence was a difficult beast to wrangle: the weaving together of scientific and romantic subplots required deftness and precision, and I was helped immeasurably by a variety of colleagues, first among them Curt Dempster, artistic director of Ensemble Studio Theatre (EST) in New York, whose opening salvo to playwrights in search of their play's motor was always the question, "What's the emergency?" Curt believed that if that could be answered, the rest of the play would unfold. In San Francisco, I teamed up with actors I knew well, led by director Mark Rucker, who helped me chart both the internal and external journeys of their characters in a way that I had been unable to do alone. With a Sloan Foundation grant awarded by EST, where

Luminescence premiered in 2005, I was able to conduct research on the play's scientific aspects, and a second grant was used to help produce it at the Magic Theatre in San Francisco in 2006.

Meanwhile, my life at A.C.T. was as busy and chaotic as ever, and I was able to function as a writer in addition to everything else in part because my (then) associate artistic director, Johanna Pfaelzer, insisted on making it possible. *Luminescence Dating* was happening at the same time that we were producing *The Black Rider*, commissioning David Mamet to adapt *The Voysey Inheritance*, hosting the Canadians with *The Overcoat*, wrangling Edward Albee with *The Goat*, and undergoing significant changes in the school. Johanna consistently gave me the breathing room and encouragement to write, convincing me that the producing tasks were not on my shoulders alone and that it was crucial for me to nurture another side of my creativity if I was to avoid becoming completely squeezed dry by the scale of the job. Because I felt guilty about every moment that I wasn't devoting full-time energy to A.C.T., I was very quiet about my writing, even with my family. It seemed like a betrayal, an activity that didn't belong in the rest of my proscribed universe. Even when the A.C.T. board, alongside the Magic's trustees, attended opening night festivities for *Luminescence* at the Magic Theatre and were vocal in their approbation, I felt shy and cautious about this new adventure. One of the few people I confided in was Sue Yung Li, the trustee who knew me best artistically and personally. And thus transpired one of the more surreal life–meets–art experiences of my life.

Shortly before the San Francisco premiere of *Luminescence*, Sue Yung invited me to her home to meet her college roommate from Smith. When I arrived at the house, an attractive woman in her seventies, holding a small dog, opened the door. "Hello, I'm Iris Cornelia Love," she said. I stared at her in wonder, as Sue Yung smiled merrily behind her. How could I explain to Love that her Smithsonian lecture thirty years before had changed my life, that I had grown up wanting to be exactly like the woman she had been, an archaeologist on a mission of discovery, and that I had just written a play inspired by her life? But it turned out she had long ago abandoned archaeology for dog training. The challenges of Knidos had been replaced by the Westminster Dog Show. I invited her to *Luminescence*, but she wasn't able to come. It was probably just as well. Her obsessive quest had become my own, and she was perfectly happy with her dogs.

Although *Luminescence Dating* was running in my own backyard, I continued to try to keep my playwriting self and my artistic director self as separate as possible. It was interesting to be a quasi-beginner again, but challenging to do so when I was also the head of a major institution; the public/private separation in my life often seemed unbridgeable. And while it's certainly vulnerable to direct a play or to stand before an audience as a producer, there is nothing quite as terrifying as revealing your passions, fears, and obsessions through your own writing, to people who know you well. But I was energized to be steadily developing my craft as a playwright. I had learned a great deal about the architecture of plays from having directed so many genres of work: from Ibsen and Sophocles I gleaned the power of detonating a secret from the past at precisely the right moment in the present; from Brecht I understood how a specific and particular encounter could become epic; from María Irene Fornés I absorbed the ways in which visual cues can shape the silent language of a play; from Pinter I learned to appreciate the claustrophobic theatricality of a single room, and from Stoppard I learned to revel in the delights of the English language.

At heart, I am a theatrical beast, I love creating events that find their essence onstage, that have a dramatic muscle to keep a story moving forward. I can usually intuit what actors will need and relish onstage, and how much can be left out of a script if one really trusts the performers. My directors have consistently opened my eyes: Robin Phillips taught me to stop staging my own plays in my head as I wrote and to trust that the story I was trying to tell could be fleshed out by a director afterwards. Maria Mileaf made me erase all my metaphors and become ruthlessly specific. Chay Yew taught me how to set up my own set of rigorous rules and then follow them consistently, and Rebecca Taichman made me dig into the backstory of my characters to flesh out their contradictions. Every time I go back into rehearsal as the director of someone else's work, I know that it fuels my own writing, and vice versa.

The summers became my precious time to develop work, and I have done so across the country, at the Sundance Institute Theatre Lab, at the O'Neill, at the Perry-Mansfield New Works Festival in Colorado, at the Orchard Project, and most notably at New York Stage and Film (housed on the Vassar College campus), which has become my second home summer after summer, play after play, and where I have always felt totally free and supported. Having physical distance from my job at A.C.T. gives me the stillness to enter areas of my imagination I am otherwise unaware of. And for me, stillness is the most elusive quality in the world. At the very end of *Luminescence Dating*, Victor says to Angela, "A kiss that good and you feel—nothing?" and Angela slowly replies, "I feel—still. Very still. Like something is about to happen." The luminous stillness that opens one's heart to the world is something I have studied via such practices as yoga and the Alexander Technique for many years, but it has never come easily to me. I long for it, but I am normally much more like a shark, feeling alive only when on the move.

One of the obvious preoccupations for me is the legacy of my mother, Marjorie, and the other formidable and almost too brilliant women amongst her female ancestors. My father's New Orleans family came from Polish peasant stock and were practical, wise, and full of their own secrets. But the expectation of genius amongst the women on my mother's side of the family was considerable and daunting. One summer, armed with tiny black-and-white photographs of the women from both sides of my family, and inspired by some reading on genetics, I began writing a play called *Waiting for the Flood*, in which Natasha, a geneticist panicked by her upcoming pregnancy, sits in her car and confronts the ghosts of her exotic female ancestors. I thought I was writing a comedy, a funny and fanciful piece filled with women clothed in forties attire emerging from the dashboard of a car speaking German, Italian, and Southern American in rapid succession. But underneath its humorous surface, the play began to get rather dark. If writing a play is about confronting your biggest fears, *Waiting for the*

Flood unearthed a plethora of feelings in the face of my family history, as well as touching upon anxieties about being a truly good parent and about the impossibility of controlling one's own destiny.

My long-standing friend and collaborator Chay Yew directed a workshop of *Flood* at New York Theatre Workshop (and then again at Roundabout Theatre Company), and every day at the end of rehearsal he would say to me, "It's all very lively and interesting, but you're writing around the hole." "What hole?" I would ask. "You have to write Natasha's mother." Every day I resisted. I said I had no interest in writing a mother-daughter play, I wanted to write about the double helix and genetics, ancestry and history. Then, the night before the public performance at Vassar, I went home, turned on my computer, and Natasha's mother, Marcia, walked into the play. She scared me to death. The scene between the mother and daughter was fierce and mean and disturbing. Who was this woman, and why was she so angry? Who was her daughter? And why were they tearing each other apart? I wrote the climactic new scene all in one go, saved it without rereading it, and before I could chicken out, called Chay and told him we'd need to find an extra actress for the reading the next day. Which we did. Of course, Chay turned out to be absolutely right—the entire journey of *Flood*, and all of Natasha's encounters with the charming and relentless women of her past built up to the moment when her mother finally appeared and confronted her. Natasha and Marcia said the kind of awful things that only mothers and daughters can say to each other, about pregnancy, mortality, abandonment, and disappointment. Marcia wasn't me and she wasn't my mother, but somehow she was the mother the play needed. She asked questions I had avoided asking, and exposed things I usually resisted thinking about, about my own past, about having children, about genetic predisposition, about race and class, love and marriage, and compromise.

The aspect of playwriting that involves the characters' backstories is slippery and fascinating; often characters will appear on the page without announcing anything about themselves, and it takes drafts and drafts to unearth who they might be. It's not that all the information has to be provided (Pinter refused to provide any backstory, and yet his characters are completely three-dimensional), but to be rounded, a character has to have a believable past. The more you dig, the more you learn, both about the play and about yourself.

I was somewhat startled when I got to the end of *Flood*. In the play's penultimate image, the women all stand at the lip of the stage, waving and calling out to their children as a flood threatens to engulf them. And then they are gone, leaving the bewildered Natasha alone, blinking in the bright sunlight of a beach in Santa Cruz. I remember sitting with Johanna Pfaelzer, Mark Linn-Baker, and Duncan Sheik at that first reading at Vassar, and we all wept as we watched those forlorn women with their hands in the air. The play was a mess, but it was a mess with some degree of originality and vitality. I felt as if a barrier had broken. I could let my imagination run wild, I could go to the darkest places in my mind, and I could trust the play to bring us out at the other end in one piece. There was real joy in that discovery.

Writing *Flood* made me realize how preoccupied I had become with ancestry and, in an odd way, with faith. My next play, *Higher*, took these issues further, in ways that surprised me. As I often say, I am a bad Jew. Although I was raised to feel very culturally Jewish, I never followed specific religious practice, and I married an agnostic Anglican who had no use for organized religion. (I had worried that my Jewish parents would be unhappy when I introduced them to my thoroughly WASP boyfriend in 1981, only to discover that with respect to Anthony, being British trumped being Jewish in my parents' eyes, because it was Churchill who had won the war and thus saved us all.) I made a halfhearted attempt to introduce my children at least minimally to Judaism, and Lexie was one of those little girls who had read every book about children in the Holocaust by the time she was twelve. But as a family, we rarely went to either temple or church. (One Christmas Eve, I even tried to persuade the family to go to midnight services at Grace Cathedral to hear the last sermon of my friend Dean Alan Jones before he retired. Anthony demurred, Lexie agreed to accompany me because midnight mass was on her "life list," and Nick rolled his eyes and announced that he refused to go to church at midnight because he didn't want to be "lied to and sleep deprived at the same time.") So it surprised me, as I began writing *Higher*, that it wrestled so actively with the desire to believe, and with the relationship of faith to art and to memory.

Higher is about a starchitect named Michael Friedman who has made his career designing visionary memorials. Michael has a gay son, Isaac, who is a deeply observant Jew and is thus appalled when he discovers that his father is competing to build a memorial on a sacred site in Israel. The other architect in the competition, unbeknownst to Michael, is his lover, Elena. Both must try to win the approbation of the elegant and sarcastic Upper East Side widow Valerie (modeled on so many of the philanthropists whom I have known over the years). The play asks questions about how we memorialize grief, about crossing international borders and presuming to understand the emotional and physical landscape of other cultures, about parents and children, and about the price of ambition. It was a piece I loved researching: I am an architecture aficionado and spent hours in the firms of friends of mine, watching pitch sessions and observing the delicate dance between architect and client that can sink or sustain a project. The director of the Contemporary Jewish Museum, Connie Wolfe, produced a reading of *Higher* in the "Yud" Gallery of their new Daniel Liebeskind building, and it was rather amazing to hear the play in such a brilliantly site-specific way.

But beyond architecture, the heartbeat of the play was about choosing to believe. Despite my lack of religious feeling, I had been wondering, in the midst of all the day-to-day struggles, why it was so difficult to find a bigger picture to hold on to. I asked my friend David Lang, the brilliant composer, how it was that after being raised as a secular Jew he suddenly became observant in his twenties. He said very simply that he had chosen to do something "hard." For him, adhering to the behavior of his ancestors was hard. Prayer was hard. Observance of dietary laws was hard. By doing these hard things, he felt connected to his history. But my own questions remained unanswered, and when I wrote the scene between Isaac and his father in *Higher* (the only scene that has remained in every draft of the play and is still the strongest writing in the piece), the conflicted feelings and confusions about belief and family came tumbling out of the mouths of this estranged father and son. One of the joys of playwriting is to set in motion a dialectic that allows all of one's own contradictory beliefs to collide in real time and with equal force. Interestingly, sometimes it's the opposing argument that gets the most air time, as Shaw demonstrates in *Major Barbara* by giving his capitalist weapons manufacturer, Andrew Undershaft, stronger arguments than his heroine, Barbara. In *Higher*, I found myself, in the mouth of Isaac, arguing for a commitment to faith that I knew I could never practice in my own life.

My resolve to keep my writing and producing lives separate dissolved in 2011 when *Higher* won the Blanche and Irving Laurie Foundation Theatre Visions Fund Award, which came with a sizeable check to support a production of the play. A.C.T. Executive Director Ellen Richard was a strong advocate for *Higher*, and with her encouragement we finally decided to produce it at Zeum, a small space near The Geary that was inadequate to the task but had been used on occasion for our conservatory and new works productions; again, the play would be directed by my trusted colleague Mark Rucker. It was the first time my A.C.T. team was completely central to the development of a play of mine, and it was far easier and less conflict laden than I had expected, though the challenge of bridging these two parts of my creative life was made even more acute by the timing of things. As it happened, I was directing an enormous production of Wajdi Mouawad's *Scorched* (a kind of Middle Eastern Greek tragedy) at The Geary at exactly the same moment that *Higher* was in rehearsal; thus the early months of 2012 were spent running down the hall from one rehearsal to another, literally switching hats midstream as I went from director to playwright and back. In the end, A.C.T. audiences seemed delighted to discover the writing aspect of my work, and *Higher* had a very successful run.

My next play emerged during one of the hardest eras I've yet faced at A.C.T. When the bottom dropped out of the economy in 2008 and we found ourselves struggling once again for survival, my professional confidence hit the skids. We had been having real success after years of change and struggle, and then suddenly all bets were off. I'm sure every responsible artistic leader felt panicked that year, as audiences and donations dried up across the country, but I went through a particularly dark period. I have always taken failure very much to heart, and I felt great sadness and despair as I wondered whether I had it in me to weather yet another storm—this one particularly enormous—and to keep my institution alive and its mission secure. I'm sure part of my bleakness had to do with turning fifty, and with watching my daughter leave home. I had come to A.C.T. as a young woman with nowhere to go but up. Now I felt middle-aged, out of steam, and adrift. I was also living through the dissolution of my professional partnership with Executive Director Heather Kitchen, something that had been under way for several years and was being exacerbated by the economic recession. While A.C.T. desperately needed new financial leadership, Heather had contributed a great deal and we knew that the change was going to be wrenching and complex. My crisis of faith in my own capacity to continue on in the face of such dire circumstances and daunting challenges broke something loose in my creative process, and suddenly, in the wee hours of the night as I thought about the future, I found myself writing something much less structured and far more exposed than anything I'd ever tried before.

In the summer of 2009 I was slated to direct *Phèdre* at the Stratford Festival, so off I went to Canada in the midst of the financial crisis. I spent three months with the finest classical actors in North America, plumbing the depths of Racine's play about passion, power, humiliation, and shame. Almost instinctively, as I was simultaneously worrying about what was happening back home and working intensely on *Phèdre*, I began writing *Kinship*, a play that mines a similar vein of passion and transgression. In *Kinship*, a successful newspaper editor becomes besotted with a young journalist in her employ. She obsessively confides in a very close older friend (based on *Phèdre*'s nurse, Oenone), who turns out to be the young man's mother. (The credit for that idea goes to playwright Morris Panych, who lived across the hall from me at Stratford and plied me with martinis while I shared the outline of my tortured new play.) I called the characters SHE, HE, and THE FRIEND, so as not to label them in any way—I just wanted to set their desires and obsessions in motion and watch the train wreck happen.

Out of the sadness and sense of failure of that time came a play that wasn't about plot or contrivance, that wasn't clever or crafted, but rather emerged almost intact from my bleak heart. It was an incredible relief to write the play, to give myself permission to give voice to those feelings of humiliation and failure, hope and hunger. Perhaps that's why *Kinship* feels more visceral and intuitive than my other plays. I took everything I had learned from directing *Mary Stuart* and *Phèdre*, from my life as a leader and from the loneliness a woman can feel in that position, and I poured it into the story of a woman who nearly wrecks her career to pursue an irrational passion for a man who turns out to be less than she had imagined. I have always been fascinated by obsession and by the lengths an obsessed person will go to in order to keep infatuation alive, and I vividly remember writing the section where SHE begins to steal things HE has left behind and hide them in her purse, just to hold on to a piece of him. I passed no judgment on the characters or their behavior, assuming that I would put this play in a drawer and never show it to anyone after purging myself of so much anxiety by writing it.

And then, nearly four years after beginning the play, a door opened where I least expected it. In the fall of 2013, while I was in Saint-Étienne doing a workshop with French acting students, the great French actress Isabelle Adjani was given *Kinship* by translator Séverine Magois, with whom I was working at the time. (She had rendered *Waiting for the Flood* into French.) For years, Adjani had been looking for a role that she felt would challenge and inspire her, and when she read *Kinship* she was convinced she'd found what she'd been looking for. She immediately said that she wanted to star in a French production of the play as soon as possible. Magois completed a stunning French version in about three weeks, signed on with enthusiasm, and off they went. I got to experience firsthand the eye-opening transformation that happens when work in one language enters the world of another. *Kinship* is a play about intimacy. Of course, in French the moment when a relationship stops being professional and crosses the line into something personal is precisely indicated in the language. Magois didn't even ask me about it—as the play moved from the scene at a speakeasy in which SHE and HE first acknowledge their love to an afternoon in the country when they are "together," the translation segued from *vous* (the formal way of saying "you" in French) to *tu* (the more intimate, personal term), and the transgression was utterly clear. Hearing my voice in French was strangely freeing. No one in Paris knew me, so I had nothing to hide. (No wonder when Beckett left Ireland he never wrote in English again!) At the same time that *Kinship* was preparing to open in Paris, we were developing it on this side of the Atlantic with the equally fascinating Cynthia Nixon. Nothing has made me happier than to know that on two continents, two powerhouse women were taking the stage to create a complex female character that I had actually invented.

As I write this chapter, I am at work on a new play called *The Rowboat Widow*, which I began on a dare to myself while in residence at the Orchard Project. Surrounded by so many inspiring and fearless twenty-somethings, I wanted to write my way to the end of a play in a week without having any foreknowledge about what form it would take. On the last day, I wanted to gather the apprentices and artists there in the mountains that week to hear the play and, in some bizarre way, "crowdsource" the ending. The play is a mystery about a man who is presumed dead and then suddenly reappears, unannounced, at his home in the Rockaways, which has been torn apart by Hurricane Sandy. There were a dozen ways the mystery could get resolved (or not), and that summer we had a joyful and inspiring time concocting possible scenarios. I have now tucked the story away in the back of my brain, where I hope it is evolving in my subconscious, ready to take on new life when I finally come up for air long enough to continue writing it.

CHAPTER 14

The Quandary of Too Many Hats

After my life-saving Canadian sojourn with *Phèdre*, in August 2009 I returned to San Francisco, and to a country in the throes of the Great Recession. I also returned to a theater in search of new leadership. A.C.T.'s board had handled Heather Kitchen's departure with incredible grace and calm, and we were about to begin the process of hiring the next executive director. Meanwhile, A.C.T. was struggling to regain its footing in precarious financial times, and I was trying once again to start over and imagine what to do next with the organization. The depth of the recession had taken us all by surprise, although of course we should've seen it coming. But between the white-hot Bay Area housing market and the excitement about an election we hoped would rescue us from the embarrassment of the Bush years, none of us quite anticipated the extent of the financial meltdown once it began.

At A.C.T. the crisis led to long and profound soul-searching about how best to go on. Naturally, many arts organizations ended up on the endangered list, reminding us all how slim our margins were and how precarious our fate. By the end of the 2008–09 season, the sizzle had disappeared from the Bay Area economy, and, like most American theaters, we were losing audiences at an alarming rate, while charitable contributions were falling precipitously. We felt inspired by Obama's election but daunted by the monumental task that lay ahead for a new president whose motto was "A crisis is a terrible thing to waste." Once again we wondered what, if anything, we could put onstage that would *matter*. I wondered whether it made sense anymore to try to produce serious theater in such a huge house. My staff was anxious and demoralized, as they watched colleagues across the field getting laid off due to the economic downturn. We had company meetings in which, despite my attempts at cheerleading and enthusiasm, I felt that nothing I could say or do was enough. I fought hard to keep the core acting company intact in spite of the funding cuts, and then wondered if I was putting my energy and resources into the right aspects of our work. Our colleagues across the bay were creating a big commercial show to the music of Green Day, while we struggled with an adaptation of Christopher Logue's poetic Trojan epic, *War Music*, which had enormous potential but collapsed onstage under the weight of its own language.

I began to feel, as I had in the past, that my particular passions were out of sync with the appetites of the times and that my personal distance from popular culture was marginalizing my theater. I watched President Obama on television night after night giving speeches to an anxious nation, and I marveled at his ability to remain cool and collected in the face of near disaster. I wondered for the millionth time whether I had it in me to be the kind of leader the situation required. In 2007, my associate artistic director Johanna Pfaelzer had returned to New York Stage and Film, just when Lexie had left for college, so, two years on, I found myself in San Francisco without two of the women I treasured most in the world. By the summer of 2009 I was also, for the first time in many years, leading the organization alone, something I had vowed I would never do again.

The change of a business partner can be highly energizing, but it is also exhausting and difficult; this is the person with whom one has to share the reins of the organization, and having disharmony at the helm makes it extremely difficult to chart a vigorous course forward in hard times. I met with Kennedy Center president and turnaround guru Michael Kaiser and listened as he proclaimed the virtues of "big ideas brilliantly marketed," and I tried to reconnect with those aspects of making theater that still mattered to me. On the surface I maintained an exuberant and optimistic outlook, but underneath it all I was miserable. I remember sitting on the set of José Rivera's beautiful *Boleros for the Disenchanted* with actress Rachel Ticotin, who had also just turned fifty and had recently sent her only daughter to college across the country, just as I had. We huddled together on a makeshift sofa and wept as we mourned our past and tried to imagine the future. Why were we still making theater? For whom? Was the relentless grind and endless barrage of criticism actually worth it? What would keep us resilient and forward-looking in the face of indifference and incomprehension?

As I tried to plot the course for A.C.T.'s future, I wrestled a great deal with the left brain–right brain duality of running a theater while trying to remain an artist. The debate over whether artistic organizations should be helmed by artists or administrators is a long-standing one and has strong proponents on both sides. There are those in our field who argue that having a leader who is not also a director (or writer or actor) is better for the managerial and fundraising aspects of the job, ensuring that the artistic director won't get pulled into the rehearsal room just when the institution needs her to be visible and externally focused. And then there are those who argue that the kind of vision required to sustain a major theater's momentum can only come from having a creative artist at the center of the organization. Given that there are extremely successful artistic directors of both types in the American theater, there is clearly no right answer to this question. I do believe that when an institution is run by an artist, the chance that artistic values and artistic passions will drive the work is higher, and that since such a huge part of the job is helping other artists succeed, it's useful to truly understand what they need and how they think. I also know that I am an adept fundraiser in part because I can clearly and passionately make the case for the art, since I am so involved in creating it. But the whiplash caused by constantly shifting from being an artist to being a CEO can be exhausting and debilitating.

As a director, one hopes to enter a rehearsal room fully prepared and with an entirely clear head, ready to devote all of one's imagination, energy, and knowledge to the creation of a new and vivid production. Now imagine how the average day of an artistic director in rehearsal unfolds. Let us say the rehearsal day is from 10:00 AM to 6:00 PM with a one-hour break in the middle. The artistic director gets to work at 8:00 AM to make sure that all the calls to New York are made to keep the season-planning process moving forward; perhaps she has an early marketing meeting or perhaps there is a breakfast with donors or with key board members to prepare for an upcoming meeting or to solicit funds for a given project, or she attends an open speech class in the school to ascertain which students will be ready to do Stoppard or Shakespeare later that season. Then she is expected to walk into rehearsal at 10:00 completely prepared for the day's work ahead, and to tune out everything else but the work at hand. But on every five-minute break, while the actors smoke or drink coffee in the sunshine on the balcony, she is proofreading grants, approving press releases, assuaging an unhappy staff member, or reviewing weekly ticket sales and expenditures.

On her one-hour lunch break, she most likely has a senior team meeting or another major fundraising task or a brainstorming session with the education department about future programming. She rushes back into the rehearsal room to pick up where she left off, trying to stay flexible and open when ideas come at her from all sides from actors, designers, and other collaborators. She tries to look decent and sound articulate on her fifteen-minute afternoon break as she is interviewed by the press about why she has chosen to produce this particular play. At the end of the rehearsal day she huddles with stage management to set the next day's schedule, before returning to her office to see what havoc has occurred in her absence and what staff crisis needs immediate triage. Then, if she has children, or a partner, or any other life, she dashes home to have dinner with the people she loves, and then once baths are taken and homework is done and conversations have abated, she sits down at her desk to read scripts for the next season, to advise a commissioned playwright on suitable next steps or to approve a design scheme for an upcoming production, to write a passionate letter to the subscribers for the next program book or to assuage an unhappy patron, to attend to the hundreds of emails she has missed all day, and to address all the administrative details that need to be taken care of if the institution is to keep running smoothly. And then it starts all over again the next morning.

Of course, many professionals in other fields have days even more packed and rigorous than that of an artistic director and are confronted by problems of far greater consequence. But there is a key difference. The part of the brain that has the executive capability to manage a huge organization is very different from that part of the brain in which the artistic impulse lies. Often, for a creative idea to happen, there has to be time, silence, stillness. It has to be possible "not to know." There has to be vulnerability, and the ability to fail. The part of me that comes alive as a writer and director is completely different from my executive self. In the years when she was A.C.T.'s associate artistic director, Johanna Pfaelzer constantly urged me to allow myself to be an artist within my own institution, assuring me not only that I would be taken care of but that the institution would survive, as well. Johanna intuitively understood that without that degree of vulnerability, the deep dive that needs to happen to write or direct a play couldn't happen. But managing to look after both sides of the job is difficult, a lament I hear over and over again from my artistic director colleagues across the country. I have often wondered if it were time to give up running a theater so that I could finally focus entirely on my own work, without feeling guilty for having abandoned my institutional responsibilities. Again and again, I have wondered whether a full-time fundraiser and producer would be better able to manage A.C.T., would be able to travel more frequently to see new work without being caught in rehearsal (to say nothing of the demands at home), would be able to lobby politicians and to court donors with more efficacy and consistency. And yet I know that I have done these things well in part because I have been so nurtured by the work.

Part of the quandary for me is that I am a natural caretaker, as many women tend to be. I have noticed that many of my male colleagues seem to spend less time at their home theaters than I do, less time holding hands, raising money, writing opening night cards and engaging in the minutiae of the organization. Perhaps that is my failing—I want everyone to be happy, I want to know what's going on, I want to turn up at every reading, every audition, and every open class, so that people know they are valued and noticed. Although I am something of a renegade in this profession, I am also a person who wants to please. Once, when I was in rehearsal with Olympia, she stopped me as I was rushing upstairs on a break to catch twenty minutes of a student project. "Stop wallpapering the kitchen!" she admonished me, meaning, "Stop attending to every detail in the organization. Let someone else do it!" Women constantly need to be reminded to resist taking on the organizational housework that they naturally end up inheriting. I have always had a hard time following that advice myself. I feel like the mayor of a small town: these are my people, and they need me.

One of the reasons I started writing again after so many years, much to the shock and dismay of my colleagues and family who all felt I already had enough to do without becoming a playwright again, was that I intuitively understood that if I didn't find an outlet for my own voice and my own stories, I risked becoming worn out and bitter, squeezed dry by the endless and competing needs of those within and outside of my theater. Ever since that eye-opening summer at the O'Neill conference when Jim Houghton not only made me read my nascent play aloud but made me stand up with all the other writers to announce myself as "Carey Perloff, Playwright," I have used my writing time to try to stay connected to my own thoughts and intuitions. The more work I have done on my own writing, the more compassion and admiration I have developed for the writers with whom I collaborate; I want the scripts to be bigger, richer, braver, and I know exactly how hard that is to accomplish. And over time, I've become more comfortable with making my own plays part of the artistic life of A.C.T.

Nevertheless, the artist/administrator dichotomy has continued to be a challenge for me. It is difficult in the American theater to wear too many hats—unlike other theatrical cultures, we tend to prefer specialization, so we have writers, actors, directors, producers, designers, choreographers, composers, but we are often anxious or confused if the lines cross and artists from one discipline begin experimenting with another. Of course it is a full-time job to be a playwright, as it is a full-time job to be a director or an artistic director. So the conflicts will never go away, and one is always stealing time from one activity to buy time for another. If I gave up the leadership of the organization, I would gain immense freedom for my own work, but I would lose the beauty of having an artistic home and a long-term relationship with the audience for whom the work exists. Such is the eternal quandary.

This was particularly true in the recession years, when the institution itself felt so precarious again. After years of artistic and financial success and the creation of an endowment for A.C.T., it suddenly felt as if nothing stood on solid ground anymore. I had to go back to square one. I had to ask, once again, what was valuable about A.C.T. to the community in which it lived. I had to figure out how I personally could be an active citizen in that community, even when I didn't have the answers. How could I help advance the life of the city from my own particular corner? How could I write something that dared to reflect what it felt like to be at the bottom of the well? How could I keep reveling in the process in spite of it all? As I had learned during my first controversial season, the most important qualities turned out to be receptivity, a sense of humor, real collaboration, and a willingness to fight the fight. I had to keep showing up until the doors started opening again. Most of all, I had to realize not only that I was never going to come up with all the solutions myself, but also that handing creative power over to other people was the most energizing decision I could make.

CHAPTER 15

San Francisco Stories

I began imagining a new kind of leadership and a new direction for A.C.T. while I was in Canada at the Stratford Festival directing *Phèdre* in the summer of 2009. It helped to be away for three months, to live alone for a while, to commit utterly to that desperate and beautiful play about passion and transgression, and to begin to write something new, far away from the eyes of anyone I knew. Being at Stratford amid those world-class classical actors renewed my fervor for acting companies and for ambitious programming, but my distance from San Francisco also helped me to see how unique my hometown was. Biking through the cornfields of Ontario every morning, I missed the quirky, adventurous spirit of San Francisco, the San Francisco values that translated into a sense of inclusiveness amidst ethnic and cultural diversity. I started to realize that if A.C.T. was going to thrive and to survive the rocky economy, it had to renew and deepen its ties to its own complicated and contradictory community. It is our job to make life richer for that wildly diverse group of people who make our city their home. It is also our job to make room for new artists and for smaller companies who could exist within the overall umbrella of A.C.T. When I returned to San Francisco, I felt revivified and somewhat hopeful about these new goals, and we slowly began to consider how we could push ourselves to really think locally. One result of this thinking was the creation of a new Education Department at A.C.T. whose job is to interact with thousands of Bay Area children every year, not only by inviting them to student matinees but also by sending teaching artists into schools to create work with a wide range of socioeconomically disadvantaged kids and, perhaps most important, by embedding two continuation high schools within A.C.T., to stimulate project-based learning through the transformative power of theater. Another was our decision to make a serious commitment to creating pieces for and about our own Bay Area audiences.

It is important to remember here that, while Bill Ball founded A.C.T. with a decidedly national focus in mind (he did not, as I have noted, choose to call his theater the "*San Francisco* Conservatory Theater"), in the early days A.C.T. had succeeded in part because Ball's work at A.C.T. was in fact intensely local, created by a standing company of actors, directors, and designers who lived and worked full time in the Bay Area. Over several decades, the audience in San Francisco came to view those artists as their own, watching the actors transform from role to role with dexterity and panache. But by the nineties, when the original company had been disbanded and A.C.T. was searching for a new identity, things had changed in the American theater. Local was no longer sexy or desirable. Resident companies had faded away, and it had become standard operating procedure for the larger regional theaters around the country to accept significant enhancement money from commercial producers in exchange for the use of their venues and their subscription audiences to try out Broadway-bound material. While this allowed large-scale musicals to be developed and previewed across the country, it risked sapping the regional theater of its artistic muscle and its local individuality. Since it is generally true that he who pays the piper calls the tune, it is inevitable that the artists working on an enhanced production are far more likely to take direction from their Broadway producers than from the nonprofit theater's artistic team (unless the theater's own artistic director is at the helm), with the result that the work ceases to have much of a local identity at all.

This is not in and of itself a bad thing; sometimes commercial collaborations can be energizing and fruitful. After all, does an audience care who calls the shots in creating a show, as long as the show is good? Can we really measure what impact the farmed-out procedure has on the vitality of individual arts communities across America? One could argue that the broad collaborations happening at theaters across the country represent a certain kind of national theater. But just as finding oil can be a dangerous discovery for any country, hitting pay dirt with a commercial production at a nonprofit theater is not typically the panacea we hope it will be. Time and again, resident theaters that become dependent upon enhancement dollars or royalties from commercial successes find themselves broke and at sea when the money dries up. The vigilance it takes to sustain a donor base, nurture and educate an audience, and manage expenses often disappears when there is money coming in from the coffers of Broadway producers and investors; thus, just as oil-rich countries from Venezuela to Libya have found themselves mired in bad governance and social unrest, nonprofit theaters can too easily lose their artistic and financial way while pursuing commercial success.

Furthermore, just as we have become attuned to the pleasures and virtues of eating food grown close to home, there is something equally important about artistic collaboration that bears some relationship to the community in which it is launched. I was inspired by reading, in Todd London's *An Ideal Theater*, the testimony of Robert Porterfield, founder of Virginia's Barter Theatre, who had the brilliant notion during the Depression of allowing his impoverished audience to barter cabbages and bacon for theater tickets. In return, more than once, Porterfield paid royalties with Virginia ham. I haven't yet gone that far, but I began to get more and more interested in the lessons theater could learn from the locavore food movement. If people travel across the country to eat California cuisine, wouldn't they also value a kind of California theater that is distinctive and specific?

A.C.T.'s collaborations with outside producers had for the most part yielded negligible results and a general feeling of dissatisfaction among the staff and artists: When the work was bad or incomplete and it came with New York money, we had limited ability either to make it better or to pull the plug. On the rare occasions when we teamed up with commercial producers to create new work (for example, David Hirson's *Wrong Mountain* or Martha Clarke's new version of *Hans Christian Andersen*), we ended up putting the work in front of an audience far sooner than it should have been seen (given the size and scope of The Geary, at any rate), and we humiliated ourselves and lost a great deal of money in the process. Our New York producing partners, much as we liked them, could walk away unscathed, but we had to face our audience the morning after and absorb the losses at the box office. So, in the wake of the recession and the discussions it triggered, we decided to commit to doing at least one project every year that was a San Francisco story, built by us, for our audience.

We had tested this ground in 2003 when we commissioned Bay Area playwright Philip Kan Gotanda to write *After the War*, a play about a Japanese American jazz musician who returns to San Francisco's Fillmore district in 1945 after internment to find his life completely upended. Philip drew on his own family's stories for *After the War*. His father, a Japanese American surgeon, had been incarcerated at the internment camp in Rohwer, Arkansas, for the duration of the war, rarely speaking to his family about it afterwards. Philip wanted to understand how the trauma of the internment camps had shaped not only Japanese American lives, but an entire city, in the postwar period, and we spent three and a half years researching and developing the piece (including a residency at the Sundance Theatre Lab). When it opened in March 2007, it was clear the tale it told resonated with both the audiences familiar with the story and those for whom it was entirely new. It was *our* story, a San Francisco story. We were overwhelmed by the passion *After the War* engendered in our audience, and by the many attendees who were coming to our theater, or any theater, for the first time.

After the War was the first of our San Francisco stories, shortly followed by *The Tosca Project*, an unusual collaboration with dancers from San Francisco Ballet. I had fallen in love with San Francisco's first-class ballet company as soon as I arrived in town, long before I could persuade anyone in my family to accompany me. (I tried to convince Lexie to take ballet classes, as I had at the Washington School of Ballet as a little girl, but she rolled her eyes when she saw all those anxious girls in tight buns and pink leotards and took up rock climbing instead.) Once I got to know some of the artists at San Francisco Ballet, I began to fantasize about ways to work with them. In the wake of *The Black Rider* and other movement-based work, I was curious about whether we could devise a movement-theater work ourselves.

It happened that, during the winter of 2004, I was working on Paul Walsh's new translation of Ibsen's *A Doll's House* with René Augesen as Nora. I needed a choreographer to stage the episode in the second act of the play when Nora dances a tarantella to distract her husband from spotting Krogstad's incriminating note in the letter box. My costume designer, Sandra Woodall, suggested I try Val Caniparoli, a choreographer for San Francisco Ballet whose *Lambarena* I had seen and admired; next thing I knew, he was in the studio with us, spinning René in sinuous loops around the room. Val amazed me. He could take nondancers, even René, who had just had neck surgery and was very fragile physically, and make them look as if dance was their natural means of expression. Val is a storyteller at heart, a character dancer with a remarkable instinct for the ways in which movement can express complex feeling without resorting to what he disdainfully refers to as "ballet mime." Indeed, his experience with *A Doll's House* was so fruitful that for San Francisco Ballet's seventy-fifth anniversary he created a ballet called *Ibsen's House* based on the complicated women of those plays.

After *A Doll's House*, Val and I started collaborating regularly. In 2005 he partnered with me on a major reimagining of *A Christmas Carol* (adapted by myself and Paul Walsh), which A.C.T. had spent several years developing; Val filled the show with movement, most memorably in the Fezziwig scene, for which he created a swirling, head-bobbing dance that always brings down the house, as well as a hilarious and charming "fruit ballet" in which children embody Spanish onions, Turkish figs, and French plums, taunting Scrooge with their Christmas abundance. In 2008, he created a sexy on-the-table dance for Susan Gibney in *'Tis Pity She's a Whore*. Val is always up for an adventure. So when Morris Panych and Wendy Gorling's seminal Canadian movement piece, *The Overcoat*, played to enormous success at A.C.T. and I invited him to see it, Val immediately said, "If you love this kind of theater, let's try to make our own version of it." The beauty of having a long-term commitment to a city and to a theater is that an idea can arise and we can say yes to it, even if we don't quite know what it will mean. Since the arrival of Head of Movement Stephen Buescher in the M.F.A. Program in 2009, our whole institution has developed an appetite for so-called "devised" work, using movement, music, and text in equal measure to collaboratively create new kinds of theater. Excited about the techniques and ideas we were developing in the school, we dove into this new adventure with relish.

Val was inspired by Ettore Scola's brilliant dance film *Le Bal*, set in a community center in provincial France, in which the sufferings and celebrations of a whole town before, during, and after World War II are told entirely though movement. For many years, Val had considered making a ballet based on *Le Bal*; now we used the idea as our jumping-off point for collective exploration. Because dancer Muriel Maffre had seen a stage version of *Le Bal* in Paris, we had many discussions about how to take the notion of a magical, complex space and transfer it to San Francisco. We had no idea what form our new piece would take, but for four years, we grabbed whatever time we could in the midst of everyone's complicated work schedules and holed up in a studio with an intrepid and highly disparate troupe of performers to experiment with ideas. The group we worked with evolved over time, including dancers Pascal Molat, Damian Smith, Muriel Maffre, Lorena Feijoo, Joanna Berman, Nol Simonse, and Yuri Possokhov and actors Jack Willis, Gregory Wallace, Rachel Ticotin, Peter Anderson, Matt McGrath, Kyle Schaefer, and Sara Hogrefe. We wanted to make a piece in which movement, though not necessarily dance, could carry the narrative with minimal text, and in which the fusion of dancers and actors was seamless and surprising.

One afternoon I found myself sitting in Tosca Café, a legendary bar in the North Beach neighborhood of San Francisco, sharing my thoughts with the bar's famous owner, Jeannette Etheredge. An Armenian refugee who had come as a child to California via Manchuria after the war, Jeannette was a balletomane and culture hound who had photos of an astonishing array of visiting film stars and ballerinas hanging across the walls of her bar. Her friendships with artists and intellectuals from around the world were legendary: everyone from Wim Wenders to Sam Shepard, from Natalia Makarova to Christopher Hitchens, came to sit in Tosca's red booths and drink spiked "cappuccinos" when they passed through San Francisco. Owing to her close relationship with the legendary dancer during the later years of his life, Jeannette had become a trustee of the Rudolf Nureyev Dance Foundation, and I had gone to her that day seeking support for our initial dance-theater workshop. As I sat in that magical treasure trove of a bar, filled with a century's worth of love, longing, drinking, and dance, I realized I had found our story. Walking back to my car, I dialed Val and said, "Let's make our piece about Tosca Café."

What would that mean? I knew that the bar was a repository of rich stories dating from its inception in 1919, when three intrepid Italians bought the café weeks before Prohibition went into effect and named it after the hit opera of their day. They cooked homemade spirits to spice up the house "cappuccino" during Prohibition, decorated the walls with giant murals of Puccini's eponymous melodrama, bought huge gold espresso machines from Italy, and installed a jukebox filled with popular Italian arias. During World War II, officers en route to the war in the Pacific lined up at the beautiful mahogany bar for one last drink, and their girls remained behind to hold the fort and dance alone to new tunes emanating from the juke. In the fifties, Tosca Café became a host to the Beat poets, for whom North Beach was the creative headquarters; it is said that William Burroughs worked on *Naked Lunch* in one of its booths, and through the large arched windows one could easily see City Lights Bookstore across the street, which Lawrence Ferlinghetti founded and where he published Allen Ginsberg's ground-breaking poem "Howl." By the time Jeannette bought the bar in 1981, Nureyev, Makarova, and a generation of refugee Russian dancers had found their way to Tosca, courtesy of Jeannette's mother, Armen Baliantz, a Russian-speaking doyenne of the arts. Jeannette's involvement with the San Francisco Film Festival brought filmmakers and celebrities to the bar; its mysterious back room (which housed the pool table of Jeannette's beloved deceased brother) is supposedly where screenwriter Philip Kaufman planned *The Right Stuff*, Joseph Brodsky wrote his first English-language poems, and many political careers were brokered. Its walls were covered with photos of the likes of the young Winona Ryder riding on the shoulders of Francis Ford Coppola. It's a space filled with extraordinary ghosts. We decided we wanted to make a piece in which the place was the subject, to create a kind of living archaeology such that the stir of a swizzle stick might bring back the sound of a voice or the footsteps of a lover long forgotten.

Our task was to figure out how to call forth the ghosts. I hired designers Darron West (sound) and Douglas Schmidt (sets) and encouraged their imagination to fuel the work from day one. With our dramaturgical team, we set about interviewing North Beach denizens, taking oral histories, and tracking down ancient newspaper articles, reading Brodsky, Kenneth Rexroth, and Hunter S. Thompson, and listening to the music on the jukebox. For our initial workshop, we decided to focus on the fifties. When the first day of rehearsal came, the actors sat on one side of the room and the dancers on the other, staring warily at each other across a great divide, wondering how on earth to begin. I brought in reams of poetry and prose, and Val taught us all to dance the Madison. We did improvisations and made drawings. The brilliant clown Peter Anderson (a Vancouver resident who had starred in *The Overcoat*) grabbed Ferlinghetti's iconic poem "I Am Waiting" and delivered it as a pungent rap, while the company improvised characters to surround it. By the end of the first week we had a small nugget of material; we went to the bar, pushed the tables aside, and performed our ten-minute creation for Jeannette, her bartenders, and a beer delivery boy who happened to appear in the middle of the showing. *The Tosca Project* was launched.

We built the piece section by section, without any clear road map of where it would end up. Every year we did a public showing and invited the audience to comment; the response was wildly partisan, as everyone seemed to have a decade or a moment in the bar that held special magic for them. From the rich stories Jeannette told us (Brodsky writing mournful poetry in a booth at the back end of the bar while his car was being towed from Columbus Avenue; ballerina Makarova meeting her businessman husband, Edward, over martinis; and Nureyev coming to visit Jeannette's mother right before he died of AIDS), we built small stories out of movement, narrating them with authentic voiceovers where necessary.

Dancers are used to starting with music, actors with text, and no one was quite used to the open canvas before us. Each day, I would bring in a new scenario or a scene to try, Val and Darron would choose music, and we'd dive in. We continued to find the differences between actors and dancers hilarious and revelatory: just seeing what sparked their imagination was fascinating. As long as the dancers had music to respond to (and to count by), they felt secure; it was, of course, second nature for them to enter "on the third eight." For the actors, counting music was like learning a foreign language, and they panicked. (At the first tech rehearsal they begged for backstage cue lights, which mystified the dancers, who sat staring at those little red lights as if they were messages from Mars and missed their entrances.) But slowly we became a cohesive unit, and as we did, we kept building the piece, decade by decade of its history.

One day I suggested a duet between a World War II sailor about to leave for war and the girl he was leaving, to be set to Rosemary Clooney singing "What'll I Do?" from which one of the loveliest sections of the piece was born. We realized that war and homecoming were themes that kept returning. We finally arrived close to the present day, with a dance of anomie and dislocation we dubbed "the Blackberry ballet," named after the ubiquitous devices the characters were carrying. By the time the first draft was finished, the piece traced a wonderful journey through time. But looking it over, we felt dissatisfied. Val and I had not set out to make a documentary; we wanted to make a dance-theater piece that, if not literally narrative, followed a strong emotional arc, like *The Overcoat*. We had huge amounts of wonderful material. But the story was still hidden.

It was at that moment that Emma Rice's methodology popped back into my mind. "*The Tosca Project?*" we asked ourselves. "What does it have for free?" The most obvious thing was right under our noses: Puccini's opera. After all, it was Puccini who gave the name to the bar. Murals of famous scenes from his opera covered the walls. The jukebox still contained old recordings of Caruso singing Cavaradossi's arias. We took a group field trip to San Francisco Opera to see a performance of *Tosca* and realized that the crosscurrents of love, jealousy, political intrigue, and memory that ran through the opera were perfect touchstones for our piece. The famous last image of a woman jumping off a parapet is part of our collective consciousness, even if we can't really remember why she jumps. We had what we needed, for free.

In our new opening scene, a woman in a red slip (danced by Sabina Allemann) walked along the bar toward the audience, smoke and fog swirling around her feet. The sound of crashing waves blended with the shrieks of her famous aria as she got closer and closer to us, reached out, blew a kiss at an unseen figure, and jumped. It was a fertile and evocative way to begin. But for whom was she reaching? When core acting company member Jack Willis, an inveterate bar denizen, came to the second public workshop, he immediately responded, "You've made a bar play without a bartender. You need to create that character, and I need to play him." So we did. The Bartender became one of the Italians who founded the bar, and we imagined that in escaping from Italy he had left behind a woman he had loved and lost. The Puccini songs on the jukebox became a tormented backdrop to his longing and his despair at losing her. His memories and hallucinations were further developed after another company member, Manoel Felciano, who began serving as a sort of unofficial dramaturg on the piece, saw an evocative video titled *Journey to the Moon* that was part of an exhibit of William Kentridge's work at San Francisco Museum of Modern Art. In the video, a sad middle-aged man obsesses about a female figure who is always just out of sight—we see her footprints, we see pencil sketches of her figure on the wall, we see him looking through every kind of lens to find her, but ultimately we see him painfully alone. It was Manoel's idea that our Bartender, having lost his love, creates the bar as a kind of homage or shrine to her. We began to imagine that her spirit was hidden in the back room, that famous private space. We imagined that the woman kept coming back to haunt him, called forth by the music, as the Bartender traveled through the decades of his life, coping less and less well with his situation. And we realized that he ultimately had to leave the bar behind in order to put that spirit to rest. The last image of the piece was the most haunting: Val created an exquisite "broom duet" in which the old Bartender, wandering through his earthquake-damaged bar, began slowly to sweep up for the last time, as "Vissi d'arte" played on the jukebox. Suddenly the Woman in Red slid across the floor, riding magically on the broom. In the swirl of two bodies and an old broom, the Woman and the Bartender finally shared a moment of love. As she kissed him and slipped away behind the jukebox, he leaned on the broom, looked up at the old neon sign of Tosca Café, and nodded to it as it slowly flickered out.

The Tosca Project was a surprising success when it opened at The Geary in June 2010, bringing together ballet audiences, theater lovers, and anyone who was passionate about San Francisco. Because it was nearly wordless, the piece invited audience members to imagine its story through their own lens. But we knew that the piece was only half finished. This is the fascinating challenge of collectively created work; since you have no preexisting script and not even necessarily a clear end goal going in, every step has to be shaped and revised on the spot and in full view, which means that often you are showing an audience a living part of your thinking process. That's part of the joy of it, and also the complexity. As soon as we saw the piece on its feet, we realized that if we were less faithful to the bar's actual history, there would be more room for the invented storytelling that was the most magical part of the piece. So when we were invited by Dennis Garnhum at Theatre Calgary to bring our work to Canada a year later, we seized the chance to go even further with the imagined sections. As potent as the image of the lost love was, we began to feel that for the piece to have real conflict and drama, there needed to be more specific flesh-and-blood characters for the Bartender to contend with. One was a musician on the lam, artfully created by Gregory Wallace, and the other, through the imagination of a visionary young actress named Annie Purcell, became a tough young street urchin right out of Chaplin's *The Kid*, who sneaks in for food (dressed as a boy), befriends the Bartender, and ends up growing up in the bar. With these additions, there was a new spine on which to hang the historical elements of the piece, along with the opportunity to create a kind of live silent movie for the early sections, something Val had always wanted to try. We were able to explore the Bartender's deep sorrow when the Kid, having grown into a woman, quarrels with him and runs away (leading to the best use of *Tosca* music in the piece, a drunken solo set to "Tre sbirri") and, finally, the joyful reunion when the Kid returns, set to a recording of Brodsky's beautiful poem "Café Trieste: San Francisco":

> To this corner of Grant and Vallejo
> I've returned like an echo
> to the lips that preferred
> then a kiss to a word.
>
> Nothing has changed here. Neither
> the furniture nor the weather.
> Things, in their absence, gain
> permanence, stain by stain.

The Canadian rehearsal process, perhaps because it was so far away from our native soil, was incredibly freeing, and the work was collaborative and joyful. Alberta, fueled by oil and gas revenues, felt comparatively flush next to the fragile U.S. economy, and being away from the tensions of the American recession was a relief. We did occasionally wonder what Albertans were going to make of our ode to San Francisco, but we needn't have worried. On the opening night of the newly renamed *Tosca Café* in Canada, we suddenly understood what San Francisco had for free across the globe: romance, mystery, anarchy, and poetry. Our textured coded journey through the emotional landscape of a place we knew so well turned out to be surprisingly universal and inclusive, and the standing ovation that greeted us on our Canadian opening night was a gift and an affirmation.

Having launched our San Francisco stories initiative so successfully, we were hungry for more. And shortly thereafter, in an act of ridiculous chutzpah, we decided to launch what would become our biggest local adventure to date, a musical based on Armistead Maupin's seminal novel *Tales of the City*, created from newspaper columns he had written and serialized in the *San Francisco Chronicle* in the seventies. *Tales* follows the adventures of a Midwestern girl named Mary Ann Singleton, who finds solace in the Barbary Lane boardinghouse of Anna Madrigal, a transsexual from Winnemucca, Nevada. The novel and its sequels are filled with wonderful characters and local atmosphere. I had met Maupin in 1993, shortly after I first arrived in San Francisco to take the helm at A.C.T.; our mutual friend Olympia Dukakis had just played Mrs. Madrigal in the PBS dramatization of *Tales*, and she wanted us to know each other. In preparation for our meeting, I reread the first book of *Tales* and immediately identified with Mary Ann, who arrives in town fresh from Cleveland without a clue how to behave or how to fit in. I was moved both by her plight and by the spirit of celebration and inclusiveness that the book finally propounds—even Mary Ann becomes a San Franciscan in the end. In those early years at A.C.T., I despaired of ever fitting in to San Francisco myself, and *Tales of the City* was a reassuring touchstone for me, as it has been for thousands of other San Francisco immigrants over the years. Rereading it, I even discovered to my delight that A.C.T. is prominently mentioned in the book; when a gay socialite is invited to a party, he replies that he can't do Wednesday because "that's our A.C.T. night." When Maupin and I met in 1993, I already had it in my mind that we should somehow try to bring his books to A.C.T.'s stage, but of course we were in no position to do anything of the kind at that time; we barely had enough money to keep the payroll going.

But the success of *Tosca Café* put wind in our sails, and bringing *Tales* to the stage became a top priority.

The version of *Tales* we launched at A.C.T. in 2011 had actually begun on a plane journey to London five years earlier, when playwright Jeff Whitty decided to watch the PBS miniseries of *Tales* during the flight. By the time he got off the plane, he had determined to make a musical of the material. In his usual intrepid way, Whitty made contact with Maupin, visited him in his San Francisco home, where they bonded immediately and decided to move forward. Whitty enlisted the help of composer/musicians Jake Shears and John Garden of the band Scissor Sisters, and began collaborating with his *Avenue Q* director, Jason Moore. In 2009, while I was in Canada directing *Phèdre* and wrestling with the future of my San Francisco theater, I got a call from an actor I loved who said he was in a reading of *Tales of the City* at the O'Neill Playwrights Conference and I should fly down immediately to see it. Although I couldn't actually get to Connecticut in time, I listened to the musical in my Stratford apartment the following week and committed immediately to producing the musical at A.C.T. In the light of all the thinking and agonizing I had been doing about A.C.T.'s future, it seemed apparent to me right away that *Tales of the City* on the Geary stage was both necessary and inevitable.

Although it represented a risky financial move, when it came time to produce *Tales* we decided to do it ourselves, without enhancement from or collaboration with commercial producers. After all, this was a San Francisco story, a sui generis and much beloved local tale, and we worried that it might end up getting watered down and betrayed in the attempt to make it palatable for a Broadway audience. And luckily, by the time the piece went into development, we had a brilliant new executive director, Ellen Richard, who was an experienced New York producer herself with the skill set and tenacity to produce a show of that scale on behalf of A.C.T. So we went ahead and raised the funds we needed to cover the considerable cost of the show (over $2 million) and launched it ourselves. Mary Ann's story struck a nerve both with longtime fans and with newcomers to *Tales*, portraying the journey so many people make in relocating to San Francisco, a city that promises release from, and experimentation with, the cultural norms of the rest of the country. The fact that a local theater company had decided to tell a story about its own local universe for an audience who was part of that universe held great appeal, as well, and the show ended up grossing almost $4.2 million (far surpassing any other show in A.C.T. history) and attracting an enthusiastic audience of more than 70,000 people.

Creating a musical out of literally dozens of plot threads and hundreds of juicy characters was an extremely challenging endeavor. As with our first pass at *Tosca Café*, we probably stayed too faithful to Maupin's original novels; we loved them and wanted to do them justice and knew that much of the audience would feel the same way. Over the course of eighteen months, we tried to figure out the spine of the piece, how to sculpt all those stories into a coherent evening in the theater. Ultimately it became about Mrs. Madrigal. With the indomitable Judy Kaye in the lead, we focused on the way in which this complicated transgender woman created her own kind of family at 28 Barbary Lane, shaping a house full of disparate people into an alternative to the outside world. Maupin was amazingly generous and open as the process evolved; he kept reminding us that, because he'd originally written the story in newspaper columns and thus had had no idea from one week to the next how the plot was going to come out, we should think freely about how to tell the story onstage.

One of the most compelling things to me was that we ended up creating a musical with extraordinary roles for women. With Mary Ann, Mrs. Madrigal, Mona, Mother Mucca, Frannie, and DeDe, *Tales of the City* gave a number of actresses terrific roles. It also told the story of gay San Francisco before AIDS, and for many contemporary audience members it was hard to believe there had been a time in the City by the Bay when gay men were not fearful for their lives whenever they had sex. Maupin's *Tales* is both ridiculously innocent and spectacularly hopeful. The centerpiece of our show was a delicate setting of "Dear Mama," the famous letter Michael Tolliver (aka Mouse) writes to his mother, in which he finally tells her he is gay. When we heard Jake Shears sing his version of that letter for the first time, everyone in the room wept; each of us could remember someone in our lives who at some moment had been forced to write a similar letter to a mother he loved but who couldn't understand him.

Tales of the City tested A.C.T.'s capacity to work on a huge scale: the production had over two hundred costumes (designed by the inimitable Beaver Bauer), a vast amount of scenery (probably too much for its own good), and a large and passionate cast. Even though most of the actors were from outside San Francisco, the entire piece had a home-grown feel that created an instant bond with the audience. Every night, as soon as the overture began playing and the words SAN FRANCISCO, 1976... were projected onto a fog-covered scrim, the crowd went wild. Is it because people just like seeing themselves? Or because different pockets of the world genuinely possess different secrets, different concerns, different ways of loving and behaving? The summer of *Tales* was the summer of the "staycation," as many Americans who were short on funds decided to forgo summer holidays in favor of playing right in their own backyards. For many people in our town, *Tales* was their local holiday, and some of them came again and again.

The reception of *Tales* confirmed our belief that locavore theater was nourishing our audience in profound ways, and we set about to find more San Francisco stories. Several seasons earlier when it played in New York, I had seen a small production of *Humor Abuse*, Lorenzo Pisoni's magical and bittersweet one-man show about growing up in San Francisco's Pickle Family Circus, and after the success of *Tales*, I resolved to do whatever I had to do to persuade Lorenzo and his director, Erica Schmidt, to develop the piece further and bring it to The Geary. The Pickles were the Bay Area's circus, after all: a legendary clown group comprised of Bill Irwin, Larry Pisoni, and Geoff Hoyle, among others, who created a subversive kind of physical comedy in the mid seventies that had enormous impact. Lorenzo is Larry Pisoni and Peggy Snider's precocious son, who literally slept in a trunk as a small child. He started performing at age two, and by the time he had grown up, had a profound story to tell.

When I approached Lorenzo about doing his show at The Geary, he initially thought I was mad; *Humor Abuse* is a one-man clown show performed by a self-professed straight man who introduces the evening with the words, "I have to warn you . . . this is a show about clowning and . . . I'm not funny." Which of course is not true. Not only is Lorenzo funny, he is complex, magical, and totally honest about his life as a child performer in the circus and the loving and difficult relationship he endured with his father, master clown Larry Pisoni. Using selections from Larry's famous acts as touchstones for milestones in their fraught relationship (a sequence in which sandbags crash to the ground, narrowly missing Lorenzo as he sidesteps each one and keeps talking, perfectly encapsulated the tensions between Pisoni father and son), *Humor Abuse* watches an artist open his eyes to the family that has shaped him, growing and struggling as a clown and as a human being until finally he has to escape in order to survive. More than anything else, the play is an ode to a father whose mantra, no matter how difficult the trick or routine proved to be, was "Do it again, Lorenzo." Not, as Lorenzo quipped, "Let me help you, son" or "Here's how the routine works." Just "Do it again." It was that kind of repetition and dedication that moved me most about Lorenzo's story.

Projected on the makeshift curtain were black-and-white photographs of a serious two-year-old boy holding his hat aloft, determined to do something, *anything*, in the circus ring that might make the audience laugh. To me, *Humor Abuse* provided the perfect metaphor for where A.C.T. was as an institution in 2012. We had survived the difficulty of the past few years by engaging in a process of introspection, ultimately making some major changes in leadership and some determined shifts in programming that reflected a renewed commitment to our city. We kept getting knocked down, and we kept "doing it again." Listening to the audience roar with laughter and then sigh with sympathy as Lorenzo charted his rocky childhood and his coming of age, it was clear to me that the most important, and most mysterious, quality one could aspire to in this most unforgiving of professions was resilience.

On opening night, Lorenzo's mother, Peggy Snider, and his father were joined in the audience by fellow clowns Geoff Hoyle and

Joan Mankin and a host of Pickle Family Circus alumni. We all wore Pickle buttons, and the lobby was filled with balloons and stilt walkers. It was like a homecoming party, a local parade, and a celebration of the future all rolled into one. The little boy had turned into a beautiful and accomplished man, and everyone in the house was bursting with pride. The fact that when the show played in Seattle later it failed to find the kind of audience it had found in San Francisco only confirmed for me the power of local storytelling for local audiences. We brought *Humor Abuse* back for an encore run, and again it packed the theater. But no performance of *Humor Abuse* was as moving as the last one of the run, when Bill Irwin, one of the great American clowns and godfather to young Lorenzo during his childhood on the road, watched the show from my house seats, his eyes filled with tears. He was overwhelmed by the way that Lorenzo had managed to transform chaos, joy, and unhappiness into a piece of buoyant art, and was moved that the story of his crazy hippy San Francisco circus from the seventies was being kept alive.

The process of trying to create work for a specific city or a specific community is slippery and fascinating; one never knows where the next story will come from. One Sunday, while reading the book review section of the *San Francisco Chronicle*, I came across a mention of a new book of Filipino American short stories called *Monstress*, by local writer Lysley Tenorio. The next day I went in search of the book and then the author, and in doing so, I discovered a rich and highly particular world. The Bay Area is home to some 350,000 Filipinos, and Tenorio's voice is a beautiful and unique echo of that community. As an experiment, we commissioned four playwrights and a composer (Philip Kan Gotanda, Sean San José, Colman Domingo, Jessica Hagedorn, and Fabian Obispo) to create theater pieces in response to the *Monstress* stories. The writers came up with totally different imaginative solutions to adapting the stories. Our goal moving forward is to weave their pieces together into some kind of immersive theater event at our new second stage, The Strand Theater, to celebrate this major part of the Bay Area community, many of whom live and work right around the corner.

By 2013, the population of San Francisco had grown to become about 34 percent Asian, and that demographic continues to expand. Even more interestingly, 21 percent of the population of the Bay Area is of Chinese descent. Not that the audience for live theater yet represents that demographic, but as part of our San Francisco stories project, it has become increasingly important to discover new ways to represent the multiplicity of Asian cultures on A.C.T.'s stages. In 2013 we produced a highly imaginative new musical by Byron Au Yong and Aaron Jafferis called *Stuck Elevator*, about an undocumented Chinese deliveryman who gets trapped in an elevator for eighty-one hours and doesn't dare to push the emergency button for fear of being discovered by the police and deported. While the true story on which this musical was based actually occurred in the Bronx, an interesting idea emerged when we produced the world premiere of the show in San Francisco. Ellen Richard wondered what would happen if we created Chinese supertitles for the show—would audiences who were not English speakers find their way to the theater? It took a long time for word to get out: we worked with every Chinese-language newspaper, blog, radio show, and website we could find, and slowly a multilingual audience began to find its way to the production. But something even more interesting started to occur at the theater. *Stuck Elevator* begins with Guang, the deliveryman, speaking and singing in his native Chinese, so at the top of the show, we deployed English supertitles to translate for the non-Chinese-speaking audience. At a certain point in his entrapment, as Guang begins to hallucinate and go deeper inside his own mind, the language of the show switches to English. At that moment, the supertitles switched to Chinese. That transition always evoked a hearty laugh of recognition and surprise from the audience. What was happening in that moment was that the entire audience, no matter the language of individual members, was united in the realization that one person's native speech is another person's hallucination.

We decided to continue our exploration of Chinese work in 2014 with the Yuan-dynasty epic *The Orphan of Zhao*, starring San Francisco native BD Wong as the doctor, Cheng Ying, who sacrifices his own child so that the orphan of a famous exterminated clan can survive. Each collaboration deepens the next one; in the case of *Zhao*, which featured a remarkable Asian American acting company and design team, we built on the success of *Stuck Elevator* by commissioning composer Byron Au Yong to create a score for the many songs in James Fenton's new version, and to hire artists such as Marie-France Arcilla (who had appeared in *Stuck Elevator*) to play the Princess. Linda Cho (costumes) and Lap Chi Chu (lighting) brought great depth of vision to the visual world of the piece, and the magical A.C.T. alumna Julyana Soelistyo returned to us after twenty years to play BD's wife. *Zhao* not only diversified our audiences (20 percent of the ticket buyers were Asian or Asian American), it took advantage of everything A.C.T. has to offer as a training institution and a locus of theater research. A year before we went into production with *Zhao*, Stephen Buescher and I held workshops with our M.F.A. students and with fight director Jonathan Rider to develop the bamboo pole fights and the physical vocabulary for the production, while Byron led investigations into the musical landscape (complete with water bowls, bones, gongs, and drums).

We rehearsed the actual production on the prebuilt set right in our scene shop, where all the artisans involved could participate every step of the way. This epic tale of sacrifice and moral dilemma was infinitely enriched by the long-term investigation possible at a place where training and performance are linked in the quest to discover new forms and reanimate ancient ones. On the final day of technical rehearsals for *Zhao*, we built a mountain out of fabric and poles, and on this mountain the aging Cheng Ying encountered the ghost of his dead son. This confluence of past and present, of grief and redemption, seemed particularly resonant on the Geary stage, a place filled with ghosts of the past and hopes for the future. The actors' bodies created a landscape on which the ghost of a dead child could be reunited with his father in a way that was both poetic and entirely real. It felt like ancient China and modern San Francisco rolled into one.

Each time we develop a new San Francisco story, we get to know a new audience, a new segment of our complicated and often fragmented town. For example, a production of Wajdi Mouawad's *Scorched* led us to the brilliant Afghan writer Khaled Hosseini, who now makes his home in the Bay Area, and to the idea of creating a new theater piece out of his shattering novel *A Thousand Splendid Suns*. We have commissioned playwright Ursula Rani Sarma to write the adaptation and will work closely with Hosseini to engage Middle Eastern communities in the Bay Area as we develop the production. Bit by bit, these kinds of intercultural connections have made A.C.T. feel more central to more peoples' lives. As audience members have started bringing us their own ideas, we have also begun to collaborate with organizations such as Litquake (an annual citywide celebration of writers and writing) and Intersection for the Arts to discover local writers who might have ideas and writing to contribute. The Bay Area has become home to some of the most important prose writers in the world today, and smaller theaters such as Word for Word and Sean San José's Campo Santo have pioneered important theatrical work inspired by that writing. These collaborations are erasing the boundaries between literature and performance, between private and public expression, in fertile ways that hold great promise for the future.

CHAPTER 16

Twitter and Me

Given the instability we all felt during the financial collapse of 2008 and the ensuing recession, I never could have predicted that by 2012 San Francisco (or at least parts of it) would again be awash in money, witnessing a second tech explosion that would have an even greater impact upon the city than the first. This time around, the tech workers decided that working in the suburban campuses of Silicon Valley was no longer as desirable, and, seemingly overnight, the companies and their employees began flooding into San Francisco. In some ways, the changes seemed miraculous, as the sudden influx of tech wealth brought an incredible boom to the cash-strapped city, but it also drove up both commercial real estate and housing prices to such a degree that long-term residents and businesses were displaced in unprecedented numbers, neighborhoods were quickly transformed, and the fabric of the city began changing beyond recognition. For A.C.T., this tech tsunami was complicated and fascinating in equal measure. Ironically, it happened to coincide with our decision to purchase The Strand, an old movie theater turned porn house that had sat abandoned for years, in the very neighborhood that was now becoming the epicenter of the tech invasion. Just as A.C.T. was finally in a position to create a second stage for the organization, something

I had wanted for twenty years, the city was being literally upended by this new and ever expanding industry. And it was moving in right next door to our new home.

Our commitment to the city and to its stories had given us a strong impetus to think seriously again about trying to acquire a smaller, second stage for A.C.T., and about putting down roots in a new neighborhood; when we bought it, The Strand represented the opportunity to do just that. We knew that in addition to the expanded programming we could do at a smaller theater, The Strand would give A.C.T. a new face, or at least a more nuanced face, vis-à-vis the city at large. Being a risk-taking nonprofit theater whose only venue is a gilded thousand-seat house was becoming a bigger and bigger challenge; it is difficult in the best of times to explain the notion of nonprofit theater to the general public, but truly challenging when your primary venue looks like a Broadway house.

While people rarely question whether ballet or opera companies require subsidy (since they are clearly not designed for the commercial marketplace), the need for support for theater is harder for the public to grasp. Theater has a commercial correlate, so it is difficult for the average audience member to understand what is fundamentally different between buying a ticket to *Wicked* at the Curran Theatre (the commercial house next door), versus buying a ticket to *Arcadia* at A.C.T. To begin with, one has to explain that the ticket price to a show at a nonprofit theater covers not only the creation of that production, but also the training of young artists, the education of schoolchildren, the sustenance of a local pool of artists and administrators, and the ability to sustain risks that a commercial enterprise simply wouldn't countenance.

A theater like A.C.T. bears little relationship to the commercial booking company that imports product from the "best of Broadway," product that has already been tested and approved in New York and is selected because it is profit making. The mission of the nonprofit theater is to nurture the art form and create a forum for a specific community; its goal is not to return a profit to its investors. How is one to engage members of the public in understanding this difference so that they will be inclined to support their local theaters? For many years, we have tried to be as transparent as possible about all of the community-based work and long-term artistic investments we have been making at A.C.T., so that people would come to understand who we are. But the gilded domain of The Geary has made telling the story of A.C.T. endlessly challenging, and one of the reasons I have longed for a second stage is my belief that, by working in an alternative performance space with a very different feel, we could overcome that obstacle and radically change the face and reputation of A.C.T.

If geography is destiny, then The Geary Theater has clearly been A.C.T.'s destiny since an extraordinary grant from the Ford Foundation enabled Bill Ball's A.C.T. to purchase it back in 1974. For decades, The Geary set the tone for A.C.T.'s work: big, elegant, classical, ambitious, extravagant, unabashed. The Geary remains a cathedral to excellence, a thrilling challenge for directors, actors, and designers. But a large gilded playhouse is not the solution for all audiences or indeed for all artists, nor should it be the only public face of a multifaceted organization with so many different kinds of programming. No matter how intimately we have tried to stage certain plays over the years, and no matter how welcoming we've tried to be, we have come to realize that there is repertoire that doesn't belong in The Geary, or at least not anymore. And while we have, over the years, pursued an ambitious artistic agenda that has included a great deal of new and experimental work, it is undoubtedly true that our ability to nurture new artists and new creative endeavors would have been far greater had we had a smaller house in which to experiment. At the same time, it is increasingly clear that some audiences crave smaller, more intimate houses for their theatrical experiences. If there is more than one entry point in a theater company's ecology, there is more opportunity to develop the kind of pluralism we long to see in our audiences.

We needed a second stage not only to broaden and deepen our audience's experience, but also to grow our artists. While we were expert in developing young actors, we had done far too little for young designers, directors, choreographers, and playwrights for whom The

Geary was simply too big to function as a launch pad. This made it difficult to help nurture the local theatrical scene and to support the next generation of artists. We were a decidedly literary, noncommercial, actor-centric, repertoire-driven nonprofit theater company housed in a gorgeous thousand-seat house that made risk taking difficult. Likewise, we had done powerful work training our M.F.A. students, but mediocre work in introducing these wonderful young artists to the public, because they had never had their own theater in which to perform. And, finally, we knew that if our community-based educational ideas were really going to flourish, we would need a central meeting place for those students and teachers. A 300-seat theater, along with a smaller flexible space, could answer most of our needs, but such a thing did not seem to exist in San Francisco. Or certainly not within our budget.

We had, over the years, rented numerous small theaters, but none that were satisfying, until one day shortly after she arrived, Ellen Richard was invited inside the old Strand Theater, which lay in a semi-ruined state in the seedy Central Market district. Built as a modest infill building called the Jewell Theater in 1917, The Strand was the same vintage as The Geary but with none of its bells and whistles. It had housed vaudeville and then film in its early life, becoming a repertory house for foreign films in the sixties and a weekly exhibitor of *The Rocky Horror Picture Show* in the seventies. By the early nineties, The Strand had become a porn house showing double features to increasingly unsavory audiences. Finally, in 2003, the theater was raided and shut down by the city of San Francisco, and it remained closed for the next nine years, falling into disrepair. Surrounded by check-cashing stores, pawn shops, and boarded-up buildings, The Strand was absorbed into the decay and blight of that benighted section of Market Street to which San Franciscans had long been accustomed, a core of urban decay and despair that until very recently has proved stubbornly resistant to change.

Ellen Richard was no stranger to real estate. While managing director at Roundabout Theatre Company in New York, she had managed to negotiate her way through the thickets of New York City bureaucracy to acquire the nightclub Studio 54 and transform it into a first-class theater for the Roundabout. She had twice relocated the Roundabout's offices, refurbished numerous performance venues, and then gone on to be part of the development of the Helen Hayes Theatre as a nonprofit space for Second Stage. So the morass of obstacles inherent in finding and developing real estate in San Francisco didn't seem to daunt her; indeed, as soon as she was hired in the summer of 2010, she set out to find us a new venue. When we first walked through the doors of The Strand to inspect what was left of the theater, the floors were littered with dead birds, the walls were smeared with filth, and the upper levels of the building were covered in graffiti trumpeting SLUMDOGS and JUNKIES FOR LIFE. But the shell of the building was perfectly adequate, and it was clear that, without destroying the original structure, we could create a simple three-hundred-seat house and have a big upstairs rehearsal room/black box looking out toward the dome of City Hall.

And so, in the spring of 2012, A.C.T. finally leapt into the void and purchased a second stage. The board was initially dubious about staking a claim in what was still an unsavory and potentially dangerous neighborhood, but the tide was turning. In 2011, the San Francisco Board of Supervisors had approved a deal that gave a six-year payroll tax holiday on new hires to any company that moved into a designated zone of the Central Market area. In exchange, it was hoped that these companies would become agents of change, revitalizing a stubbornly destitute urban core. The companies within the payroll tax exemption zone signed community benefit agreements outlining ways in which they would work to better their new neighborhood, and very quickly the techno-hipsters started moving in. Twitter took over several floors at the top of the old Furniture Mart on Market between 9th and 10th, and other companies followed suit. Inspired by this burst of activity and believing that Central Market was the neighborhood for A.C.T. to invest in, a generous and brave trustee named Jeff Ubben bought the ruined Strand in February 2012 and donated it to A.C.T. for redevelopment.

Spurred on by the tax exemption, adventurous corporations such as Dolby Sound, One King's Lane, Benchmark Capital, and Spotify snapped up property in Central Market, while A.C.T. became the major nonprofit to enter the fray. Through another trustee, Abby Schnair, we were able to secure the services of Skidmore, Owings & Merrill in designing our new theater, and our willing and openhearted architect Michael Duncan worked tirelessly with us as we began to articulate a vision. Almost twenty years after the Geary reconstruction, I found myself once again in the byzantine world of historical preservation and city politics. Although The Strand is not a landmarked building, there were enough special interest groups with a passion for old movie houses and early-twentieth-century architecture to cause design hiccups all along the way, most notably when we were told that we had to memorialize the crumbling and unsafe interior marble staircase by creating a permanent "scar" on the new floor of the theater to mark where the stairs had been.

Duncan's scheme was to divide the old space in half, retaining the south side as an intimate theater and capturing the north side as lobby and café space, with a large event space/black box theater on the top two floors facing City Hall. Central to Duncan's concept of transparency and welcome was a double-story lobby with huge windows and an interior LED screen that could project a wide variety of content and colors to light up the theater and illuminate the street all the way across UN Plaza. As we watched the designs evolve, we were mindful of the fact that in The Geary we already had a Cadillac; what we wanted at The Strand was a VW—a simple, functional, welcoming space that could be run inexpensively and didn't feel intimidating to walk into. We were acutely aware of the many second stages that had been built across America over the past decade and had proved to be as expensive to run as the main house, with far less revenue potential; we didn't want to make that mistake at The Strand. But how exactly would it function? And for whom? As we met every week to move the design process forward, the vexing question of the relationship of live theater to the neighborhood to which we were moving—with its street-level poverty and the insular and powerful tech worlds surrounding us—became central to our thinking. Why put a live theater next to Dolby Sound? What might induce a twenty-something Twitter worker who had everything he or she could want up in that elevated campus to descend to the street and see a play? And how would the longtime inhabitants of the neighborhood react to a shiny new art complex appearing in their midst? What did we all have in common? How could we coexist?

The question of the relationship of modern technology to the ancient impulses of live theater is a complex one about which much has been written. There are those who believe that theater has to mirror the technological prowess of its age, and indeed recent advances in sound, lighting, and projection technology have changed the way we think about storytelling and theatrical experience, just as they did in the Victorian era. Why build scenery for a multi-location play, for example, when you can evoke the whole world with projections? Why train actors to project heightened language across a thousand seats when you can use microphones instead? There are huge advantages and concomitant disadvantages to our reliance upon technology in the contemporary theater, but, at its most basic, theater is a form of storytelling in which live actor meets live audience member in a kind of intimate transaction that triggers the imagination in new ways. The one relatively constant phenomenon is that live theater usually involves experiencing something in a group and *as* a group. This is what makes it potent. Aside from attending sports events or going to church, few occasions remain to us in which people of different ages, backgrounds, and predilections find themselves sitting side by side experiencing something together in real time; still, we know that collective experience can be both enriching and comforting.

The tech industry tends to be obsessed with speed. The goal is to do everything faster, more efficiently, more "disruptively," and with less interference. "Change" is the mantra. At its best, an artistic experience is, by contrast, immersive. It slows down our consciousness in profound ways, functioning more the way dreams do. And just as dreams are mysterious but neurologically necessary journeys that restore and reset our frazzled brains, immersion in a piece of art can briefly stop time and let air into our overcharged and time-crunched minds. The deepest and most fundamental tools of theater have remained unchanged for thousands of years: a live actor telling a vivid story to a real audience in real time. Each performance is unique, unrepeatable. When theater really works on an audience, things start to seep in—you get behind the eyes of a character, you begin to understand how someone thinks, you lose yourself in the melody of a voice, you feel desire, you release. I am convinced that after the immersive experience of a play, when you reenter your quotidian life, there is a new suppleness of thinking that creates room for thoughts, feelings, ideas that one couldn't have predicted. Indeed, one of the biggest hits in recent A.C.T. history was a production I directed of Glen Berger's hypnotically written *Underneath the Lintel*, a solo play about a mysterious man who takes us on a surreal quest for identity, with only a few transformative props and some adjustable lights as storytelling aids. Watching *Lintel* was like sitting around a campfire listening to a shaggy-dog story slowly unfold; actor David Strathairn turned his spectators into wide-eyed children caught up in the magic of what would come next. For ninety minutes, we were all in the same room, in the same space, held captive by a singular imagination.

We know from experience that, when it works, theater can provide the means to sustain and enrich one's mental and emotional health. But given the lack of arts education today at every level of the educational system, from kindergarten to university, and given the extremely lucrative benefits of devoting a life to coding or derivatives trading, the choice to engage with live theater isn't even on most people's radar screens anymore. This has shifted radically in just the last decade. In his hilarious memoir *Little Failure*, writer Gary Shteyngart describes spending his Wall Street lunch breaks devouring books: "In 1996, people still read books and the city could support an extra branch of the legendary Strand [bookstore] in the Financial District, which is to say that stockbrokers, secretaries, government functionaries—*everybody* back then was expected to have some kind of inner life." So what happens to "inner life" in an era when it doesn't get you a job and isn't on the curriculum? How do you encourage people to believe that the encounter with a live work of art might have resonance in their lives? That encounter takes time, inclination, and permission. The arts venue has to feel welcoming enough for a range of people to feel drawn to enter. On one side of our new Strand Theater is an impoverished neighborhood whose inhabitants are barely making it, on the other side are tech workers toiling eighteen-hour days to stay ahead of the competition; neither group is going to naturally gravitate to a play. So I know that in developing The Strand, audience building isn't going to be simple. I want multiple generations to find a home there, including our own core audience (whom we should never take for granted in our drive to attract newer and younger audiences). One of my interests in opening The Strand is to figure out if and whether multiple and seemingly disconnected audiences can come to embrace The Strand as their theater.

We had the opportunity to test this out when we began using our small Costume Shop space next to The Strand to host community groups and to produce new shows and M.F.A. Program projects. In 2011, when we opened the doors of that forty-nine-seat space at the front of the facility where we build our costumes, it was fascinating to see how quickly audiences found their way there, in spite of the uninviting climate of the surrounding streets. An enormous range of nonprofits took advantage of our free space-sharing program to perform: from Awesöme Orchestra Collective to Lorraine Hansberry Theatre, from the Magic Theatre to Singers of the Street. Each group had its own followers, and soon the word began to spread that something fun was happening at The Costume Shop. I felt as if, after so many years, A.C.T. was returning to something that Ed Hastings had tried so hard to do in the eighties, to be part of the broader ecology of local theater and to help launch and nurture new companies and new artistic efforts. The journey from the proud isolation of A.C.T.'s early years to a more collaborative position in the Bay Area theater community has been a long one, and one can only hope that The Strand will offer infinitely more possibilities for real artistic exchange.

At its best, theater can function as the equivalent of the corner bar, a place where people can gather and feel at home, where when you walk in the bartender knows right away who you are and what you're drinking. On a recent night at The Geary, a young woman who had recently relocated to San Francisco came to see our production of *The Normal Heart* and was in line behind a couple who were clearly longtime subscribers. She heard one of our ushers greet the subscribers, asking them how their summer had been and showing them to their seats without looking at their tickets. I feared the young woman would feel disdain for this old-fashioned theater with its longtime subscribers, but the opposite was true. She said afterwards to her friend, an M.F.A. Program student at A.C.T., that she hoped someday to get to the point where the ushers knew her name and welcomed her with the same enthusiasm as the long-term subscribers. That interests me. In our online lives, we are accustomed to algorithms that make us feel that our preferences are known and important, but when we walk into a theater or a symphony hall, we are often like strangers in a strange land. Would it make us come to our local theater more readily if we were known, recognized, personalized?

This was one of many questions circling through my mind when I made my first foray to the new headquarters of Twitter, one block from The Strand, in the spring of 2013. Rusty Rueff, then president of A.C.T.'s board, had arranged a meeting with Twitter CEO Dick Costolo, who seemed a good person to start with, as he had spoken proudly and publicly about taking improvisation classes at Chicago's Second City early in his career and thus presumably had a predilection for live theater. On the appointed day, Rusty, A.C.T. Trustee Antonio Lucio, and I gathered to prepare for our meeting at a new coffee spot across the street from Twitter. Café Mavelous is run by an intrepid man named Phillip Ma, who hoped that the combination of really good coffee and no Wi-Fi might lure exhausted tech workers to enter his doors and have a (god forbid) real, as opposed to virtual, conversation. It took two years for Ma's café to catch on, but it was packed the morning we gathered there to plot our strategy. We wanted to ask Twitter to make a contribution to the Strand campaign, possibly in exchange for acquiring naming rights to the lobby, and we had prepared boards showing our massive video screen displaying Twitter's logo and tweet stream. The idea didn't seem such a crazy pipe dream at the time; for decades, we have had generous support from traditional corporations such as banks and utility companies, and we naïvely believed that this was an excellent moment for the tech companies to follow suit. We knew that one of the things Twitter was focusing on was how to drive specific audiences to specific venues via Twitter, and we thought The Strand might prove to be a useful laboratory.

When we arrived in the lobby of Twitter HQ, I was struck by the absence of any visual reference to the company at the ground level, and by the security procedures required to ascend. You can't tweet your way up; you have to gain admission the old-fashioned way, waiting patiently while a guard matches your driver's license to a name on a list. My board president assured me that I would be overwhelmed by the forward-thinking vibe when we got to the ninth floor, so it amused me that the receptionist who greeted us as we got off the elevator was exactly like the well-coiffed, miniskirted receptionists at most law firms and corporate offices. "Welcome to Twitter. Let me show you around," she enthused before asking us to sign a nondisclosure form on her iPad. "This is the yogurt bar. This is the granola bar. It's *awesome*." She assured us that part of Twitter's "awesomeness" was being able to bring your bike to work, as well as your dog, both of which definitely rate on the scale of desirable things.

We had discovered that, alas, Costolo had been called out of town (this was not long before Twitter's IPO), and we met with one of his colleagues instead. The meeting took place in an all-white corner room; like most tech companies, Twitter doesn't believe in private offices, and most of the space is communal. That made our task harder. Throughout my long fundraising career, I've always found it helpful to sit in a prospect's office and take a look at the images, books, and trinkets that line the shelves, gathering clues as to what he or she cares about before asking for support. If there is common ground, there is something to build upon. Such was not the case at Twitter. Our host sat in an unadorned room that betrayed nothing about his background or interests. When we pulled out our photographs of The Strand, he looked somewhat surprised to discover that there would be a *theater* right down the street from his headquarters, and I wondered how often he ever left Twitter HQ to explore the neighborhood. The tech companies work extremely long hours and provide nearly everything anyone could want or need in-house—from food to dentistry to massage—with the apparent result that employees spend most of their long workdays inside the building. As Allison Arieff wrote in the *New York Times* in December 2013: "Tech tenants now fill 22 percent of all occupied office space in San Francisco—and represented a whopping 61 percent of all office leasing in the city last year. But they might as well have stayed in their suburban corporate settings for all the interacting they do with the outside world. The oft-referred-to 'serendipitous encounters' that supposedly drive the engine of innovation tend to happen only with others who work for the same company."

Determined to find some point of connection, we talked about our dreams and hopes for the new theater, and asked him how he thought we might be valuable to Twitter, in terms of our auditorium (for speeches and meetings), our audience, and our neighborhood building. He thought it all looked . . . well . . . *awesome*. When we left forty-five minutes later, he graciously promised to consider our request and to get back to us soon. On the street, Rusty and Antonio were ebullient. "What a great meeting—he gave us forty-five minutes!" Apparently, the golden rule at Twitter is "No meeting more than thirty minutes." This was the world of 140 characters, after all. I came away feeling somewhat discouraged: it was clear that we were speaking a completely different language from this new industry next door, and indeed it is proving to be the case that the nonprofit cultural institutions in San Francisco and the technology-based companies we hope to engage with are like two radically different and often mutually suspicious tribes who have a great deal to learn about each other's customs, appetites, values, and ways of working if we are going to coexist happily in this city that we have all chosen to inhabit. How do we who believe in live theater move forward in tandem with an industry that is suspicious of large nonprofits (often rightly so), eager to engage only when there is a technical problem to be solved, and unaccustomed to writing checks so that someone else can do the creative work that they often think they can do better and faster? We don't seem to be disruptive enough appeal to an industry that values breaking the pattern above all else. Yet, truth be told, every theatrical production is a start-up, every rehearsal an attempt to create meaning out of chaos, exactly as if one were writing code. The synergies must be there somewhere.

I have not found answers to these conflicts yet, but there are signs that some kind of dialogue is beginning to emerge in the brave new world of contemporary San Francisco. I remain convinced that the yang of technology's yin is live experience, narrative, character, immersion. Both can exist, if we can find ambassadors who carry the spark of one part of the culture back to the other. All of us have an investment in education, in the vibrancy and safety of the city, and in juicy experiences. We recently sent the cast of Shaw's *Major Barbara* to the offices of the customer service software company Zendesk to observe the behavior of workers in the controlled and pristine world of tech, in preparation for the scene in Undershaft's munitions factory. The Zendesk workers were delighted to have a company of actors in their midst and were extremely welcoming; it was fascinating to share with them the thinking behind Shaw's radical play, which questions whether employment alone is enough to nourish men's souls, particularly if that employment involves the fabrication of bombs. The practice of isolating workers in a controlled environment so as to extract every ounce of labor is vividly depicted in *Major Barbara*; the comparison with their own "utopian" workplace was interesting and challenging food for thought for the Zendesk workers, just as spending a day at Zendesk headquarters was rich fodder for our actors.

Much will be discovered once The Strand is actually open for business. If nothing else, our new theater's proximity to the epicenter of tech culture has forced me to reaffirm the core values that drew me to theater in the first place. A great play operates at the intersection of feeling and ideas, and at that crossroads, magical things can happen. To return to Shaw, when that great playwright wanted his audience to understand and respond to the causes of poverty in a capitalist world, he created a work of art in which we identify not only with the underclass but also with the passions and arguments of the industrialists themselves. We engage with Barbara and Undershaft's beliefs because they arouse our emotions as well as stimulate our intelligence. This is perhaps why a lay audience often grasps (and retains) more about politics and economics from a good play than from an academic lecture. Neurologically speaking, we are discovering that the part of the brain known as the amygdala performs a primary role in determining what we remember. Emotion-arousing information increases amygdalar activity, which in turn correlates with long-term memory and retention. (Interestingly, the amygdalae light up during sports events as strongly as at aesthetic experiences, so perhaps Brecht's correlation of theater with boxing was prescient!) A student will retain the substance of a lesson far more successfully if that lesson triggers an emotional response connected to the information being imparted. This is one reason why arts education has such consistent benefits, and why it is worth fighting for. This is why speed and efficiency cannot be our only gods, and why it is dangerous when the development of emotional intelligence is neglected. It turns out that what we *feel* is at least as important as what we know.

If the landscape of our thinking has been forever changed by the tech industry, then we in the theater have to change with it. Sometimes that change is wrenching, sometimes it is invigorating and even, surprisingly, fun. I was recently part of a hackathon at the imaginative Orchard Project in the Catskill Mountains. The idea was to bring together theater workers and software developers to explore ways in which theater and technology could partner to achieve certain goals. One thing that became immediately clear was the longing that young artists have to connect with each other, coupled with their inability to figure out how to do so; thus they imagined apps that would help them find compatible friends in new cities, search for new collaborators, and wake them up to new ideas. My favorite of the hackathon ideas centered around crowd-sourcing local stories. There were schemes for interactive scavenger hunts around the theme of a play and for shared videos of movement ideas that could become a dance;

there was even a prototype for an app aimed at aspiring playwrights that would provide a writing prompt each day. The possibilities were endless, like finding a thousand new ways to make a meal. My hope is that the meal itself will remain important. No matter how we distill a complex set of tastes into edible foam or discover the perfect temperature to cook sous vide, we still in the end want to sit down at a table with a group of people and eat together. We are social beings and citizens of the world, and human connectivity takes time and energy. The dream is that The Strand will become a place to gather and be nourished in real time, no matter what the app is that gets people there to begin with.

CHAPTER 17

Canons to the Right, Canons to the Left

In August 2013, in the midst of our Strand campaign, I got an urgent call from Marco Barricelli, by then artistic director of Shakespeare Santa Cruz. That morning, the dean of the arts at UC Santa Cruz had abruptly closed down Marco's theater. Shakespeare Santa Cruz was an excellent small professional theater that had been drawing audiences to its beautiful redwood glen to see outdoor Shakespeare for thirty-two years, so the news that it had suddenly been shut down was shocking and rather frightening. Aside from the fact that it was run by a beloved comrade and former A.C.T. core company member, I was disturbed because Shakespeare Santa Cruz had upheld a high standard of classical theater in the Bay Area, with beautifully performed productions at accessible prices. But an open letter to the UC Santa Cruz community declared:

> UC Santa Cruz announced today that this will be the final season for Shakespeare Santa Cruz (SSC), the professional repertory company in residence at the campus. The current season, the 32nd since the festival debuted on campus in 1981, will conclude this year following the annual holiday show in December.

"The campus has provided Shakespeare Santa Cruz with a large amount of financial support in hopes that the company could become more financially self-sustaining," said David Yager, UCSC dean of the arts. "Unfortunately, with each passing season, it has become clearer that this goal is not attainable."

Such a letter is bound to put fear into the heart of any artistic director, and I felt a sense of foreboding, not only for Shakespeare Santa Cruz, but for all of us in the arts. Aside from the fact that Shakespeare Santa Cruz had always been required to raise the bulk of its own annual funding and had done so admirably, to be suddenly informed that the mission of your institution is no longer worth the investment is chilling in the best of times. But to be told this by a parent company that was not a for-profit corporation or a disgruntled board of trustees but an institution of higher learning was particularly disturbing. Surely when it came to culture wars we were meant to be on the same side? Responses to Dean Yager's letter began to pour in to the local press, including one from Hayden White, famed UC Santa Cruz professor of the history of consciousness: "Presumably, our programs in literature, philosophy, and history must soon follow the fate of Shakespeare if pay-as-you-go is the only criterion to be used to evaluate what is euphemistically called the 'development' of our campus."

Why was this happening? Was this merely an isolated episode, the response of a financially strapped public university to a seemingly expendable program? Or was this symptomatic of something larger? And if so, why? Why was having a vibrant theater on campus no longer deemed worthy of investment? And how was this connected to the way that theater is being taught at universities today? These questions began to haunt me.

Exposure to professional artists making work of a high standard can be the beginning of a lifelong devotion to the arts, and this was an obvious benefit that Shakespeare Santa Cruz provided to the UC Santa Cruz students and to the field at large. Yet one of the things that annoyed UC Santa Cruz the most was having to pay the salaries of professional artists in the summer. "Why do you need to hire so many professionals?" the administration had repeatedly asked Barricelli. "Why can't you use students?" To which he had replied, "Why do you need professional physicians or trained lawyers at UC Santa Cruz? Why can't you just use students?" Clearly universities exist to engage their students in rigorous work, but without the presence of working professionals to guide that work, the results can be negligible. So, at the moment when live theater could desperately use advocacy and intellectual support, and academe could use the infusion of creative energy that professional theater could help to provide, the question to ask would seem to be: How might universities and the nonprofit theater find a more successful way of collaborating?

After all, many of the same impulses that launched the resident nonprofit theater movement in America spawned radical new thinking about theater on college campuses, and this new thinking in turn inspired new theater journals and new ways of thinking about the dramatic act. But this thinking was based on a deep knowledge of what had come before. Had Peter Brook not known the Shakespeare canon by heart, he never would have decamped to Paris to start his radical new international troupe at the Théâtre des Bouffes du Nord, riding the wave of his visionary reimagining of *A Midsummer Night's Dream*. Jerzy Grotowski's deep knowledge of both literature and spiritual texts underlay all of his profound experiments in form. One of Brook's most seminal collaborators was an academic, the brilliant Polish theater critic Jan Kott; the acme of Kott's scholarly work was its realization in the hands of professional theater geniuses like Brook and Lev Dodin. But I can't think of a single academic today who has that kind of deep working relationship with a professional artist.

The situation is becoming dire, because not only have cuts in funding and a focus on teaching to the test eviscerated arts education in elementary and high schools, but fewer and fewer college students are choosing to study humanities today. As a result, the world of literature, let alone dramatic literature, has become unfamiliar to most people under forty. One can no longer assume that a college graduate will have read *King Lear*, *Hedda Gabler*, or *Oedipus Tyrannos*, or even

227

contemporary classics like August Wilson's *Joe Turner Has Come and Gone* or Tennessee Williams's *A Streetcar Named Desire*. At my own alma mater, Stanford University, the appetite for entrepreneurship is so enormous that undergraduates are provided a venture fund to which they can apply for start-up ideas, but (according to the *Stanford Report*) less than 9 percent of the student population majors in the humanities. As of 2013, Stanford students are required to take courses within various "capacities," including "aesthetic and interpretive inquiry" and "creative expression," so perhaps this will make a difference. However, it seems clear that if access to, and appreciation of, culture is a value to our society, then nonprofit arts organizations are going to have to help do the job of stimulating lifelong learning and creating user-friendly ways to explore the work. Fewer and fewer universities perform this function anymore, and even when they try, debt-burdened students are often too busy taking career-building classes to pay much attention.

The notion of a liberal arts education was never a utilitarian one; rather, it was based on the idea that if you expose students to great works of literature, philosophy, history, and art, they will learn how to think beyond their own narrow experience, they will develop language skills that allow complex ideas to be articulated, and they will have a larger appetite for global culture through the empathy that comes with experiencing fictional characters. In other words, the study of art, literature, and history exposes students to the "why," just as science exposes them to the "how." This exposure is one way to place ourselves in the context of the larger universe of which we are a part, and to give meaning to the vast amounts of data we continue to collect. It is also a way to feel less alone. An ongoing relationship to any number of artistic experiences creates a kind of framing device for a life; it connects the dots and provides context for personal experience. It has been said that if we don't find a way to tell our own stories, our stories will end up telling us. In other words, narrative is the way we make sense of our lives, and drama is a pungent and immediate form of narrative.

I think often of the example of Alan Stein, the board chair who first brought me to A.C.T. It was Alan who heroically stepped forward and launched the Geary capital campaign when A.C.T.'s prospects were bleak, and I often wondered why this lively and successful businessman cared so much about the theater that he would give up years of his life, to say nothing of considerable resources, to save it. But his educational experience was telling. By his own account, Alan was a poor boy from Philadelphia who got into Columbia University on a basketball scholarship. At Columbia, even today, every single student (including the engineers) takes part in a Core Curriculum that has been in place for seventy-five years (and which my son, Nicholas, is currently in the midst of as a Columbia sophomore). The centerpiece of the Core is a two-part course called Lit Hum (Literature and the Humanities) and Contemporary Civilization. Lit Hum begins with the *Iliad* and works its way through seminal works of literature from Dante and Virgil to Cervantes, Shakespeare, and Austen; Contemporary Civilization pursues intellectual history (from Aristotle to Locke to Marx) with equal vigor, focusing on twice-weekly in-depth discussions in which the major moral, philosophical, and aesthetic questions raised in the books are debated and wrestled with.

These courses changed Alan's life. He went on to become an extremely successful investment banker, but I would hazard that what has truly given his life meaning over the years, aside from his family, is his relationship to the arts, serving for many years on the boards of SFMOMA, California College of the Arts, and A.C.T. No one had to lure him into a gallery to persuade him to collect, or convince him of the value of sitting through a play—the habit was in his blood because he had been exposed to the humanities in a serious and rigorous way at a young age. The Alan Stein experience epitomizes two truths that have come to be accepted in the study of arts participation today: first, that sustained involvement is the key to deep satisfaction with the arts, and second, that gateway experiences that introduce a participant to the arts at a young age are crucial and hard to replace.

It is, of course, impossible to know what is going to spark the next brilliant idea or nurture a more civil and civilized society, but in the absence of exposure to great writing, it's no wonder that our language

229

is so easily debased, that we traffic in endless clichés about "level setting," "disruption," and "innovation," and that we use verbs as nouns (as in, "What is the solve on this problem?") or nouns as verbs ("We have to scaffold our vision") in ways that flatten our thinking and deaden our ears to the nuances of articulate speech. Dramatic literature, from Lorca to Caryl Churchill, revitalizes and defamiliarizes our language and forces it to remain supple and alive. Shakespeare alone invented hundreds of words in the English language: in his appetite to express the human condition as he saw it, he was constantly at a loss for the mot juste and thus created new words in a rush of invention that has enriched the way we speak and think even today. As George Orwell so brilliantly articulated, a flexible and living language is the key to a functioning democracy. This is why theatrical and literary language is so valuable: We can only think as creatively and richly as we can speak, and the more narrow our language becomes, the more narrow our thinking. If students don't learn to parse complex and heightened language in school, when and how will they learn it? If they are only bombarded by the off-the-shelf clichés of popular culture as transmitted through the media, is it any wonder that their thinking becomes lazy and derivative? Ambiguity is gold. If one is able to navigate the conflicted behavior and shifting morality of a three-dimensional literary or dramatic character, one becomes more adept at recognizing complexity and contradictions in one's own human relations. Nothing made me happier than a recent newspaper article arguing that reading Chekhov is the best preparation for a successful date night: the rich complexity of his characters and their subtle longings demand a nuanced reading that helps prepare one for the true mystery of encountering, and even loving, another human being.

So why is the rigorous analysis of art and literature so rare, even in a university setting? At Stanford, the introductory course in the Department of Theater and Performance Studies is described in the course catalogue as follows:

> Approaching theater as presentational form of organization, this class *shifts study of theater from the context of literature to that of*

performance [my italics]. It offers an overview of performance across disciplines: from theater and other performing arts, to law, management, sports, and new technologies. In this interdisciplinary exploration, performance emerges as a model that cuts across diverse branches of contemporary culture, from sports events, to social dances, to political protests, to the organization of a workplace.

This led me to wonder, if theater as a performative act is no different from a legal trial or a sports match, why should it even be worthy of study? Is it not an ancient art form worthy of disciplined regard in and of itself? If not, should we be surprised that major universities like Stanford have only a handful of drama majors, while the vast majority of undergraduates are engaged with "serious" subjects like engineering and computer science, where there is a body of knowledge to master? The course I just described is labeled introductory. Suppose this were the only course a Stanford undergraduate ever took in drama. Would it encourage him or her to ever seek out a play, to become an active theatergoer, to learn to understand and value the power of drama?

What if, instead of this kind of theoretical look at the performance act, students were taught that the structure that sustains a play is as specific, rigorous, and worthy of investigation as the structure that supports a circuit board or a bridge? The fundamental rules of conflict and resolution, of rising action and denouement, of exposition and revelation, are as complex and difficult to master as those of STEM disciplines, yet they are rarely taught or taken seriously. It is far more fashionable to discuss the performativity of the sports arena than to analyze a play. And when plays *are* read and discussed, the discourse tends to make value judgments about the characters as if they were real human beings and not complex literary creations.

Drama exists at the crossroads of emotion and intellect; it is not merely a soft subject to balance out the rigor of a "real" education. Alas, again and again we are the victims of our own pedagogy: if drama class only asks whether you like a character or how theater resembles every other kind of performative act, there is no reason to assume that respect for the discipline will be achieved. Drama is an intensely challenging and difficult art form to conquer. You know if you've written code that makes a program run, but how do you know if you've created a theatrical event that has traction and durability? The latter may be more difficult to quantify, yet the effort is not in vain. If students were asked to understand the architecture of a play in the way that they understand the architecture of a nucleus or a chemical compound, things would start to get more interesting.

My disappointment with the relationship between professional theater and academe is particularly acute because of the many years I spent trying to forge a long-term relationship between A.C.T. and Stanford. Given the enormous intellectual riches that Stanford has to offer, I hoped to bring our M.F.A. Program under Stanford's umbrella the way that Trinity Repertory Company had so successfully merged its graduate acting program with Brown University some years before. The Brown/Trinity Rep M.F.A. model seemed a brilliant one for sustainability and for a deeper relationship between theory and practice in our field, and I deeply admired what I had learned about it from my colleague Oskar Eustis, then artistic director of Trinity Rep. I felt that such a relationship between A.C.T. and Stanford would not only be a way to ensure the long-term excellence of A.C.T.'s extraordinary acting program but would also deepen Stanford's relationship to contemporary culture by bringing a diverse group of some of the finest young artists in America today to the Stanford campus. At one time Stanford, like many universities, had a very robust relationship to professional theater; in the sixties, it housed a remarkable cadre of actors including the great Gerald Hiken, and the Stanford Repertory Theatre produced such significant work that the outside public regularly flocked to the campus to see theater. In a 1960 article in *Theatre Arts* magazine, Bay Area critic Stanley Eichelbaum described the exciting work being produced at Stanford and San Francisco State:

The college groups, because of their advanced facilities, their institutional money, and their unlimited free labor force, are the envy of the commercial little theatres. . . . Stanford maintains a program that features paid professional stars; the school has been visited by a group including Douglas Watson, Aline MacMahon, Jessica Tandy, and Hume Cronyn.

For some time, the local newspapers . . . have given [resident] productions regular coverage.

It was no coincidence that Stanford invited Bill Ball's fledgling American Conservatory Theater to a deeply appreciative campus in 1966 to perform with his new company, and it was the opportunity to see his work at Stanford that led San Francisco's civic leaders to invite A.C.T. to San Francisco on a permanent basis. I hoped that my idea of bringing A.C.T.'s M.F.A. Program to the Stanford campus was worth pursuing in light of the earlier history between the two institutions. What if the Bay Area could be home to a cutting-edge experiment in the relationship of practical theater training to the daily lives of undergraduates who might be studying a wide range of other disciplines? If nothing else, it might encourage future biologists or engineers to become appreciative audience members and supporters of the arts in their later lives.

For many reasons, this idea never came to fruition, although Stanford has embarked upon an exciting arts expansion that includes a new symphony hall and several major art buildings. So I have to admit to feeling a certain puzzlement when I read a recent (October 2013) article in the *San Francisco Chronicle* about Stanford's latest effort to engage students in theater:

Mona Thompson wanted to have glow-in-the-dark kickball in the rec yard of Alcatraz, or perhaps throw someone off a boat in the middle of the Bay.

Andrew Evans contemplated locking participants in prison cells after taking their cell phones, wallets, and keys. . . .

These were just a few outside-of-the-box ideas thrown out in brainstorming sessions for *Alcatraz: Art Behind Bars*, an immersive theatrical experience that will take place on the island Oct. 30.

The project is part of the ReDesigning Theater Project, an initiative at Stanford instigated about a year ago by Carole Shorenstein Hays of SHN [Shorenstein Hays Nederlander, the entity that books Broadway tours into three commercial theaters in San Francisco], who also inspired *Alcatraz: Art Behind Bars.*

"The thing we are trying to do at a very high level is to create a new theatrical experience for people in their 20s and 30s who aren't going to other shows," said Jeff Kessler, a member of the design team who recently graduated from Stanford with a master's in mechanical engineering.

This article was published about two months after the news about the demise of Shakespeare Santa Cruz was announced. The irony was not lost upon me that Stanford's latest experiment, made for those who disdain traditional theater, was paid for by the leader of commercial theater in San Francisco. I wondered what those "other shows" were that Stanford students weren't going to? What opportunity had they had to be broadly educated about the theater and how it functions, before it was decided to try "at a very high level" to "create a new theatrical experience" for them? Is it not a truism that there is no originality without a deep knowledge of the past? And is that knowledge not in part the responsibility of the university to impart?

In the wake of all of this, I was infinitely heartened by an essay written by the outgoing president of the Mellon Foundation, Don Randel, in which he made the simple but beautiful point that, for an undergraduate, every idea encountered for the first time is by definition a new idea. It matters not whether that idea comes from Plato or from Dawkins; a great and lasting idea is as vigorous and worthy of exploration today as when it was conceived. If in our breathless appetite for the instrumental and the innovative we fail to keep one eye on the richness of the past, we risk becoming an expendable, disposable culture. Which is why we must fight for a healthy balance of classical and contemporary work and for performance practices that grow out of the best paradigms of the past while experimenting with new ways to engage the audience. We should vigorously nurture that engagement with the emotional complexity and moral ambiguity that drama can provide. Otherwise we risk becoming trivial and forgettable.

CHAPTER 18

Small Experiments of Radical Intent

Where does that leave us? For twenty years I have participated in cultural battles that change and evolve but never really get won. Maybe that's part of the beauty of this hybrid art form that is both intensely private and necessarily public, that needs fertile imagination and ferocious lobbying, that always seems about to become extinct but keeps reimagining itself just in the nick of time. My husband is fond of quoting the diplomat George Kennan, who famously warned that foreign policy was "more like gardening than architecture," meaning that no matter how good a structure one thinks one has built, weeding and watering can never stop, and seemingly solid forms have an odd habit of suddenly disintegrating or changing. This perception is also true of making theater. Again and again, as artistic director of A.C.T., I've believed I have succeeded in overhauling the system, restructuring the staff, revitalizing the work, or reimagining our producing and audience-engagement models in order to create an ever more flexible and creative dramatic engine. And then we hit a wall and the process begins again. In reality, a theater company is an organism that is constantly evolving, filled with complicated, opinionated people who are immersed in the maddeningly imprecise enterprise of making theater and hoping someone comes. Just as in academe the humanities feel they must compete with scientific studies by quantifying and systematizing their discipline in ways that are inimical to its actual impulses, so, too, in the contemporary theater we have resorted to justifying our existence by pointing to all the extrinsic markers that reveal our worth. In a sense, this has been necessary; throughout the nineties, as arts funding came under attack in an increasingly hostile political climate, we developed, in the name of survival, sophisticated analyses of the instrumental value of the arts to American culture: We learned to demonstrate how much the arts contribute to the national economy, to the campaign for literacy, to safer neighborhoods. We have learned to demonstrate a strong return on investment and to talk in terms of measurable impact. We coined terms like "creative placemaking" to argue that embedding theaters and performing arts groups in at-risk communities could bring social cohesion and safety to mean streets. We demonstrated how many people the arts employ and what kinds of benefits they receive. We proved that access to the arts improves student test scores, reduces truancy, and stimulates active citizenship. And we packaged all of this data in elegant strategic plans that we rolled out to demonstrate to donors, supporters, and politicians that we had a coherent vision and a clear road map of where we were going. As a sign of the times, in 2006 the William and Flora Hewlett Foundation created the Nonprofit Marketplace Initiative, the goal of which was to persuade 10 percent of individual donors to be more evidence based in their charitable giving, promoting measurable outcomes and a stricter rating system for charities.

But it has gradually become clear that these extrinsic markers, while crucially important, cannot tell the whole story of why theater *matters*, why it has survived for thousands of years against the assault of new technologies, fractured attention spans, and woefully underfunded resources. As Bonnie Marranca articulates so beautifully in *Ecologies of Theater*: "The materialist turn in criticism and art-making and the hyperpoliticization of culture have failed to acknowledge the extraordinary range of human subjectivity, especially the spiritual energy that constitutes an individual life and its creative acts. . . . The new philistinism . . . has distorted the role of art in a life, in a society, to suit its utilitarian goals." Marranca urges us to remember the value of "engagement with art for its own intrinsic sensual value and creation of other worlds." Indeed, in the attempt to resurrect a fuller dialogue about the value of art to our culture, in recent years we have begun to return to the much more difficult and, to my mind, more central argument about the intrinsic value of the arts, and to recognize that metrics can't fully explain why the creative enterprise is so crucial to our society. In a startling reversal, the Hewlett Foundation in 2014 declared a moratorium on its metrics-based charity models when it recognized that, no matter how much data is available, donors tend to give from the heart, not the head.

This returns us, in part, to the discussion about mission, about aesthetic, and about voice. A landmark 2004 RAND Corporation study titled *Gifts of the Muse*, commissioned by The Wallace Foundation, made a powerful case for reframing the debate about the value of the arts by encouraging us to address benefits that are, in the words of RAND's research brief, "less amenable than the instrumental benefits to the increasingly results-oriented, quantitative approach that characterizes public policy analysis." Those of us for whom the arts are part of our lives understand intrinsic value intuitively: we flock to concerts or galleries or theaters for the visceral mind-opening pleasure the experience can provide, not in order to improve our test scores or broaden the economic base of our towns, much as we appreciate those results. Olympia Dukakis thinks of actors as "ministers of the interior," mining the deepest part of their inner lives to bring forth emotional and intellectual truths for an audience to experience, to recognize, and to think deeply about. José Antonio Abreu, the visionary conductor, economist, activist, and politician who helped create Venezuela's El Sistema music education program, speaks of an "affluence of the spirit" that comes from exposure to the arts. Most important for young children, he says, is access to beauty, because when that happens, "material poverty is being defeated by the spiritual affluence. . . . The latter can provide the physical condition, the ethical principles, and the emotional and intellectual tools necessary when overcoming the former."

Any artistic creation involves both some form of vivid personal experience or epiphany on the part of the artist, and the capacity to communicate that personal epiphany through a given artistic medium. What we experience when we watch a piece of theater or hear a piece of music is an intensely private universe being transmitted through a public forum. The social bonding that happens when we as an audience share such an experience is a very particular one. We have all experienced that personal universe through our own lens, but by artistic transformation, it can be translated into a form that allows us to more objectively absorb its meaning. The result is that we attain, at least for the brief spell that we are in the theater, a sense of social communion with a group of people and, at best, a sense of communal meaning or communal mythology. I think back to the crucial role that Greek tragedy played in reflecting back to fifth-century BCE Athenians a narrative and mythology about their own political situation. Theater was how democracy told its story to itself, embedded in a common mythology that helped the public view turbulent current events with a more eternal lens.

Since the landscape that surrounds it is constantly changing, the theater itself is necessarily a living organism that exists inside the larger environment of its city or community. As we plan our seasons and commission new work, we always try to guess the direction that environment is going to go, but needless to say, our chances of being accurate are slim. This is why it was so fascinating for me to meet Richard Evans, an arts consultant who runs a company called Emc-Arts that focuses on innovation. Anyone who knows me knows the general antipathy I have for consultants of any stripe, but Richard is unique. He uses none of the platitudinous language of self-help books and business models; he is only interested in creative and operational flexibility. His company tries to help organizations understand what it means to build innovation into the very fabric of what they do. And in order to achieve this, he proposes doing "small experiments of radical intent." Not huge overhauls that could put the entire operation at risk, but not such piddling changes that the basic operation remains the same. He recognizes that in our obsession with strategic planning we often fail to take the simplest steps forward until every detail and repercussion has been ironed out, by which point the step is probably irrelevant and in need of rethinking. He questions the value of "best practices" when trying something entirely new (basing much of this thinking on David Snowden's fascinating Cynefin Framework, which asks decision makers to recognize what kind of system they are operating inside of at any given moment, and to trust that relying on "experts" is not always the most successful choice when one is experimenting in a new environment).

Evans urged us to consider the kind of small but powerful steps that could fail utterly and still move the organization forward; thus, for example, he encouraged us to pursue our radical notion of creating an El Sistema–like educational program for theater. El Sistema is a system for musical education that has proven to be extraordinarily effective across social and class lines in Venezuela; the proposition we put before ourselves at A.C.T. was to see whether such a system of mentoring, rigorous daily participation, and family observation could be practically applied to the American theater. We had begun approaching this question as if it were part of a comprehensive strategic plan, studying the history and practice of El Sistema, consulting with experts, and attempting to build a five-year model, when Evans encouraged us to dare to make a "small experiment with radical intent" and just *do* it. As I write this chapter, various parties in A.C.T.'s education and artistic wings have come together to brainstorm about creating a single "nucleo" as a tiny test nodule of a much bigger idea. There is a great deal to be learned here: We have no idea whether the kind of consistent four-hours-per-day six-days-per-week immersion that Venezuelan children have been willing to make in their musical education will be remotely possible for American children, and whether the discipline of music making will prove to be more suitable to intensive youth training than the much more subjective enterprise of theater making. As our Young Conservatory Director Craig Slaight is fond of saying, in the theater our instrument is our self, and the use of "self" in practicing one's craft is a complex and challenging thing. But our small experiment with radical intent will teach us a great deal relatively quickly, and from it will evolve some emergent practices that we can use as we move forward, without putting the entire operation at risk.

This vision for art making appeals to me since at heart I am an off-off-Broadway artist housed in a huge regional theater. I always long for the kind of nimbleness and speed of change that was possible in my early career at CSC, where we were too small to really matter. All over our contemporary culture, we have been handed examples of large corporations and entities that have been deemed too big to fail. This is a horrifying thought. In the arts, at least, no organization should be considered eternal, and much is being written today about whether we should more willingly let struggling institutions fail. Given the decline in both earned and unearned income over the past decade, along with questions of ongoing artistic relevance, many of our major arts institutions will indeed be at risk of failure in the next decade or two; witness the demise of New York City Opera and of San Jose Repertory Theatre. Institutional funders such as the James Irvine Foundation in California are encouraging arts groups to survive by radically rethinking their producing models to include audience participation as a key component of their work, recognizing that until audiences have a gateway experience into an art form, they are unlikely to choose to go see the work, no matter what the incentive.

This makes a certain degree of sense: In countries such as England, where amateur theater is a thriving force, many audience members have participated in plays themselves and know what is involved. My own father-in-law has been an active member of his local Lapworth Players for thirty years; thus when he goes to see a play at the Royal Shakespeare Company, his other "local" theater, he has a knowledge of the art form that dramatically increases his appreciation of professional work.

Whether one can actually kickstart that kind of participation through foundation grants is an open question. The point is that, if we are going to survive as a field, we are going to have to undertake these small experiments of radical intent again and again as we search for ways to matter. One way of not becoming too big to fail is by ensuring that our larger arts institutions are constantly spawning smaller things: new companies, new collaborations, new opportunities for artists to pursue their own visions within a larger umbrella. It is no longer necessary or indeed valuable to have every idea, to do everything oneself, and to prove that one is different from every other arts organization in town; as a field we are beginning to realize that it is more interesting to figure out how we are alike, how we function as a single complex ecology, how we let the best ideas rise to the top no matter where they come from. This is difficult to sustain in a large institution, but not impossible; it requires a degree of openness to the world beyond one's doors, and an insatiable appetite to learn.

I feel as if my career to date has been a series of small experiments of radical intent. It was never my intention or desire to become a producer; rather, I dreamed of being Peter Brook and creating visionary productions of classical plays. But I realized that the only way to have the opportunity to direct the plays I wanted to direct was to control the means of production and run the theater myself. My first years at CSC were filled with desperate experimentation and endless errors. I learned to produce by doing it, stalking anyone I knew with money to become a donor, writing the promotional copy myself, using whatever means of persuasion I could muster to lure major actors and directors to my tiny downtown theater. It is ever thus.

At least in my case it was entirely fortuitous and profoundly lucky that, with the offer from A.C.T., I landed in a city and at a theater so congenial to my tastes, personality, and predilections. Even so, there's no template for success. Many people in the American theater go to graduate school to prepare themselves for the profession, but I'm not sure (particularly in the case of artistic directors) whether anything truly prepares you other than doing it. And because the field is constantly changing, the most valuable predictor for success seems to be resilience, combined with a pugnacious determination to stick to one's guns and to fight for those things one cares about the most. In preparing a recent speech to our M.F.A. graduates, I was reminded of the fact that the word "resilience" comes from the Latin *resilire*: "to leap back" or "to leap again." Merriam-Webster defines it as "the ability to become strong, healthy, or successful again after something bad happens" or "the ability of something to return to its original shape after it has been pulled, stretched, pressed, or bent." I suppose resilience is a practice like anything else, and I am convinced that leaping back is something that needs to be learned and relearned throughout one's career, particularly if that career is in the theater.

CHAPTER 19

Serving and Subverting:
Theater and Community
or "How Do You Open the Doors?"

The challenges I had faced at CSC paled in comparison to the enormity of the task at A.C.T. when I arrived, although in both cases I inherited organizations whose founders had tragically imploded and yet who had set a bar for artistic excellence that was indisputably high. In my early days at A.C.T., the legacy of Bill Ball's idealism helped to keep me inspired, despite the fact that the institution he founded had become insular, defensive, and extremely precarious financially. I had been hired to reverse the troubled course of the organization, so my first decade at the helm was far more about change than about continuity. But as I reimagined A.C.T.'s repertoire, reinvented the core company, restructured the M.F.A. program, and tried to reinvigorate the board, I often wondered whether we were indeed keeping what was precious about Ball's legacy alive. After twenty years at the helm, I still believe that the vigorous devotion to great classical literature, the development of muscular new plays, the ongoing coexistence of training and performance, and the centrality of transformative acting are tent poles from which to hang a great theater. So it was with complete fascination that I recently discovered a manifesto, hidden in a drawer for many years, written to justify the dissolution of Ball's San Francisco board of directors, the C.A.A.C.T. (California Association for the American Conservatory Theatre).

I found this document in the summer of 2013, just as I was finishing the first draft of this book, when soaring San Francisco rents (the result of the current tech boom) forced A.C.T. to consolidate its office and studio space from three floors to two. While cleaning out files and boxes in preparation for the move, I came across a typed essay that both shocked and enlightened me about the institution I had helmed for twenty years. It was a rough draft of an article written in 1983 by Dennis Powers (and published in May 1984 by *American Arts* magazine), in defense of Ball's reorganization of the operations of A.C.T., and in particular his rationale for operating without a local fundraising board. Ball had made this move in order to prevent the trustees from unduly influencing the policies and choices of the A.C.T. management, and this article was apparently written to publicly explain his thinking.

Ball's original vision for a theater entirely governed by artists and paid for by individuals who had no relationship to the working life of the theater was a pipe dream that would undoubtedly have died a very swift death had not the Ford and Rockefeller foundations stepped in in 1965–67, and underwritten the first seasons of A.C.T. in Pittsburgh and then in San Francisco. But almost twenty years into Ball's tenure, the dearth of consistent funding and the lack of strong community support continued to plague A.C.T. "Every eighteen months or so I'd have to Indian wrestle with some power mogul who decided he'd like to dabble in the arts," Ball asserted. He bristled at the interference of wealthy donors who in his opinion knew nothing about running a theater. And so finally, in the early eighties, the board was dissolved, the "moguls" departed, and Ball brought fundraising under the jurisdiction of the staff. In many ways, this was the beginning of the end for Ball; his ongoing hostility to board interference and his paranoia about being sabotaged by interfering trustees led him to undercut the very fundraising body that could have kept A.C.T. solvent, and these emotions ultimately helped bring about his demise as artistic director.

The document we found was a typewritten draft, which someone named Margot had marked up in urgent penciled notes across the margins; on the cover she had scrawled: "Dear Bill, I have made *many* marks on this, since I think it is *imperative* that no old arguments be disenterred [sic] and no bitterness at past problems be aired." The article begins by quoting Ball's description of a fictional board meeting at which the president, in light of ongoing financial problems at the theater, urges the organization to stop programming high-brow classics and instead opt for a few big, upbeat musicals, particularly musicals starring his corpulent wife. Obviously this fictional scenario is meant as a joke, but the article is not a lighthearted one, it is a cry of despair. In it, Ball goes on to chart what he imagines to be the attitude of board members to a theater's various fortunes over the course of twenty years:

> First Year: The newly formed board is flamboyant and enthusiastic as it discovers "how incredibly generous people can be." . . . Fifteenth year: "Couldn't we turn the experimental theatre into a disco? FIRE THE ARTISTIC DIRECTOR." Sixteenth year: "Couldn't we borrow some money on the theatre mortgage?" Seventeenth year: "Couldn't we make a TV deal or send one of our hits to Broadway every year like Joe Papp does?" Eighteenth year: "Couldn't we sell the air rights over the theater to a Japanese corporation?" Nineteenth year: "If we could only make the theater part of the new downtown real estate development. . . ." Twentieth year: "FIRE THE ARTISTIC DIRECTOR!"

Throughout his tenure, Bill Ball was tormented by the fact that the means of production were not in his own hands and that, due to fiscal constraints, he was beholden to people whose knowledge of theater was negligible but whose power over his artistic choices was considerable. It didn't seem to occur to him that the solution was to make a commitment to educate his board about what he valued; his response was to try to keep the civilians as far away from the art as possible. He insisted that he didn't want artistic freedom if that didn't include control over the theater's purse strings, telling the sad tale of his experience at Lincoln Center Theater when he was directing *Tartuffe* just as its artistic directors Robert Whitehead and Elia Kazan were being fired: "When the scenery for *Tartuffe* was delivered, there were no knobs on the doors, because the board had cut off all expenditures while the set construction was still in progress. You may have all the artistic freedom in the world, but how do you open the doors?"

Originally, Ball had envisioned creating a board "national in scope and composed of working theater professionals who would guide the theater in the light of their practical experience and dedication to the art. There would be local fundraising board drawn from social, political, and corporate sectors of the community, but its members would have no control over such matters as theatre policy, personnel, or day-to-day management." Of course that notion ultimately had no traction; in the long run, civic-minded individuals will not write checks for institutions over which they have absolutely no control or with which they have no real dialogue.

It was a surreal and sobering experience to read what Ball had arrived at almost twenty years after founding A.C.T., just when I was celebrating my own twentieth anniversary at his institution. Ball's cry of anguish felt frighteningly familiar to me, as did his profound discouragement that the creative process is always and inevitably held hostage to the constraints of money and the marketplace. "Now, for the first time, I feel we've freed ourselves from the language, the structure, and the psychology of profit-making," he proclaimed as he walked away from his entire funding base. Reading it over, I felt both horrified and moved by his assessment of the situation and by his solutions. Horrified at the self-destructive myopia that had led someone as brilliant as Bill Ball to push his beautiful creation to the brink of disaster in a desperate search for purity and control, but moved by the sustaining power of his vision. After all, his utopian idea of an artist-led organization dedicated to the future of the art form was powerful enough that it had survived his demise and the subsequent thirty years; it was the legacy I had inherited and was so committed to carrying forward.

There is not a strategy on Ball's mock list of board solutions, from Broadway transfers to real estate deals to the sale of air rights to firing the artistic director, that has not been tried at nearly every American regional theater in the past fifty years, as organizations across the country struggle to stay afloat, stay relevant, and stay solvent. Perhaps that very struggle is what keeps us vibrant. It certainly keeps us humble. In the thirty years since Powers's article was written, our field has learned a great deal about the relationship of a nonprofit to its own community, and we are much less frightened about transparency and less precious about protecting the work from the rapacity of boards and outside critics. So much of my own time with my board is involved in discussions about the work, about the ideas behind the work, the ways to create outreach around the work, and the artists making the work, in the belief that the more deeply individual trustees understand our thinking, the more they will fight to help us support the vision. Every board meeting at A.C.T. features an artistic forum in which the trustees engage in frank conversation with a guest artist. I have never, in my twenty years at A.C.T., been told by a trustee that I couldn't produce a play or shouldn't pursue a given artistic agenda. The best illustration of how far artist-board relations at A.C.T. have come since the dissolution of C.A.A.C.T. in 1981 is an event introduced by Board Chair Nancy Livingston in 2011 that is now part of each annual meeting of the A.C.T. board, at which our artistic team distributes scenes from the upcoming season's plays, and board members are cast in the roles and invited to perform for each other. What I initially feared would be an exercise in futility turned out to be an inspired idea. The trustees relish the chance to perform bits of those challenging plays as part of this exercise, while at the same time discovering what talent and training it takes to make sense of dramatic literature and sustain a scene. So they get to experience the work in a visceral way, and at the same time they develop respect for the craft and for the artists who perform it professionally.

A part of me feels heartened by how far not only A.C.T. but the field as a whole has moved since Powers articulated Ball's despair in 1983. The article reminded me why, even in 1992 when I arrived at A.C.T. and thought I was coming to an institution with a twenty-five-year history, I was really taking over a start-up with little board history or governance. That was Ball's legacy. A.C.T. was maverick to the core, for better and for worse. Another part of me will always envy Ball's courage in throwing down the gauntlet and demanding artistic freedom. I envy his proud assertion that artists are not children but should be permitted to be in charge of their own destinies. I envy his belief that excellent training will yield thrilling performances and that great literature will remain great no matter how the times change around it. I envy the clarity of his vision and his certainty about who the enemy is and what the fight is really for.

Thirty years later, the opposite problem prevails. We (the leaders of American theaters) have become cowardly, careful people, so frightened of offending anyone (from our boards to our donors to our audiences) that we rarely take a stand on anything. This may explain why we have precious few national spokespeople in our field, few cultural leaders who are truly willing and able to speak out on behalf of the American theater, few individuals to whom the public at large can turn for a larger vision about the role of the arts in the culture. Perhaps artistic directors have ceded that task to writers, such as August Wilson and Tony Kushner, which in and of itself is no bad thing. But within the ranks of the leadership of the field, where are our voices? Why are we so silent? What are we so scared of? Is it that in this age of viral communication, a slight misstep can be magnified out of all proportion and threaten to destroy us? Is it that funding is so unpredictable that we don't dare forgo a single opportunity for support by alienating anyone along the way? Is it that we are so obsessed with sustaining our institutions that we have forgotten why we created them to begin with? Didn't we go into the arts to be provocative, to make a few waves as well as to make beauty, to assert what we believe and explore what we love? Wasn't it up to us to set the artistic bar and then strive to keep it high? Have we become so addicted to mere survival, to celebrity, or to institutional security that we have forgotten our own value?

What will it take to get us to speak with the eloquence and passion of our theatrical forebears, like Zelda Fichandler and Bill Ball? That, as I see it, is our challenge in the new millennium. We have an urgent need to rescue our visions and dreams before they become diluted and small. First we need to believe that our work is exciting, fresh, and well executed. But then we need to find pathways to connect that work to people for whom it will *matter*. We must always remember, as Lorca said, that our task is to offer a cup of beauty to the public so that, in drinking, they will understand themselves.

Understanding always comes back to the self. An artist's life is an examined life. Yet a life in the arts is peculiar in that the private quest to understand oneself is often undertaken in a very public way. This is why artists have such a hard time with criticism, because it is not just about our work but ultimately about ourselves. In writing the first draft of this book, I was determined to stay away from anything I felt was too personal. Slowly it became clear that the intersection of personal feeling with public expression is where the story is. From the trenches, it is never easy to discern the qualities that keep one going, or the meaning of the decisions and choices one has made. But the process of writing this book has allowed me to confront and consider many of my own appetites, obsessions, predilections, and fears. Interestingly, I didn't expect the female angle to figure so strongly until I realized that for a woman to see herself as the center of a narrative is a difficult and unusual task. We are so used to being supporting players that we feel bashful when we take center stage. Or I certainly did. I couldn't fathom why anyone would be interested in my own mad struggles as a working mother or my creative excavations of female behavior, until I realized that, at least in my profession, these stories rarely get told. As a culture we tend to remember male successes and female failures, so that women have to succeed over and over again just to stay in the game. And once we have survived, women have to remember to talk about what we've learned, so that there is a mirror for the women right behind us.

When all is said and done, it's important to acknowledge that for me the game has been, for the most part, intensely pleasurable. I decided to write about my life in the American theater because, despite every obstacle, the field continues to give me such visceral satisfaction. As much of an outlier as I often feel I am, I have managed to find enough kindred spirits to continue to explore the kind of beauty and theatrical magic that excites me. I am also outraged frequently enough to remind myself that there are things in this field worth fighting for. And so, between a quest for beauty and ongoing explosions of outrage, I keep on.

What will the next step of the journey be? I am no longer an emerging artist, even if I often feel like one inside. I no longer have my beloved children at home to balance out my working life, but I have a husband of thirty years who is as hungry for the next set of adventures as I am. A.C.T. has a strong enough staff and infrastructure that I can say yes to a Hungarian theater festival or a Parisian production of my play or a research trip to Shanghai without compromising my theater or my family. Does that mean the next decade of my life will be more global? Perhaps. Or perhaps it will be more local, as we use the new Strand to experiment with how theater intersects with community? Perhaps it will be more introspective, as I go deeper down the rabbit hole of my own unanswered questions. I have been around long enough to know that all predictions are futile, and that by the time this book is published, the landscape of my life will have shifted a dozen times over. What doesn't change is the basic DNA. For better or for worse, I am an enthusiast. When I find someone or something that sparks my imagination, I fall in love. I am intensely loyal to the work and the artists I admire. And far too judgmental of those I don't. After all, I am the daughter of a literary critic.

Martha Graham often talked about the "divine dissatisfaction" of the artist. I feel that every day. I am a restless soul who can't stand still, constantly in search of the serenity that enlightened people seem to have for free. But somehow I am also always ready to get up and do it again. Critical buffeting and self-imposed doubts only make me even more eager to get back into the ring. That's where the joy is. "Do it again, Lorenzo." May that always be my mantra.

Appendix

STATEMENT OF PURPOSE OF THE AMERICAN CONSERVATORY
THEATER FOUNDATION

1. WHEREAS: The United States is the only country in the civilized world without a national conservatory of theater art, and there is no immediate likelihood of one being created within our existing theatrical structures;

2. The commercial theater is so heavily burdened with the pressures of immediate projects, that it cannot be expected to provide development and training for theater artists;

3. Such training as exists in universities and professional schools often suffers from inadequate standards and is often limited by the highly individualistic stamp of one teacher or method;

4. There is no consistently available link for young professionals of these schools and the competitive commercial theater;

5. The creative artists in many professional theater structures often find their work limited or dominated by institutionalism, financial or pedagogic interference, or the personal whim of a proprietary interest;

6. The theatrical trade unions generally refuse or are unable to use their power to initiate constructive programs toward revitalizing the theater;

7. The metropolitan theater audience consists mainly of hit-followers; the minority of thoughtful theater lovers is offered little in the way of a sustained, meaningful repertoire;

8. A handful of drama critics find themselves in a position to shape the canons of theater art and the tastes of the entire nation; that their mere opinion may make or break the self-esteem, progress, and longevity of an artist or company;

9. The exaggerated values of "fame and fortune" and the panicky competitiveness accompanying them have intimidated most the-

atrical artists to the point of paralysis; these myths have misled others in the conviction that their work has achieved an incontestable excellence, that their venerated talents are no longer in need of training and extension;

10. Every day, innovators announce new theater projects, each determined in his own way to solve the problems of today's theater; but lacking valid experience and research they are frequently unaware that their formulas for tomorrow's theater have already proven yesterday's mistakes;

THEREFORE WE RESOLVE TO FOUND:
THE AMERICAN CONSERVATORY THEATER

1. As a nonprofit tax-exempt educational institution resembling the European concept of Conservatory—adapted so that development and performances are integral and inseparable parts of the professional's creative life. Training and production shall be indigenous, the one to the other, not working as separate programs with separated personnel. All participants in the Conservatory— as in a ballet company—will always be in training;

2. To bring together the finest directors, authors, playwrights, actors, and educators in the theater arts to provide comprehensive advanced training to a large professional company and to make this aggregate training available to representatives of regional theaters and educators in university and professional schools of drama;

3. To restore to the creative artist himself the right of leadership in shaping and fulfilling his own potential;

4. To determine the qualifications for membership and welcome as participants in the Conservatory any union person who demonstrates creative ability and who agrees to participate in the triple role of student, instructor, and production artist. It shall not, however, demonstrate prejudice against gifted young talent merely because they are not union members;

5. To engage artists on long contracts so that within an explorative atmosphere, with reasonable security, the adventuresome artist may test his potential;

6. To structure the Conservatory-Theater to insure the maximum freedom from proprietary interference, and to vest in the artistic directors of the Conservatory the authority to determine the continuity and policies of the Foundation;

7. To build and rely completely upon a subscribed membership audience, offering a meaningful repertoire at a popular, accessible ($4.95 top) price scale;

8. To enlist the cooperation of national leaders, publishers, editors, and theater critics themselves in an experiment by which television and journalistic reviewing will be limited to exclude both praise and disparagement of the repertory performances for a period of three years; in return, the Conservatory-Theater will agree to limit advertising to exclude "quotes" from any source;

9. To found the AMERICAN CONSERVATORY THEATER upon the observed and reported experience of all related theater projects; principles derived from research and experience collated from former theater projects with the aim to avert the misjudgments that have caused so many projects to founder; to leave provision for expansion and adjustment with the Charter and By-Laws; to encourage, through future programs (already drafted) the growth of playwriting, criticism, design, architecture, opera, mime, and theater literature; to provide a receptacle for the focus of isolated theater projects and to aid all efforts towards unity and economy in the national theater.

DEFINITION

THE AMERICAN CONSERVATORY THEATER combines the concept of resident repertory theater with the classic concept of continuous training, study, and practice as an integral and inseparable part of the performer's life.

THE AMERICAN CONSERVATORY THEATER is simultaneously an educational and performing organization. The purpose in the first three years is to provide actors, craftsmen, directors, and designers with a triple-pronged program. Each participant in the program will

Develop his own artistic potential through study
Teach the younger professionals
Perform wide repertoire

As the project is aimed at broadening the expressive ability of the actor and director, all available techniques for acting and directing will be used as sources. An eclectic program will be explored with a wide range of theory and experiment, while performance will serve to apply and test techniques.

The training program of the Conservatory will be concurrent with the program of presentations. Training will be woven into the rehearsal pattern by stage managers specifically engaged for the purpose of preparing the daily schedule and assignments of personnel (*Estudientenlieder*).

Our goal is to awaken in the theater artist his maximum versatility and expressiveness.

Bibliography

Abreu, José Antonio. Acceptance Speech, The Right Livelihood Award (December 7, 2001). www.rightlivelihood.org/abreu_speech.html.

Arieff, Allison. "What Tech Hasn't Learned from Urban Planning." *The New York Times* (December 13, 2013).

Billington, Michael. *The Life and Work of Harold Pinter*. London: Faber and Faber, 1996.

Blau, Herbert. *The Impossible Theater: A Manifesto*. New York: Macmillan, 1964.

Brecht, Bertolt. "Zum Einzug des Berliner Ensemble in das Theater am Schiffbauerdamm" (1954). In Frederic Ewen, *Bertolt Brecht: His Life, His Art, and His Times*. New York: Citadel Press, 1967.

Brodsky, Joseph. "Café Trieste: San Francisco." In *Collected Poems in English*. New York: Macmillan, 2002.

Brook, Peter. *The Empty Space*. New York: Atheneum, 1968.

Burroughs, William S. "Robert Wilson." In *Robert Wilson's Vision: An Exhibition of Works by Robert Wilson with a Sound Environment by Hans Peter Kuhn*, edited by Trevor Fairbrother. New York: Harry N. Abrams, 1991.

Eichelbaum, Stanley. "Theatre USA: San Francisco." *Theatre Arts* (March 1960).

Esslin, Martin. *The Theatre of the Absurd*. New York: Anchor Books, 1961.

Fichandler, Zelda. "Whither (or Wither) Art?" *American Theatre* (May/June 2003).

Foye, Raymond. "The War Universe." In *Burroughs Live: The Collected Interviews of William S. Burroughs 1960–1997*, edited by Sylvère Lotringer. Los Angeles and New York: Semiotext(e), 2001.

García Lorca, Federico. "The poem the song the picture." Quoted in Susan C. Haedicke, "The Challenge of Participation: Audiences at Living Stage Theatre Company," in *Audience Participation: Essays on Inclusion in Performance*, edited by Susan Kattwinkel. Westport, CT: Praeger Publishers, 2003.

Grotowski, Jerzy. *Towards a Poor Theatre*. New York: Simon and Schuster, 1968.

Gussow, Mel. *Conversations with Stoppard*. New York: Grove Press, 1995.

Ho, Cathy Lang. "Robert Wilson Sees the Light." *Architect* (February 2000).

London, Todd. *An Ideal Theater: Founding Visions for a New American Art.* New York: Theatre Communications Group, 2013.

Marranca, Bonnie. *Ecologies of Theater: Essays at the Century Turning.* Baltimore and London: The Johns Hopkins University Press, 1996.

Marks, Jonathan. "An Interview with Robert Wilson: Constructions in Space and Time." *The A.R.T. News* (February 1985), reprinted in American Conservatory Theater, *Words on Plays: The Black Rider* (2004).

Pinter, Harold. "Writing for the Theatre." In Harold Pinter, *Complete Works: One.* New York: Grove Press, 1977.

McCarthy, Kevin F., Elizabeth H. Ondaatje, Laura Zakaras, and Arthur Brooks. *Gifts of the Muse: Reframing the Debate about the Benefits of the Arts.* Santa Monica, CA: RAND Corporation, 2004.

Perloff, Carey. "Introduction." In *Sophocles' Elektra,* by Ezra Pound and Rudd Fleming. New York: New Directions, 1990.

———. *Kinship.* Paris: L'avant-scène théâtre (December 15, 2014).

———. *Luminescence Dating.* New York: Dramatists Play Service, 2007.

———. "Pinter in Rehearsal: From *The Birthday Party* to *Mountain Language.*" In *Pinter at Sixty.* Bloomington, IN: Indiana University Press, 1993.

Powers, Dennis. "Power, Politics, and Purse Strings: Revolution in the West." *American Arts* (May 1984).

Quigley, Austin E. *The Pinter Problem.* Princeton, NJ: Princeton University Press, 1975.

RAND Corporation. "Reframing the Debate about the Value of the Arts." Santa Monica, CA: RAND Corporation, 2005. www.wallacefoundation.org/knowledge-center/audience-development-for-the-arts/key-research/Documents/Gifts-of-the-Muse-RAND-Research-Brief.pdf.

Rappaport, Scott. "Shakespeare Santa Cruz to End 32-Year Run Due to Budget Problems." University of California, Santa Cruz Newscenter (August 26, 2013). http://news.ucsc.edu/2013/08/shakespeare-release.html.

Sandberg, Sheryl. *Lean In: Women, Work, and the Will to Lead.* New York: Knopf, 2013.

Schwab, Katharine. "Alcatraz Experiment Tries to Turn Audience into Community." *San Francisco Chronicle* (October 21, 2013).

Shteyngart, Gary. *Little Failure: A Memoir.* New York: Random House, 2014.

Stoppard, Tom. "On Turning Out to Be Jewish." *Talk* (September 1999).

Sullivan, John. "Carey Nation." *SF Weekly* (July 26, 1995).

Taylor, Marland. "Review: *The Colossus of Rhodes.*" *Variety* (August 6, 2001).

Teachout, Terry. "Beckett's Explicit Excess." *Wall Street Journal* (May 25, 2012).

Walters, John L. "Storm in a Pawnshop." *The Guardian* (May 20, 2004).

White, Hayden. "Should Have Directed Efforts at Saving SSC." In "As You See It, Aug. 29, 2013: Shakespeare Santa Cruz a Precious Jewel." *Santa Cruz Sentinel* (August 28, 2013). http://www.santacruzsentinel.com/letters/ci_23969731/you-see-it-aug-29-2013-shakespeare-santa.

Wilk, John R. *The Creation of an Ensemble: The First Years of the American Conservatory Theater.* Carbondale and Edwardsville, IL: Southern Illinois University Press, 1986.

Winn, Steven. "A Director Shakes Up Unshockable San Francisco." *The New York Times* (June 13, 1993).

Index

Carey Perloff was born in Washington, DC, the daughter of Joseph Perloff, a pediatric cardiologist from New Orleans, and Marjorie Perloff, a literary critic and Austrian refugee. Her dream from a young age was to become an archaeologist and discover the next Troy; this led her to study ancient Greek at Stanford and then to migrate to the theater, where she first learned to direct by staging Greek tragedies outdoors while studying theatrical modernism with Martin Esslin. She graduated Phi Beta Kappa in classics and comparative literature in 1980, went on a Fulbright Fellowship to Oxford—where she met her British husband, Anthony Giles—fell in love with the work of Harold Pinter and Samuel Beckett, and moved to New York to begin her directing career. At age twenty-seven, she was hired to run Classic Stage Company, which she saved from financial ruin by staging vigorous productions of unusual classics and new work with major actors, including the American premieres of Pinter's *Mountain Language* and Tony Harrison's *Phaedra Britannica*, the world premiere of Ezra Pound's *Elektra*, and many others. Perloff was the youngest person ever to be hired to run a major LORT theater when A.C.T. chose her in 1992 to become its third artistic director. She took over a ruined building and a demoralized and broke institution and set about bringing it back to life. She's had deep collaborations with Tom Stoppard, Philip Kan Gotanda, Robert Wilson, Frank Galati, and Timberlake Wertenbaker; with major actors such as Bill Irwin, David Strathairn, BD Wong, and Olympia Dukakis; and with other notable artists from around the world, making A.C.T. a true destination for passionate, literate, and diverse theater. In addition, Perloff has written a number of award-winning plays, including *Luminescence Dating, Higher*, and *Kinship*; has taught for many years in A.C.T.'s acclaimed M.F.A. Program and at universities around the country; and has directed dozens of major reinterpretations of classical plays, from *Hecuba* to *'Tis Pity She's a Whore*, as well as world premieres of new work. She helped rebuild A.C.T.'s Geary Theater after it suffered massive damage in the 1989 Loma Prieta earthquake and is now involved in opening The Strand, a new performing venue and a long-dreamed-of second stage for A.C.T. Perloff writes and lectures regularly about the American theater and about issues in culture and contemporary life that are close to her heart. She and her husband have two children: Alexandra, who graduated from Harvard in art history and worked in Paris for three years before attending Yale Law School, and Nicholas, who attends Columbia University and is perhaps best known as the electronic music producer Flaxo.

AWARDS

1982 Los Angeles Drama Critics Circle Award for Best Production for *Greek* (L.A. Theatre Works)

1986 Theatre Communications Group Observership Grant

1987 National Theatre Conference Award to a Theatrician with Outstanding Career Promise

1987 U.S./International Theatre Institute Representative to Theater der Welt, Stuttgart, Germany

1988 OBIE Award to CSC Repertory for Artistic Excellence

1990 Drama-Logue Award for Best Production for *The Collection* (Mark Taper Forum)

1990 Citation of Honor from the League of Professional Theater Women in New York

1994 Koret Israel Prize

1996 Drama-Logue Award for Best Production for *The Rose Tattoo* (A.C.T.)

1997 Jujamcyn Theaters Award to A.C.T. for outstanding contribution to the development of creative talent for the theater

1999 Lucille Lortel Award to CSC Repertory for Outstanding Body of Work (thirty-two years of excellence in the field)

2000 Elliot Norton Prize for Outstanding Production by a Large Resident Company for *Mary Stuart* (Huntington Theatre Company)

2001 American Theatre Critics Circle Award nomination for Best New Play for *The Colossus of Rhodes*

2002 The Susan Smith Blackburn Prize finalist for *The Colossus of Rhodes*

2002 Heideman Award/National Ten-Minute Play Contest for *The Morning After* (Actors Theatre of Louisville)

2005 Ensemble Studio Theatre/Alfred P. Sloan Science and Technology Project Commissioning Award for *Luminescence Dating*

2011 Chevalier des Arts et des Lettres, government of France

2012 Blanche and Irving Laurie Theatre Visions Fund Award for *Higher*